MASTER IT
Textbook

Von

Dipl.-Hdl., akad. geprüfter Übersetzer

Klaus Kirschning

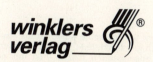

Vorwort

Das Lehrbuch „MASTER IT" ist hauptsächlich für den Unterricht an berufsbildenden Schulen bestimmt, die zum Abschluss „Mittlere Reife/Fachschulreife" führen. Es ist so konzipiert, dass den unterschiedlichen Vorkenntnissen der Schüler an diesen Schulen Rechnung getragen wird.

In dem Buch sind Themen aus dem Alltags- und Berufsleben sowie aus dem soziokulturellen und wirtschaftlichen Bereich behandelt. Es sind darin außerdem gesellschaftliche Probleme angesprochen, mit denen junge Leute immer wieder konfrontiert werden.

Das Buch hat einen breit angelegten Übungsteil, der hauptsächlich der Schulung der schriftlichen und mündlichen Kommunikationsfähigkeit dient. Er enthält diverse comprehension tests, picture stories, letter-writing, dialogues in class, comments u. a. Im Grammatikteil der einzelnen „Units" sind wichtige grammatische Strukturen leicht verständlich erklärt; sie werden anhand zahlreicher „Exercises" geübt. Das begleitende Tonträgermaterial dient der Schulung der Aussprache und des Hörverständnisses (listening comprehension).

Ab der 5. Auflage erscheint zu dem Lehrbuch (Textbook) ein Workbook, um sprachliche Fertigkeiten und eigenständiges Arbeiten der Schülerinnen und Schüler noch intensiver schulen zu können. Das Workbook ist so konzipiert, dass die Themen der einzelnen „Units" weiter ausgebaut und die im Grammatikteil verarbeitete Grammatik durch weitere „Exercises" ergänzt wurden. Neu ist außerdem, dass das Vokabelverzeichnis in das Lehrbuch integriert wurde.

In der 5. Auflage des Buches wurden Texte aktualisiert, neu bearbeitet oder neue hinzugenommen; dies gilt auch für die „Exercises" in den comprehension tests. Grammatische Erklärungen wurden weiter verfeinert, die Übungen hierzu zum großen Teil neu bearbeitet.

Ich möchte an dieser Stelle den Kolleginnen und Kollegen herzlich danken, die mir für die Neubearbeitung des Buches wertvolle Anregungen gegeben haben. Mein Dank gilt außerdem Mrs Catherine Schwerin (M. A.) für die Durchsicht der fremdsprachlichen Texte.

Frühjahr 2002   Verfasser und Verlag

5., neu bearbeitete Auflage, 2002
© Winklers Verlag
im Westermann Schulbuchverlag GmbH
Postfach 11 15 52, 64230 Darmstadt
http://www.winklers.de
Druck: westermann druck GmbH, Braunschweig
ISBN 3-8045-**4246**-8

Dieses Werk und einzelne Teile daraus sind urheberrechtlich geschützt. Jede Nutzung – außer in den gesetzlich zugelassenen Fällen – ist nur mit vorheriger schriftlicher Einwilligung des Verlages zulässig.

Contents

READING MATTER COMPREHENSION TESTS	PAGE	GRAMMAR AND EXERCISES	PAGE
1. Working for Fowler & Co	7	the plural of the nouns	9
Jobs/Activities	8	the cardinal/ordinal numbers (1)	9
		the present simple	9
		question tags	10
2. What to do at the weekend?	12	the definite article (1)	15
Theatres/Cinemas/Shows/Concerts	14	the indefinite article (1)	15
		the present continuous	15
		the present simple and continuous (Comparison)	16
		the possessive adjectives	17
3. By caravan to the seaside	18	the imperative	20
Nationalities	19	the demonstrative adjectives	21
This is Mr Fox speaking	19	irregular plurals of the nouns (1)	21
4. Great Britain and its geography	22	the cardinal numbers (2)	25
The British Isles	23	Arithmetic	26
Do you like learning English?	25	How to translate "null" into English	26
		Prices	27
		What time is it?	27
5. Making travel enquiries to London	29	the personal pronouns	32
Picture story	31	How to translate the German "es" into English	33
To Aberdeen by train	31	the word order (1)	33
6. Short scenes from everyday life	34	the past simple	38
English and American money	37	the word order (2)	39
7. Sightseeing in London	40	the past continuous	44
Having lunch at a self-service restaurant	43	the possessive pronouns	45
Taking the underground	44		
8. Always trouble with the boss and the parents	47	the "of"-genitive	50
A letter to Sally	50	the "s"-genitive	51
		the demonstrative adjectives/pronouns	52
9. Let's go to Harrods	54	interrogative and negative sentences	57
Here you can buy everything – from a pin to an elephant	56	How to translate "nicht wahr" into English (1)	57
Picture story	56		

10. An exciting football match	59	the interrogative pronouns	62
Big sporting events in Britain	61	interrogative sentences with interrogative pronouns	63
		the ordinal numbers (2)	63
		fractions/the date	64
11. Going on a tour of South England	65	the "will"-future	68
A Mini, please!	67	the adjective (1)	69
What do the following road signs mean?	67	(the comparison with "er/est", "more/most")	69
12. Having an accident	71	the "going to"-future	73
Where does it hurt?	73	the present continuous	73
		the adjective (2) (irregular comparison)	75
		older/oldest/elder/eldest	75
		next – nearest	75
		last – latest	75
13. Some aspects of modern British life	76	the conditional	79
Changing eating habits	78	adjectives in comparison (as, the ... the, than, etc.)	80
		many – much	81
14. A visit to an English school	82	the present perfect simple	85
Some other aspects of English schools	84	the present perfect continuous	86
Talking about exams	84	since – for	87
		ago – before	87
15. What to do after school?	88	the past perfect	90
Jobs/activities	89	the adverb (1)	91
Still a man's world?	90	during-while	91
16. Communicating in business	92	the relative pronouns	95
Advertisement	93	relative clauses without a relative pronoun	96
Making an enquiry by e-mail	93	some – any	97
Submitting a quotation by fax	94		
17. The Media	98	the definite article (2)	101
The Times, please!	98	the indefinite article (2)	103
Horoscope	99	every	103
Astrology	100	each	104
Watching TV in Great Britain	100		
BBC1 (extracts from the programme)	100		
Listening to the radio	101		
18. How Great Britain is governed	105	the passive voice (1)	108
The Monarchy	105	ich auch	109

The House of Commons 105
The House of Lords 105
The Prime Minister 105
Election campaign 107

ich auch nicht 110

19. A bloody day 111
No longer war in Northern Ireland? 113

the passive voice (2) 114
How to translate the German "man"
into English 115

**20. Great Britain and its ethnic
minorities** 116
A glance at the Commonwealth
of Nations 118

revision of the most important tenses 119
irregular verbs (siehe auch Seite 191) 120

**21. Let's have a look at the British
economy** 121
Visiting a car company 123

the adverb (2) 124
the word order (3) 125
irregular plurals (2) 126

**22. Is the world facing an environ-
mental catastrophe?** 127
What can the government and we do
to fight pollution? 128
Energy – important for all of us 128

the reflexive pronouns 129
the adverb (3) 130
little – few 131

23. Social aspects of Great Britain 132
A discussion about trade unions in
Britain 132
Social services in Great Britain 134
Talking about shorter working hours 134

the modal auxiliaries 135
general rules 135
can – to be able 136

24. Britain and the world 138
Towards a united Europe 139

may – to be allowed / to be permitted 140
both – as well as 141

25. New York 142
Would you like to live in the
city or in the country? 145

must – to have to, to be obliged to,
to be compelled to, etc. 145

26. Impressions of the United States 147
Impressions of the USA (continued) .. 149

will 149
I'd like, to want, to intend, etc., ... 149
need – dare 151

27. Some aspects of modern American life .. 152
Schools and sport in the USA 154

shall 154
to be said to, to be to, should, ought to 155

Specific texts dealing with commerce and trade

1. Working in an export firm 157
2. At the port of London (Shipping goods) 158
3. A business talk 159
4. A business letter (Making a counterproposal) 160
5. A business letter (Making a complaint) 161
6. Visitors at the Hanover Fair 162
7. What do you know about modern communications systems? ... 163
8. How a house is built 165
   Tradesmen 165
   Tools 166
9. A farmer's activities 166
10. Sarah learns how to cook 167

For further study

1. The prepositions 170
2. The conjunctions 172
3. The if – clauses 173
4. The indirect speech 176
5. The infinitive 178
6. The participle/the gerund 181/183

Short forms of the auxiliary verbs 188
Conjugation table 189
List of the irregular verbs 191
Key to pronunciation and stress 267
Grammatical terms 268
List of grammatical subjects 270

Vocabulary 194
How to find the words in the vocabulary 271

1 Working for Fowler & Co

This is Ms Freeman. She has a fulltime job with Fowler & Co. She is a typist and types business letters. She is 23 years old and has a small flat in London. She likes cooking, playing tennis and travelling.

Mr Jackson is the sales manager of Fowler & Co. He telephones businessmen, offers his products and sells them. He is 32 years old, married and has a son and a daughter. His hobbies are reading, playing squash and driving his car.

Mike Pillow is a computer specialist. He is a programmer and a real computer freak. He is 25 years old and lives with two friends in a little house in a London surburb. His hobbies are cycling, swimming and collecting stamps.

Alice Hudson is 18 years old and a junior clerk with Fowler & Co. She has to do all the work that a beginner has to do. She sorts the correspondence, posts business letters, etc. She is engaged to Mike Jones, a nice chap. She likes knitting and dancing.

COMPREHENSION TESTS

1 Have a look at the text and answer the following questions:

1. Who is this?
2. How old are they?
3. What are their jobs?
4. What kind of work do they do?
5. Where do Ms Freeman and Mike live?
6. What are their hobbies?

2 Complete the following sentences:

1. Ms Freeman is a ... and has a ... job.
2. She is 23 years ... .
3. She has a small ... in London.
4. Mike Pillow is a ... computer ... .
5. He lives in a London ... .
6. Alice Hudson is ... to Mike Jones.
7. Mike, her fiancé, is a nice ... .
8. Mr Jackson is a ... and has a son and a ... .

3 Rewrite the words adding (einfügen) **the missing** (fehlen) **letters.**

t.p.st, s.les man.ger, to be ma.ied, to be eng.ged, c.cling, trave.ing, d.ghter, to progra.e, s.b.rb, st.mp, corr.spond.nce, kni.ing, to c.ll.ct

4 JOBS / ACTIVITIES – What do these people do?

Mr Harris is a ... .
He drives a Ford and likes his job.

Michael is a ... .
He has a lovely voice and a lot of fans.

Jimmy is a … . He repairs cars and does the usual inspections on them.

Mrs Simon is a … in a London store. She works in the radio and TV department and sells TV sets and video recorders.

VOCABULARY AIDS
car mechanic, shop assistant, taxi driver, pop star

GRAMMAR AND EXERCISES

THE PLURAL OF THE NOUNS – Der Plural der Substantive

car	– car**s**
uncle	– uncle**s**
teacher	– teacher**s**

Der Plural des Substantivs wird in der Regel durch Anhängen von „**s**" gebildet.

THE CARDINAL NUMBERS (1)
(Die Grundzahlen)

one	six
two	seven
three	eight
four	nine
five	ten

THE ORDINAL NUMBERS (1)
(Die Ordnungszahlen)

first	(1st)	sixth	(6th)
second	(2nd)	seventh	(7th)
third	(3rd)	eighth	(8th)
fourth	(4th)	ninth	(9th)
fifth	(5th)	tenth	(10th)

THE PRESENT SIMPLE – TO BE – Das einfache Präsens/Gegenwart

I	am	a student	**SHORT FORMS**	I'm	I'm not	(aren't I)?[1]		**SHORT FORMS**
you	are	a student		you're	you aren't	aren't you?		
he				he's	he	isn't he?		
she }	is	a student		she's	she } isn't	isn't she?		
it				it's	it	isn't it?		
we	are	students		we're	we aren't	aren't we?		
you	are	students		you're	you aren't	aren't you?		
they	are	students		they're	they aren't	aren't they		

[1] Für „am I not" gibt es keine Kurzform; stattdessen verwendet der Engländer in der Umgangssprache als Ersatz „aren't I".

Question tags – Bestätigungsfragen

Susan is a typist,
↑
(Aussagesatz)

isn't she?
↑
(Bestätigungsfrage)

Susan ist Stenotypistin,
nicht wahr?

Bei der Übersetzung von „**nicht wahr**" wird, wenn das Prädikat im Aussagesatz „**to be**" (hier: „**is**") ist, das **Verb** in der Bestätigungsfrage **wiederholt**.

Auf einen **bejahten** Aussagesatz folgt in der Regel eine **verneinte** Bestätigungsfrage in der „**short form**" des Verbs (hier: **isn't she**).

5 Fill in the forms of to "be":

PATTERN
You ... a blank clerk, ... you?　　　　You **are** a blank clerk, **aren't** you?
Yes, ... No, ...　　　　　　　　　　Yes, **I am**. No, **I am not**.

1. Sally ... 35 years old, ... she?
   Yes, ... No, ...
2. Bob ... single, ... he?
   Yes, ... No, ...
3. You ... German, ... you?
   Yes, ... No, ...
4. They ... English, ... they?
   Yes, ... No, ...
5. Susan ... married, ... she?
   Yes, ... No, ...
6. She ... pretty, ... she?
   Yes, ... No, ...
7. Your hobbies ... reading and travelling, ... they?
   Yes, ... No, ...
8. Mike and Maureen ... at the disco, ... they?
   Yes, ... No, ...
9. You ... a student, ... you?
   Yes, ... No, ...
10. Roy ... a teacher at the Technical College in Manchester, ... he?
    Yes, ... No, ...

THE PRESENT SIMPLE – TO HAVE – (TO HAVE GOT)
(Das einfache Präsens/Gegenwart)

I	have	(got) a car	I've	I haven't	haven't I
you	have	(got) a car	you've	you haven't	haven't you?
he	has	(got) a car	he's[1]	he hasn't	hasn't he?
she	has	(got) a car	she's[1]	she hasn't	hasn't she?
it	has	(got) a car	it's[1]	it hasn't	hasn't it?
we	have	(got) a car	we've	we haven't	haven't we?
you	have	(got) a car	you've	you haven't	haven't you?
they	have	(got) a car	they've	they haven't	haven't they?

Der Engländer verwendet in der Umgangssprache statt „**I have, you have**" usw. auch „**I have got, you have got**" usw., wenn es sich bei „**haben**" um einen **Besitz** handelt.

---

[1] Diese Kurzformen werden nur verwendet, wenn keine Verwechslung mit anderen Hilfsverben möglich ist. (z. B. he's = he is, it's = it is)

6 Fill in the forms of "to have got":

Statt „to have got" kann man auch „to have" verwenden. Dann muss man aber mit „doesn't he? No, he doesn't" antworten.

PATTERN

Mr Fox ... two sons, ... he?
Yes, ... No, ...

Mr Fox **has got** two sons, **hasn't he**?
Yes, **he has**. No, he **hasn't**.

1. The Hunters ... a beautiful house, ... they?
   Yes, ... No, ...
2. Mr Hunter ... a nice car, ... he?
   Yes, ... No, ...
3. The Hunters ... two children, Andrew and Joan, ... they?
   Yes, ... No, ...
4. Andrew ... a girlfriend whose name is Irene, ... he?
   Yes, ... No, ...
5. Joan ... a cat who is called Kitty, ... she?
   Yes, ... No, ...
6. Andrew ... a dog who is called Rex, ... he?
   Yes, ... No, ...
7. Both ... a television set, ... they?
   Yes, ... No, ...
8. Joan ... a video recorder, too ... she?
   Yes, ... No, ...
9. Andrew ... an interesting job, ... he?
   Yes, ... No, ...
10. He ... a MINI, ... he?
    Yes, ... No, ...

THE PRESENT SIMPLE OF THE FULL VERBS
(Das einfache Präsens der Vollverben)

I	work	for Brown & Co
you	work	for Brown & Co
he	work**s**	for Brown & Co
she	work**s**	for Brown & Co
it	work**s**	for Brown & Co
we	work	for Brown & Co
you	work	for Brown & Co
they	work	for Brown & Co

MAN MERKE SICH

1. Die Vollverben erhalten in der **3. Person Singular Present simple** ein **„s"**.

2. Die Verben, die auf einen **Zischlaut** enden, erhalten in der **3. Person Singular Present simple** ein **„es"**. (he wash**es**, he finish**es**)

3. Vollverben, die auf **„y"** enden, verwandeln das **„y"** in der **3. Person Singular Present simple** in ein **„i"** und erhalten die Endung **„es"**, wenn dem **„y"** ein **Konsonant** vorangeht. (to study – he stud**ies**, aber: he play**s**)

Susan **has** an interesting job.
Mr Harris **teaches** French and German.
Books **are** very instructive.
Is Jack a drinker? Yes, he **is**.
Anne **goes** jogging every morning.

Man verwendet das **„Present simple"** zur Bezeichnung eines **gegenwärtigen Zustandes**, einer **allgemein gültigen Tatsache** oder einer **Gewohnheit**.

ETWAS IST IMMER / STÄNDIG SO

7 Fill in the following words:

to go (2)	to have (2)	to call on	to leave
to telephone	to take	to dictate	to get up
to watch	to prepare		

1. Mr Chapman ... at six o'clock.
2. Mrs Chapman ... breakfast.
3. For breakfast they ... cornflakes, bacon and eggs.
4. At seven o'clock Mr Chapman ... for his office.
5. He ... there by underground while his children ... the bus.
6. In his office Mr Chapman ... customers, ... letters and so on.
7. At one o'clock he ... lunch in a restaurant.
8. In the afternoon he often ... customers.
9. In the evening the Chapmans often ... for a walk.
10. Their son Eric usually ... TV after dinner.

2   What to do at the weekend?

Weekend at last! People are glad that it is there and that they can do what they want – go to the cinema, practise sport, visit friends or relax.

There is, for instance, Oliver, an apprentice. He has a date with his girlfriend. On Saturday night they usually go to the disco where they always have a lot of fun.

Miriam is a nurse. She lives in Luton where life is rather boring. Therefore she often drives down to London on Saturday or Sunday. She likes to walk in Hyde Park; in the evening she usually goes to the cinema or theatre or visits a show.

Mark, a Londoner, often spends the weekend in his cottage in the country where life is not so hectic. He likes to work around the house. He paints, puts up wallpaper, builds cupboards and so on. He buys the material which he needs for this work in the nearby "DO IT YOURSELF" shop.

Sarah is a stewardess. She likes to play tennis and golf and to visit horse races. She mostly spends her free time on the golf course or tennis court.

COMPREHENSION TESTS

1 Have a look at the text and answer the following questions:

1. What are people glad about?
2. Why are they glad about it?
3. What do Oliver and his girlfriend do on Saturday?
4. What does Miriam like to do when in London?
5. Where does Mark mostly spend the weekend?
6. What does he like to do in his free time?

2 Are these statements (Angaben) right or wrong?

1. Oliver is a junior clerk.
2. Miriam lives in Bristol.
3. Mark is a Londoner.
4. He buys wallpaper and so on in the nearby supermarket.
5. Sarah often goes to the golf course.

3 Explain in your own words:

1. A **disco** is a place where … .
2. A **"do it yourself"** shop is a shop where … .
3. **Free time** is the time when … .

4 What's the right thing to say?

1. **Is Liz at the cinema?**
   a) That's great.
   b) Let's have a drink.
   c) Yes, she is.
2. **What's the film like?**
   a) It is very good.
   b) Okay.
   c) My goodness!
3. **You have a date with Alan tomorrow?**
   a) That's funny.
   b) I'm all right.
   c) That's no business of yours.
4. **You like to work around the house, don't you?**
   a) Let's do it.
   b) That's true.
   c) Damn!

5 Reproduce the contents of "What to do at the weekend" in your own words.

6 THEATRES / CINEMAS / SHOWS / CONCERTS

ADELPHI 02073440055
on-line.www.chicagomusical.com
Josefina Gabrielle, Sacha Distel
CHICAGO
WINNER! AN OUTSTANDING MUSICAL!

ROYAL OPERA HOUSE
Tel. & Fax: 09061992 035
The Royal Ballet
ROMEO & JULIET
A MAGNIFICENT BALLET PRODUCTION

SKY CINEMA
02041903784
A SIMPLE PLAN
starring Bill Paxton
A THRILLER! ACTION PACKED, EXPLOSIVE!

OLD VIC 2079287616
From tonight for two weeks
HAMLET
Directed by Yuri Lyubimov
BRILLIANT ARTISTRY, ATMOSPHERIC POWER

COMEDY THEATRE
02073691731
Booking fees, Groups
UNDER THE DOCTOR
By Peter Tilbury
Cancel your engagement!
You will laugh till you cry.
Mon–Fri at 8.00, Sat/Sun at 5.00 & 8.30

Answer the following questions:

1. What is shown at the Royal Opera House, the Adelphi and the Old Vic?
2. What do the advertisements say about:
   – the musical "Chicago"?
   – the production of "Under the doctor"?
   – the production of "Hamlet"?
   – the film "A simple plan"?
3. When do performances at the Comedy Theatre take place?
4. Who is the leading actor/actress in the musical "Chicago"?

GRAMMAR AND EXERCISES

THE DEFINITE ARTICLE (1) – Der bestimmte Artikel

the camera the television set the computer	Im Englischen heißt der bestimmte Artikel für alle drei Geschlechter „the".

1. the bus
   the plane
2. the university
   the Europeans
3. the airport
   the opera
4. the hour
   the honour
	Der bestimmte Artikel lautet:
	[ðə] 1. vor einem **Konsonanten** (Mitlaut)
	        2. vor einem **konsonantisch** anlautenden **Vokal**
	[ði]¹ 3. vor einem Vokal (Selbstlaut)
	        4. vor einem **stummen** „h"

THE INDEFINITE ARTICLE (1) – Der unbestimmte Artikel

a student a watch a camera a European a university a house [haʊs]	Im Englischen heißt der unbestimmte Artikel für alle drei Geschlechter **vor einem Wort mit konsonantischem Anlaut** (gesprochenem Konsonant): „a"
an uncle an eye an hour [ˈaʊəʳ] an honour [ˈɑnəʳ]	Im Englischen heißt der unbestimmte Artikel für alle drei Geschlechter **vor vokalischem Anlaut** (gesprochenem Vokal): „an"

7 Fill in the definite and indefinite articles. Read the words.

... boyfriend	... uncle	... aunt	... mechanic
... American	... European	... hairdresser	... exporter
... university	... penfriend	... businessman	... Englishman

THE PRESENT CONTINUOUS – Die Verlaufsform im Präsens

I	am	writing a letter	Man bildet das „**present continuous**" mit:	
you	are	writing a letter		
he she it }	is	writing a letter	**PRESENT** **von** **TO BE** +	**ING-FORM** **des Verbs**
we	are	writing a letter		
you	are	writing a letter		
they	are	writing a letter		

---

1 ðiː – strong form

Andrew **is playing** tennis.
Andrew spielt gerade Tennis.

Sarah **is watching** a video.
Sarah sieht sich gerade einen Videofilm an.

Man verwendet das „**present continuous**" bei **Handlungen**, **Tätigkeiten** oder **Vorgängen**, die

GERADE ABLAUFEN/ GESCHEHEN

und bei denen die zeitliche Dauer **begrenzt** ist.

THE PRESENT SIMPLE AND CONTINUOUS – COMPARISON
(Das einfache Präsens und dessen Verlaufsform – Vergleich)

Susan **is phoning** Mark. *Susan ruft gerade Mark an.*	Susan **phones** Mark every day. *Susan ruft Mark jeden Tag an.*
John **is going** to his yoga course. *John geht gerade zum Jogakurs.*	John **goes** to his yoga course once a week. *John geht einmal in der Woche zum Jogakurs.*
ES GESCHIEHT GERADE ETWAS/ JEMAND TUT GERADE ETWAS!	**ETWAS IST STÄNDIG SO/ JEMAND TUT ETWAS STÄNDIG!**

MAN MERKE SICH

Folgende Verben bilden normalerweise **keine** Verlaufsform:

to see, to feel, to hope, to understand, to love, to know, to think, to want, to wish, to cost

8 Make sentences according to the pattern. Use the "present continuous".

PATTERN
Mike (to flirt) with Maureen (Sarah).
Is Mike **flirting** with Maureen?
No, he is **flirting** with Sarah.

1. Andrew (to play) squash (badminton).
2. Jack (to have) a drink with Richard (Ronald).
3. Father (to read) THE TIMES (THE SUN).
4. Anne (to go) for a walk (jogging).
5. Mr Turner and his son (to watch) the sports news (the talk show).
6. Mrs Rider (to listen) to the weather forecast (pop concert).
7. Alice and Howard (to drive) to Eastbourne (Torquay).
8. Helen (to read) a love story (thriller).
9. She (to write) a business letter (love letter).
10. They (to send) a fax to Hillman & Co (an e-mail).

9 Put the verbs in brackets into the correct present tense:

1. Steve and Simon .... chess. Don't disturb them. (to play)
2. Steve and Simon often .... chess at the weekend. (to play)
3. Mandy usually .... crossword puzzles in her free time. (to do)
4. Mandy.... a crossword puzzle. Don't be so noisy. (to do)
5. Mrs Gibbs .... shopping. She will be back soon. (to go)
6. Mrs Gibbs usually .... shopping after breakfast. (to go)
7. Henry .... for his office at half past seven in the morning. (to leave)
8. Sarah .... at the fitness centre "FIT" once a week. (to work out)
9. Roger isn't in. He .... his bike. (to ride)
10. Jimmy .... his car. Wait a moment, please. (to wash)

THE POSSESSIVE ADJECTIVES (DETERMINERS)
(Die adjektivischen Possessivpronomen/die Possessivbegleiter)

I	wash	**my**	car		we	wash	**our**	cars
you	wash	**your**	car		you	wash	**your**	cars
he	washes	**his**	car		they	wash	**their**	cars
she	washes	**her**	car					
it	washes	**its**	car		➤ **it's** = it is		**its** = sein (pronoun)	

10 Fill in a possessive adjective:

PATTERN

Does Dorothy show Brian ... new Discman?
Yes, ... No, ...
Does Dorothy show Brian **her** new Discman?
Yes, **she does**.   No, **she doesn't**.

1. Do they show Miriam ... new house?
   Yes, ...   No, ...
2. Does Dennis give Janet ... scooter?
   Yes, ...   No, ...
3. Does Marilyn show Nicole ... new wristwatch.
   Yes, ...   No, ...
4. Is this ... telephone number?
   Yes, ...   No, ...
5. Do they give Ann ... addresses?
   Yes, ...   No, ...
6. Do Peggy and Trevor show Irene ... new flat? Yes, ...   No, ...
7. Is this ... wallet?
   Yes, ...   No, ...
8. Are these ... credit cards?
   Yes, ... No, ...
9. Is that ... mobile phone?
   Yes, ...   No, ...
10. Does Alan show Alice ... new computer?
    Yes, ... No, ...

3   By caravan to the seaside

Mike Hunter, who is an electrician and lives in a small flat on the outskirts of London, has a caravan and usually spends his holidays in Britain or abroad. As Monday next is a bank holiday, he and his girlfriend Susan decide to spend the weekend at a caravan site in Brighton.

On Friday afternoon they leave for this lovely seaside resort. They take the motorway, listen to the radio on the way and arrive there at about 7 p.m. At the caravan site there are a lot of foreigners who come from France, Belgium, the Netherlands, Germany, Denmark and even from Switzerland. The people in the tent beside them are Germans. They soon make friends with them.

In the morning they usually go to the beach, have a swim in the sea, surf or read magazines. At lunchtime they either go to McDonald's or to the nearby snack bar where they have a hamburger, hot dog or a cheeseburger. After that they go to the beach, do their shopping or drive along the lovely coast with its many places of interest. In the evening Susan does the cooking which is one of her hobbies.

TIFFANY BAR	
Hamburger	£1.25
Hot dogs	£1.05
Cheeseburger	£1.40
Eggburger	£1.50
Chips	£0.65
Milkshakes	£0.80
Coca Cola	£0.50

Before they go to the disco or to a pub, they stroll along the promenade where they often can see the sunset. If there is a show on, they don't miss it.

As there is a lot of traffic back to London, especially at weekends, they decide to leave Brighton early in the afternoon.

COMPREHENSION TESTS

1 Have a look at the text and answer the following questions:

1. Where does Mike Hunter live?
2. Who is Susan?
3. Where does Mike usually spend his holidays?
4. What do they listen to on the way to Brighton?
5. Where do the foreigners come from?
6. What do they usually do in the morning/afternoon and in the evening?
7. Why do they leave for London early in the afternoon?

2 Are these statements correct? If not, correct them.

1. Mike Hunter is a car mechanic.
2. They take the A 25 to Bournemouth.
3. They make friends with some Germans.
4. They often have a hamburger in the nearby snack bar.
5. In the evening they have dinner at a restaurant.

3 Fill in the correct preposition(s):

1. They spend the weekend ... the caravan site ... Brighton.
2. Mike lives ... a flat ... the outskirts of London.
3. ... Friday they leave ... Brighton.
4. They listen ... the radio.
5. The people in the tent ... them are Germans.
6. ... the evening Susan does the cooking.
7. There is a lot ... traffic ... the morning.
8. Most of the foreigners come ... France and Germany.

4 Have a look at the "Tiffany Bar" (page 18) and at the main radio stations.

1. How much is/are: a hamburger, cheeseburger, chips and milkshakes?
2. Which radio station(s) do you like best?

> **THE MAIN RADIO STATIONS**
> There are four BBC stations:
>
> RADIO 1 pop music
> RADIO 2 light music, sport, entertainment
> RADIO 3 classical music
> RADIO 4 news, comedies, radio plays

5 NATIONALITIES

1. Where do these people come from?
2. What's their nationality?
3. What languages do they speak?

6 THIS IS MR FOX SPEAKING
Listen to the cassette and answer the following questions:
Actor/actress: Mr Fox, Mrs Brown

1. Who's phoning?
2. Who does he want to speak to?
3. Is Maureen in?
4. When will she be back?
5. What does John Fox ask Mrs Brown to do?

> **VOCABULARY AIDS**
>
> to take a message for sb
> *jmdm. etw. ausrichten*
>
> to make a date with sb
> *sich mit jmdm. verabreden*

GRAMMAR AND EXERCISES

THE IMPERATIVE – Der Imperativ, die Befehlsform

Singular	Plural
be – sei!	**be** – seid!
have – habe!	**have** – habt!
ask – frage!	**ask** – fragt!
play – spiele!	**play** – spielt!

1. **Der Imperativ lautet wie der Infinitiv** (aber ohne „to").
2. Er ist für Singular und Plural **gleich**.
3. Das Pronomen **„Sie"** (Gehen **Sie** nach Hause!) wird im Englischen weggelassen.

Shut your books, please.
Schließen Sie bitte Ihre Bücher!
(Schließt bitte ...!)
Be careful.
Seien Sie vorsichtig!
Seid (sei) vorsichtig!

Der Imperativ wird bei einer **Aufforderung** an jemanden, bei einem **Ausruf, Rat, Befehl, Verbot** oder einer **Ermahnung** angewendet. Zur Milderung eines Befehls, Verbots usw. setzt man **„please"** hinzu.

Don't be so foolish.
Seien Sie (sei) nicht so töricht!
Don't worry.
Machen Sie sich (Mach dir) keine Sorgen!

Der Engländer umschreibt den **verneinten Imperativ** mit „to do"; ebenfalls die Hilfsverben „to have" und „to be".

Let's do it.
Lass(t) es uns tun!

„**Lass(t) uns, wir wollen**" wird im Englischen mit „**let us (let's)**" ausgedrückt.

| **Be** quiet! | *Sei(d) ruhig!* |
| **Shut up!** | *Halt(et) den Mund!* |

Das **Ausrufezeichen** steht beim Imperativ nur bei einem **strikten Befehl** oder einem **Ausruf** (mit erhobenem Zeigefinger).

7 Make sentence according to the pattern:

PATTERN 1	PATTERN 2
– to do it once again	– to do it once again
Do it once again.	**Let's do it once again.**
Do it once again, please.	

What does Mr Jenkins say to Michael?

1. to spell the word
2. to translate the sentence into English
3. to open the window
4. to try it once again
5. to sit down
6. to be quiet

1. to play cricket
2. to go to Roy's party
3. to have a dance
4. to have a swim
5. to have a smoke
6. to leave now

THE DEMONSTRATIVE ADJECTIVES (DETERMINERS)
(Die adjektivischen Demonstrativpronomen/ die Demonstrativbegleiter)

Singular	Plural
this car	**these** cars
dieses Auto	*diese Autos*
that car	**those** cars
jenes Auto	*jene Autos*
this football	**these** footballs
that football	**those** footballs

Die **adjektivischen Demonstrativpronomen** beziehen sich auf **Personen** und **Sachen**.

Man gebraucht „**this**" und „**these**", wenn sich Personen oder Sachen in **unmittelbarer Nähe** befinden, „**that**" und „**those**", wenn sie **weiter entfernt** sind.

8 Fill in a demonstrative adjective:

PATTERN
Is ... your cheque card?
Yes, ... No, ...

Is **this (that)** your cheque card?
Yes, **it is.** No, **it isn't.**

1. Is ... woman French?
Yes, ... No, ...
2. Are ... gentlemen British?
Yes, ... No, ...
3. You know ... people, don't you?
Yes, ... No, ...
4. ... tourists come from Italy, don't they?
Yes, ... No, ...
5. Is ... your e-mail address?
Yes, ... No, ...
6. Is ... your credit card?
Yes, ... No, ...
7. Is ... your mobile phone?
Yes, ... No, ...
8. Are ... your passports?
Yes, ... No, ...
9. Is ... your identity card?
Yes, ... No, ...
10. Is ... your travel bag?
Yes, ... No, ...

IRREGULAR PLURALS OF THE NOUNS (1)
(Unregelmäßige Plurale der Substantive)

kni**f**e – kni**v**es *Messer*	potat**o** – potat**oes** *Kartoffel*	child – child**ren** *Kind*	foot – feet *Fuß*
wi**f**e – wi**v**es *Frau*	negr**o** – negr**oes** *Neger*	m**ou**se – m**i**ce *Maus*	t**oo**th – t**ee**th *Zahn*
cal**f** – cal**v**es *Kalb*	g**oo**se – g**ee**se *Gans*	m**a**n – m**e**n *Mann*	w**o**man – w**o**men *Frau*
lea**f** – lea**v**es *Blatt*			

9 Put the nouns in brackets and in bold type into the plural:

PATTERN
What is Janet doing? (to play with – her **child**)
Janet is playing with her **children**.

1. Who is Roger talking to?
(this **woman**)
2. What is Oliver doing?
(to wash – his **foot**)
3. What is Milly doing?
(to catch – the **mouse**)
4. What are you looking for? (the **calf**)
5. Who are these people? (**Englishman**)
6. What did Mr Brown buy at the grocer's. (**tomato**)
7. What is Mum doing?
(to peel – the **potato**)
8. What is Diana doing?
(to sharpen – the **knife**)
9. What do dentists do?
(to pull out – **tooth**)
10. What is Jane doing?
(to sweep up – the **leaf**)

4   Great Britain and its geography

I'm certain you know quite a lot about the geography of Great Britain. Let's see whether you can answer the following questions. If you have any difficulties, have a look at the map or consult a dictionary.

- What's the capital of Great Britain?
- How many people live in Great Britain? (30/50/70 million)
- What's Great Britain surrounded by in the north, east, south and west?
- Which are the countries of Great Britain and the United Kingdom?
- Name the capitals of Scotland, Wales and the Irish Republic.
- Name some cities in Great Britain.
- Name important rivers in Great Britain.
- What are the mountains in Scotland called?
- Which are the most important ports?
- What are Oxford and Cambridge known for?
- What are Liverpool and Loch Ness known for?
- Name well-known seaside resorts in Britain.
- What connects Britain and France now?

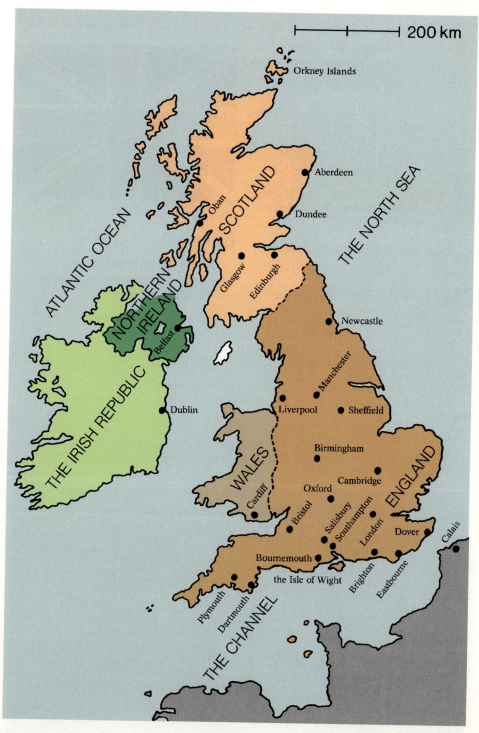

The British Islands

COMPREHENSION TESTS

1 Are the following statements correct? If not, correct them.

1. Great Britain has about 50 million inhabitants.
2. Great Britain consists of England and Scotland.
3. London is situated on the Thames.
4. Glasgow is situated on the Clyde.
5. The Highlands are situated in England.
6. The Beatles come from Manchester.
7. Ireland consists of the Irish Republic and Northern Ireland.
8. The Isle of Wight and the Orkney Islands are situated in the Channel.

Union Jack

2 Rewrite the words adding the missing letter(s):

Edinburg ., i . le, mount . n, cit . s, Un . ted Kingd . m, ri . er, import . nt, to be s . rrounded, seas . de r . sort, Great Brit . n, to be situ . ted, Sco . land, inhabit . nts

3 ATTENTION, PLEASE!

The following words sound (klingen) the same in English. Find the others.

for	four
their	....
too	....
by	....
sea	....
whether	....

4 What's correct?

1. Was the Channel Tunnel (Kanaltunnel) opened in 1972, 1994 or 1998?
2. Does the Channel Tunnel run from Folkstone to Calais or from Eastbourne to Cherbourg?

5 DO YOU LIKE LEARNING ENGLISH?

important, help, language, letters, countries

English is, as you know, the world ... . (1) It is spoken not only in the United Kingdom but also in those ... (2) which belong to the Commonwealth of Nations (Canada, India, Australia, etc.). As the world language, English also plays an ... (3) role in business life. Businessmen, no matter whether Norwegians, Dutch, Japanese, etc. often write business ... (4) in English. As a tourist, as well, you will find that it is a great ... (5) in foreign countries if you can speak English.

I hope you will enjoy learning English with this book.

1. Fill in the gaps with one of the words in bold type (Fettschrift).
2. Read the text.
3. Translate the text into German.
4. Ask questions on the text and answer them.

GRAMMAR AND EXERCISES

THE CARDINAL NUMBERS (2)

11 eleven	16 sixteen	21 twenty-one	60 sixty
12 twelve	17 seventeen	22 twenty-two	70 seventy
13 thirteen	18 eighteen	30 thirty	80 eighty
14 fourteen	19 nineteen	40 forty	90 ninety
15 fifteen	20 twenty	50 fifty	100 a (one) hundred

1000	**a (one) thousand**
1034	**a (one) thousand and thirty-four**
6745	**six thousand seven hundred and forty-five**
1 Million	**a (one) million**
1 Milliarde	**a (one) thousand million**
	amerikanisch: **a billion**

forty-four
fifty-five

1. Zwischen Zehnern und Einern steht ein **Bindestrich**.

five hundred **and** three
three hundred **and** seventy-seven

2. Bei Zahlen über 100 steht vor Zehnern oder Einern „**and**".

ENGLISCH	DEUTSCH
1 (eins)	1
7 (sieben)	7
3.5 miles	3,5
4,675,312	4.675.312 bzw. 4675312

3. **andersartige Schreibweisen**:
„Eins" (handschriftlich) ohne Aufstrich.
„Sieben" ohne Querstrich.
Der Engländer setzt an die Stelle, wo der Deutsche ein Komma setzt, einen Punkt (Dezimalzahlen).
Zum leichteren Lesen der Zahlen verwendet der Engländer Kommata.

6 Arithmetic

What is five plus four? Five plus four is nine.	**Addition**
What is twelve minus six? Twelve minus six is six.	**Subtraction**
What is three times nine? Three times nine is twenty-seven.	**Multiplication**
What is forty divided by eight? Forty divided by eight is five.	**Division**

How to translate "null" into English

five minus five leaves nought	„**nought**" zur Bezeichnung eines Zahlenwertes
four degrees (Grad) below zero	„**zero**" auf dem Thermometer oder einer Skala
the score (Spielstand) is three nil	„**nil**" beim Sport und Statistiken
dial the number 502416 five oh two four one six	„**0**" bei Fernsprechnummern „**oh**" (ou), wenn es ausgeschrieben wird.

Add:	**Subtract:**	**Multiply:**	**Divide:**
15 + 8 = ?	25 − 9 = ?	5 x 8 = ?	32 ÷ 4 = ?
124 + 12 = ?	44 − 18 = ?	9 x 12 = ?	48 ÷ 6 = ?
544 + 14 = ?	136 − 19 = ?	8 x 16 = ?	63 ÷ 7 = ?
792 + 27 = ?	318 − 37 = ?	4 x 13 = ?	88 ÷ 11 = ?
978 + 78 = ?	409 − 66 = ?	12 x 6 = ?	96 ÷ 12 = ?

7 PRICES

What's that?   How much is it?

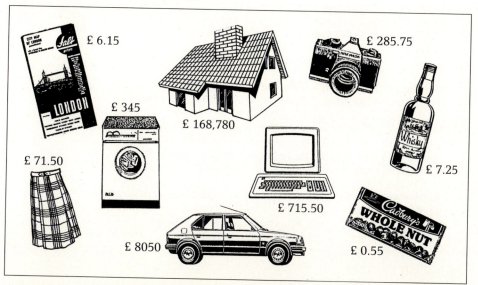

VOCABULARY AIDS

kilt — Schottenrock
washing machine — Waschmaschine
a guide to London — ein Londoner Fremdenführer

8 What time is it?

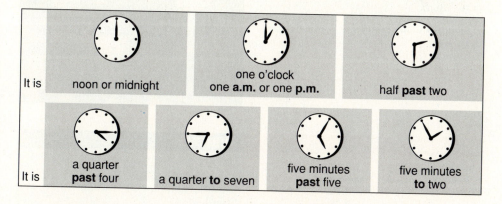

It is: noon or midnight | one o'clock one **a.m.** or one **p.m.** | half **past** two

It is: a quarter **past** four | a quarter **to** seven | five minutes **past** five | five minutes **to** two

MAN MERKE SICH

1. Die Zeitangaben der **ersten halben Stunde** bezieht man auf die **vorhergehende Stunde**.
   09:10 Uhr   ten minutes **past** nine in the morning/evening

2. Die Zeitangaben **der zweiten halben Stunde** bezieht man auf die **folgende Stunde**.
   09:50 Uhr   ten minutes **to** ten

3. Die Uhrzeit kann auch folgendermaßen angegeben werden:
   09:50 Uhr   **nine fifty**   09:10   **nine ten**

   Um Verwechslungen zu vermeiden, werden die Stunden gekennzeichnet:
   von **0 - 12** Uhr durch **a.m.** (ante meridiem = <u>vor</u> Mittag)
   von **12 - 24** Uhr durch **p.m.** (post meridiem = <u>nach</u> Mittag)
   8.00 **a.m.** = acht Uhr vormittags   8.00 **p.m.** = acht Uhr abends

4. Bei der Angabe von Uhrzeiten im **Bahn-** und **Flugverkehr** gebraucht man die **24-Stunden-Uhr:**
   The train leaves at   14.00   fourteen hundred hours
                          16.05   sixteen oh five / 15.15   fifteen fifteen

9 Read the times of departure and arrival:

Example:

The train to Edinburgh leaves at 6.15 a.m., etc.

The train from Oxford arrives at 12.27 p.m., etc.

DEPARTURES		ARRIVALS	
Edinburgh	6.15	Oxford	12.27
Bristol	7.45	Manchester	14.35
Dover	8.12	Cardiff	15.46
Newcastle	8.55	Sheffield	18.01
Eastbourne	9.05	Birmingham	20.44
Liverpool	10.30	Harwich	21.25
Aberdeen	11.00	Brighton	22.15
Glasgow	11.23	Paris	23.11

5   Making travel enquiries to London

An American teacher who is on holiday in Hamburg enquires about trips to London in a travel agency.

American	Good morning.
Clerk	Good morning, sir. What can I do for you?
American	I'd like to go to London over the weekend. What's the best way to get there?
Clerk	That depends. You can go by ship on the MS Admiral of Scandinavia from Cuxhaven to Harwich and on to London by train. From Hamburg you can take the train to the Hook of Holland or to Ostend where you can catch the ferry to Harwich or Dover. Of course, you can also fly.
American	How much is a second-class return ticket to London via Ostend, and how much is it by ship from Cuxhaven?
Clerk	A return ticket to London via Ostend costs about 240 euros, and by ship from Cuxhaven about 220 euros.[1]
American	How long does it take to get there by ship or by train?
Clerk	It takes about 20 hours by ship and about 21 hours by train via Ostend.
American	That's quite a time.
Clerk	Well, there are companies which offer cheap charter flights including bed and breakfast. Have a look at this brochure.
American	The rates are really cheap. Please book a single room in the Senator Hotel from Friday to Sunday.
Clerk	All right. The total price is 320 euros. (The clerk phones the airline company.) You are lucky. There are still some seats vacant on the plane and some free rooms in the hotel. The plane leaves at 8.30 a.m. You must be at the airport one hour before takeoff at the latest. You check in at the British Airways desk where you get your tickets and the hotel voucher.

American: Thank you. Goodbye.

Clerk: Goodbye. Have a pleasant trip.

[1] The rates depend on the season, class and the bugth of the stay.

COMPREHENSION TESTS

1 Have a look at the text and answer the following questions:

1. What is the American teacher doing in Hamburg?
2. What does he enquire about in a travel agency?
3. How can you get from Hamburg to London?
4. How much is a return ticket from Hamburg to London via Ostend
5. Where does the American teacher check in?
6. What does he get there?

Flight No Aircraft Class	BR 944 B11 Y	BR 948 B11 Y	BR 952 B11 Y	BR 956 B11 Y
Edingburgh dep.	0800 🍴	1300 🍴	1700 🍴	2000 🍴
London (Gatwick) arr.	0915	1415	1815	2115

2 Complete the following sentences:

1. In Ostend you can ... the ferry to Dover.
2. It ... about 20 hours to go by ship ... Cuxhaven ... Harwich.
3. The American teacher has to be at the airport one hour before ... .
4. There are companies which offer cheap ... flights to London.
5. The ... are really cheap.
6. You are... . There are still some seats ... on the plane.

3 Explain in your own words the words underlined:

1. A <u>travel agency</u> is a place where you can ... .
2. A <u>hotel</u> is a place where ... .
3. <u>to be vacant</u> means that ... .
4. <u>to be cheap</u> means that ... .

4 Reproduce the contents of "Making travel enquiries to London" in your own words.

5 What services do travel agencies offer?

Here you can:
- rent cars
- book package holidays
- book do-it-yourself holidays
- insure your luggage
- book tickets for the theatre
- see video films
- enquire about the times of departure and arrival of trains/planes

Is that right or wrong?

6 Picture story

VOCABULARY AIDS

to go up and down the quay (Kai), kiosk, passengers (Passagiere), to board the ship, sweets, disco, information signs (Hinweisschilder)

1. Interpret the pictures in your own words.
2. Find a suitable title for the story.

7 TO ABERDEEN BY TRAIN

fine, to take, to leave, direct, to reserve

Sally	Good morning.
Clerk	Good morning.
Sally	What time do trains ... (1) for Aberdeen?
Clerk	There's a train at 8.23 a.m., one at 2.15 p.m. and another at 7.30 p.m.
Sally	Do I have to change?
Clerk	No. These are ... (2) trains.
Sally	How much is a second-class return ticket?
Clerk	£28.70. (It is the super saver ticket.)
Sally	That's ... (3) I'd like to ... (4) a seat on the 8.23 tomorrow.
Clerk	All right. Here is your ticket.
Sally	How long does it ... (5) to get to Aberdeen?
Clerk	About 8 1/2 hours.
Sally	Which platform does the train leave from?
Clerk	Platform 2.
Sally	Thank you.

1. Complete the sentences by using one of the words given above.
2. Read the text.
3. Pick out the most important questions in the dialogue text.
4. Act out the dialogue in class.

GRAMMAR AND EXERCISES

THE PERSONAL PRONOUNS – Die Personalpronomen

SUBJEKT „Wer"-Fall			DIREKTES OBJEKT „Wen"-Fall			INDIREKTES OBJEKT „Wem"-Fall		
I	am	reading		me	mich		to me	mir
you	are	reading		you	dich		to you	dir
he	is	reading		him	ihn		to him	ihm
she	is	reading	he knows	her	sie	he gives it	to her	ihr
it	is	reading		it	es		to it	ihm
we	are	reading		us	uns		to us	uns
you	are	reading		you	euch, Sie		to you	euch, Ihnen
they	are	reading		them	sie		to them	ihnen

This is Mr Hopkins.
He is a teacher.

This is our baby.
Isn't **he (she)** funny?

That's Puss. Isn't **she** a nice cat?

My watch is slow; **it** is slow.
Meine Uhr geht nach; sie geht nach.

This car costs a lot of money;
it costs a lot of money.
Er (Wagen) kostet sehr viel Geld.

Der Engländer gebraucht je nach Geschlecht „he" und „she"
a) bei **Personen**,
b) bei **child** und **baby**
   (bei allgemeinen Aussagen „it"),
c) bei **Tieren**, wenn eine **persönliche** Beziehung besteht, sonst „it".

Der Engländer gebraucht bei **Sachen** das Personalpronomen
„it".
Im Deutschen steht auch „er", „sie".

8 Replace the nouns in brackets by a personal pronoun:

PATTERN
I can't find my purse (Portmonee)
I can't find ... .
I can't find **it**.

Harry is sending Mary an e-mail.
Harry is sending ... to ... .
Harry is sending **it to her.**

1. Kevin enters a store.
   He enters ... .
2. Eric buys cigarettes at a kiosk.
   He buys ... at a kiosk.
3. Tim enters Barclays Bank.
   He enters ... .
4. He cashes two traveller's cheques.
   He cashes ... .
5. Marilyn changes euros into pounds.
   She changes ... into pounds.
6. Janet buys two postal orders at the post office.
   She buys ... at the post office.
7. Arthur makes a trunk call to Glasgow in a telephone box.
   He makes ... in a telephone box.
8. He puts coins into the slot and then dials the area code for Glasgow.
   He puts ... into the slot and then ... .
9. Ann gives Susan the map of New York.
   She gives ... to ... .
10. A guide shows the tourists Manhattan.
    He shows ... to ... .

9 HOW TO TRANSLATE THE GERMAN "ES" INTO ENGLISH:

he, she, they, it, there

PATTERN

Who is that woman?
... my wife.
She is my wife.

Translate the following sentences into English:

1. Wer ist dieser Herr?
   Es ist mein Mann.
2. Wer sind diese Damen?
   Es sind meine Kolleginnen.
3. Wer ist dieser Junge?
   Es ist mein Freund.
4. Wer ist dies?
   Es ist Mr Newman.
5. Wer sind diese Mädchen?
   Es sind meine Töchter.
6. Wer ist das?
   Es ist unser Lehrer.
7. Wer ist die Schauspielerin dort?
   Es ist Julia Roberts.
8. Wer sind die Leute dort?
   Es sind die Rolling Stones.

THE WORD ORDER (1) – Die Wortstellung

1. **Harold** — **plays** — **cricket.**
   Subjekt — *Prädikat* — *direktes Objekt („Wen"-Fall)*

   Grundwortstellung

   S — P — O

2. **Harold** — **gives** — **Sarah** — **his CD player.**
   Subjekt — *Prädikat* — *indirektes Objekt („Wem"-Fall)* — *direktes Objekt*

   Harold — **gives** — **his CD player** — **to Sarah.**
   Subjekt — *Prädikat* — *direktes Objekt* — *indirektes Objekt*

MAN MERKE SICH

a) Das am **stärksten** betonte Objekt steht am **Ende**.

b) Steht das **indirekte Objekt** (indirect object) **hinter** dem **direkten Objekt** (direct object), so wird es mit „**to**" gebildet.

---

10 Make sentences according to the pattern:

PATTERN

Nicole is showing **her boyfriend** the sights of Paris.
Nicole is showing the **sights of Paris to her boyfriend.**

1. Philip is showing his girlfriend the skyline of New York.
2. I often write Ronald love letters.
3. William is sending Mr Sherman an express letter.
4. Alan often tells his friends stories.
5. Father gives James pocket money at the weekend.
6. Mabel is showing Bobby her new Walkman.
7. I have lent Sheila five pounds.
8. The waiter is showing Mrs Brian the menu.
9. The waiter hands Mr Brian the bill.
10. Mr Brian gives the waiter a good tip.

6 Short scenes from everyday life

Mr Harris from Toronto wanted to visit the trade fair in London. After the plane had landed at Heathrow Airport, he first went to the Tourist Office.

Mr Harris	Excuse me. Can you tell me where the Tourist Office is?
Constable	Yes, sir. It's only three minutes' walk from here. Go straight on. When you reach the traffic lights, turn left and carry on until you reach the underground station. The Tourist Office is just opposite.

(At the taxi rank)

Mr Harris	Good morning. I'd like to go to the Regent Hotel. I'm in a hurry.
Taxi driver	All right, sir.
Mr Harris	How long does it take to get there?
Taxi driver	Well, about 20 minutes. We're in the middle of the rush hour.

(They arrive at the Regent Hotel.)

Mr Harris	What's the fare?
Taxi driver	£7.25.
Mr Harris	Here you are. Keep the change.
Taxi driver	Thank you, sir.

(In the hotel)

Mr Harris	Good morning. My name is Harris. Do you have any vacancies?

Receptionist	What sort of room would you like? A single or a double?
Mr Harris	A single room with breakfast.
Receptionist	That's no problem.
Mr Harris	How much is it per night?
Receptionist	Forty-eight pounds a day including breakfast.
Mr Harris	I'll take it.
Receptionist	All right, sir. How long will you be staying?
Mr Harris	Three days.
	What time do you serve breakfast?
Receptionist	From 7.00 to 10.00.
Mr Harris	What's today's exchange rate of the euro to the pound?
Receptionist	It's 1,68 euros.
Mr Harris	I'd like to cash this traveller's cheque.
Receptionist	All right, sir. May I see your passport?
Mr Harris	Yes. Here you are.
	Do you have any stamps?
Receptionist	Yes, we do.
Mr Harris	How much does it cost to send a letter to Germany.
Receptionist	36 pence.
Mr Harris	Give me two, please.
Receptionist	Here you are.
	(After three days)
Mr Harris	Will you please make up my bill and call a taxi for me for 10 o'clock?
Receptionist	All right, sir.
Mr Harris	Thank you.

COMPREHENSION TESTS

1 Have a look at the text and answer the following questions:

1. What does Mr Harris ask the constable?
2. What does the constable answer?
3. Where does taxi driver take Mr Harris?
4. Why does it take so long to get there?
5. What do you have to present if you want to cash a traveller's cheque?
6. What does Mr Harris ask the receptionist to do after a week's stay?

2 Act out the dialogue in class.

3 Complete the following sentences:

1. The tourist office is only three minutes' ... from here.
2. When you ... the traffic lights, turn left and ... until you reach the underground station.
3. The tourist office is just ... .
4. He asks the receptionist, "Do you have any ... ?"
5. Keep the ... .
6. What's the ... rate of the pound to the euro?

4 Fill in the correct preposition(s):

1. When do trains leave ... Harwich?
2. How much is a second-class return ticket ... Bristol?
3. Will you reserve a seat ... me ... the morning train.
4. Which platform does the train ... Glasgow leave ... ?
5. Is there a plane ... Manchester tonight?
6. I'll have a look ... the timetable.
7. Passengers must be ... the airport one hour ... takeoff.
8. The airport bus leaves ... 10.45 a.m.

5 Fill in one of the following adjectives opposite in meaning:

stupid, impolite, small, ugly, slow, fast

1. This gentleman is polite.   That one is ...
2. Maureen is pretty.   Claire is ...
3. Tim is intelligent.   Jack is ...
4. Roy is tall.   Hans is ...
5. This car is fast.   That is ...
6. This watch is slow.   That is ...

6 ENGLISH AND AMERICAN MONEY

The monetary unit of the United Kingdom is the pound (£) and that of the United States is the US dollar ($). The pound sterling has 100 pence. The following notes are in circulation: £5, £10, £20, £50. The US dollar has one hundred cents. American notes are: $1, $5, $10, $20, $50, $100, $500 and $1000.

1. Read the text: "English and American money".
2. Translate the text into German.
3. Ask questions on the text and answer them.
4. What is/was the monetary unit of:
   – Canada   – Italy
   – Australia   – Denmark
   – India   – Sweden
   – Japan   – Norway
   – France   – Belgium
   – Spain   – The Netherlands

Some foreign currencies

Canada
kanad. Dollar – Canadian dollar

Australia
austral. Dollar – Australian dollar

India
Rupie – rupee

Japan
Yen – yen

France – euro
franz. Franken – French franc

Spain – euro
Peseta – peseta

Italy – euro
ital. Lira – lira

Denmark
dän. Krone – Danish crown

Sweden
schwed. Krone – Swedish crown

Belgium – euro
belg. Franken – Belgian franc

The Netherlands – euro
holl. Gulden – Dutch guilder

Norway
norw. Krone – Norwegian crown

GRAMMAR AND EXERCISES

THE PAST SIMPLE – Das einfache Imperfekt / Vergangenheit

to be	to have	to ask	to go
I was *ich war* you were	I had *ich hatte* you had	I asked *ich fragte* you asked	I went *ich ging* you went
he she } was it	he she } had it	he she } asked it	he she } went it
we were you were they were	we had you had they had	we asked you asked they asked	we went you went they went

I **bought** the car last week.
We **saw** this film yesterday.
Bob **was born** on 5 May, 1972.
Anne **died** three years ago.

Der Engländer gebraucht das „past", wenn eine Handlung **abgeschlossen** ist und **zur Gegenwart keine Beziehung mehr hat**. Die abgeschlossene Handlung ist oft erkennbar an: **last week, last month, last year, yesterday, the day before yesterday, on Monday, in April**, etc.

MAN MERKE SICH

1. Das „**past**" der regelmäßigen Verben wird durch Anhängen der Endung „**ed**" an die Grundform (Infinitiv) des Verbs gebildet.

2. Bei den unregelmäßigen Verben ist die **2. Form** der Stammformen das „**past**". (to go – **went** – gone)

3. Das stumme „**e**" entfällt beim Anhängen der Endung „**ed**". (to arrive – arrived)

4. Nach **kurzem, betontem** Konsonanten wird der einfache Endkonsonant **verdoppelt**, wenn die Betonung auf der **2. Silbe** liegt. (to prefer, etc.) He prefe**rr**ed.

7 What's the past tense of:
(If you don't know, have a look on page 191.)

to begin	....	to meet	....	to see	....
to buy	....	to pay	....	to speak	....
to catch	....	to read	....	to take	....
to do	....	to sell	....	to tell	....
to give	....	to send	....	to try	....
to make	....	to say	....	to write	....

8 Make sentences according to the pattern. Use the past simple:

PATTERN

What did Ted (Alice, they) do last night? **to watch a show on BBC1**
Ted (Alice, they) watched a show on BBC1.

1. to play bingo in a pub
2. to go dancing
3. to make love to Nancy
4. to go swimming in the pool
5. to have a picnic in the forest
6. to take one's dog for walkies
7. to do the cooking
8. to collect stamps
9. to go to the football stadium
10. to work on the computer

THE WORD ORDER (2)

I met him **in London**. Ort	Die adverbiale Bestimmung des Ortes steht **am Ende**, aber auch am Anfang des Satzes.
I met him **last night**. Zeit	Die adverbiale Bestimmung der Zeit **steht am Ende**, aber auch am Anfang des Satzes.
I met him **in London last night**. Ort Zeit	Die adverbiale Bestimmung des **Ortes** steht **vor** der Umstandsbestimmung der **Zeit**.
Last night I met him **in London**. Zeit Ort	Die adverbiale Bestimmung der Zeit kann auch am **Anfang** des Satzes stehen.

9 Make complete sentences using the following words and expressions. Use the past simple.

PATTERN

The ferry / at 9 a.m. / to arrive / in Dover
The ferry arrived in Dover at 9 a.m.

1. The plane / at 7.50 p.m. / to take off / from San Francisco
2. We / at the Delta Airlines' desk / to check in / one hour before takeoff
3. A young couple / to smuggle / gold watches / to try / into the United States
4. The customs official / the suitcases / to examine / in the office
5. Roy and Alice / a caravan / to rent / on Monday / at a car-rental firm
6. They / the freeway / to take / to Los Angeles
7. They / to visit / on the way / their American friends / in Santa Barbara
8. They / after that / to drive / to the National Parks
9. They / an accident / from the Grand Canyon / twenty miles / to have
10. An ambulance / to hospital / to take / them

7 Sightseeing in London

Have you been to London yet? If not, you will, I am sure, go there as soon as possible. Let's see what Andreas and Heike, two German tourists, got to see when in London.

The day after their arrival they first went on a sightseeing tour around this lively city. The bus first passed Piccadilly Circus with its famous neon signs and its statue of Eros. There were a lot of youngsters sitting around the statue. It is said that in summer there are more foreigners than Londoners at Piccadilly Circus.

After that they reached Trafalgar Square where they got out. Some people took photos of Nelson's column or fed the many, many pigeons there. After a short break they continued the tour. They passed Buckingham Palace, the residence of the Royal Family. At Hyde Park they had another break. At Speakers' Corner, where anybody can make a speech, there were a lot of people who listened to a soapbox orator. In his speech he wanted the return of the death penalty.

From Hyde Park they turned into Oxford Street, London's busiest shopping street. Then they reached Downing Street and had a look at No 10, the residence of the British Prime Minister. From there they walked to Big Ben and the Houses of Parliament. Some tourists visited Westminster Abbey, which is just opposite, and is the coronation church of English kings and queens.

After lunch they continued sightseeing. They went to Westminster Bridge and from there on a boat trip to the City of London. They fully enjoyed it. After an hours' trip they arrived at the Tower of London, which once served as a prison and as the Royal Residence. It is a museum now. When in the Tower, you should not miss having a look at the crown jewels.

After their visit to the Tower they got onto the bus again. They passed the Bank of England and saw St Paul's Cathedral where once the wedding ceremony of Prince Charles and Lady Diana took place. At four o'clock they reached the Docklands with its many skyscrapers, high-tech companies, banks, insurance and newspaper companies. Here the sightseeing tour ended.

In the evening they went to one of the famous London pubs, which have an atmosphere of their own. It is easy to get to know other people there and the dry but fantastic British humour.

COMPREHENSION TESTS

1 Have a look at the text. Are these statements right? If not correct them.

1. Nelson's column is at Piccadilly Circus.
2. At Speakers' Corner a soapbox orator made a speech about crime and how to fight it.
3. No 10 Downing Street is the residence of the Prime Minister.
4. The Docklands is the entertainment district of London.
5. The Tower is the residence of the Royal Family.

2 Rewrite the words adding the missing letter(s):

ins . r . nce compan . s, c . r . nat . on, fam . s, orat . r, d . th pen . lty, pr . s . n, the b . s . est sho . ing str . t, off . ci . l, we . ing cer . m . ny, to make a sp . ch, cr . wn j . w . ls, to enj . y, sk . scr . per

3 Reproduce the contents of the text "Sightseeing in London".

4 Find the nouns which correspond to the following verbs:

1. to begin   ....
2. to express ....
3. to pay   ....
4. to serve   ....
5. to arrive ....
6. to visit   ....

5 What would be the correct answer?

1. **Did you go to Madame Tussaud's wax cabinet?**
   Try it again / I was there on Wednesday / that can't be true

2. **Did it rain in London yesterday?**
   It's all nonsense (Unsinn) / I'm fed up with it / (ich bin es satt) / it was raining cats and dogs (Bindfäden gießen)

3. **Was the sightseeing tour interesting?**
   It was great / it makes me sick / you are right

4. **Is Mr Sherman a good reporter?**
   It's time to go / he is a top man / my goodness!

42

424642

6 HAVING LUNCH AT A SELF-SERVICE RESTAURANT

During the break of the sightseeing tour, Andreas and Heike had lunch at a self-service restaurant.

Menu

Starters

1 Tomato soup	145p	3 Vegetable soup	130p
2 Chicken soup	155p	4 Oxtail soup	145p

Specialities of the house

5 *Hamburger*, fried onion rings and French fried potatoes   145p

6 *Bacon and eggs* (2 fried eggs, 3 rashers of bacon) grilled tomato, French fried potatoes   225p

7 *Three grilled pork sausages*, beans and mashed potatoes   205p

8 *Fried chicken* with salad and French fried potatoes   255p

9 *Fried filet of plaice* and potato salad   265p

10 *Two lamb cutlets* with garden peas and French fried potatoes   395p

11 *Grilled steak* with pineapple, salad and French fried potatoes   475p

12 *Roast beef*, Yorkshire pudding, mashed potatoes or French fried potatoes   445p

Afters

13 *Peaches and cream*   110p

14 *Pineapple and cream*   110p

15 *Fruit salad and cream*   125p

16 *Vanilla ice cream* with chocolate sauce   135p

17 *Ice cream:* strawberry, vanilla or chocolate   65p

Beverages

18 *Coffee*, black or white   75p

19 *Coffee* with cream   90p

20 *Cappuccino*   125p

21 *Espresso*   130p

22 *Pot of tea* with milk or lemon   85p

23 *Hot chocolate*   85p

24 *Soft drinks:* Pepsi Cola, Orange, Lemon, etc.   70p

Answer the following questions:

What did Heike have for lunch?		What did Andreas have?		What would you like to have?	
1. ...	14. ...	4. ...	16. ...	...	...
9. ...	22. ...	11. ...	20. ...	...	...

7 Taking the underground

Listen to the cassette and answer the following questions:
Actors: Mr Roberts, receptionist, clerk

1. What does Mr Roberts decide to do in the morning?
2. Who tells him how to get to Selfridges?
3. How can he get to Selfridges?
4. Why does he go by underground?
5. Where does he have to change?
6. Where does he get out?
7. What does he buy at the ticket office?
8. Where's the Bakerloo Line?

VOCABULARY AIDS
to decide to do sth
sich entschließen, etw. zu tun
to enquire - sich erkundigen
receptionist - Empfangschef

The underground

GRAMMAR AND EXERCISES

THE PAST CONTINUOUS – Die Verlaufsform im Imperfekt

I	was writing	a letter
you	were writing	a letter
he		
she	was writing	a letter
it		
we	were writing	a letter
you	were writing	a letter
they	were writing	a letter

Simon and Jack **were playing** chess when I arrived.
Simon und Jack spielten (gerade) Schach, als ich kam.

Sheila **was sending** a fax to Mr Pitt when Bobby phoned her.
Sheila faxte (gerade) Mr Pitt, als Bobby anrief.

While Jack **was watching** the talk show, I **was dropping** a line to Ann.
Während sich Jack die Talkshow ansah, schrieb ich an Ann ein paar Zeilen.

Man bildet das „**past continuous**" mit:

„PAST" von **to be** + ING-Form des Verbs

Man gebraucht das „**past continuous**", wenn eine **zeitlich begrenzte** Handlung (Hintergrundhandlung) **gerade** in der Vergangenheit lief, als eine **neue** begann.

Was geschah gerade, als etwas Neues begann?

Der Satz, in dem die neue Handlung beginnt und der meist durch „**when**" eingeleitet ist, steht im „**past simple**".

Soll **hervorgehoben** werden, dass **beide** Handlungen **gleichzeitig** in der Vergangenheit ablaufen, so steht in **beiden Sätzen** das „**past continuous**". Dies ist vor allem bei „**while**"-Sätzen der Fall. (Verben ohne Verlaufsform siehe Seite 16)

8 Answer the following questions according to the pattern. Use the "past continuous".

> **PATTERN**
> What were you doing when Roy arrived?
>
> – to play badminton with Harry
>
> I **was playing** badminton with Harry when Roy arrived.

1. What were you doing when Jack arrived?
   – to do one's homework
   – to quarrel with Susan
   – to read a detective story
2. What were they doing when you arrived?
   – to watch a video
   – to dance a waltz
   – to crack jokes
3. What was Mark doing when Ann arrived?
   – to phone Maureen
   – to take photos of his dog
   – to do a crossword puzzle

9 Put the verbs in brackets into the correct tenses:

> **PATTERN**
> When Tracy (to listen) to the weather forecast, she (to have) a cup of tea.
>
> When Tracy **was listening** to the weather forecast, she **had** a cup of tea.

1. I (to do) the football pools when the postman (to come).
2. Sarah (to go) to the solarium when it (to begin) to thunder.
3. While I (to play) cards, William (to puke).
4. Janet (to go) to McDonald's when she (to meet) Eileen.
5. While we (to stroll) around the shopping centre, it (to begin) to snow.
6. When I (to leave) Selfridges, I (to catch) sight of a beautiful woman.
7. While I (to try on) the jeans, the alarm system (to ring).
8. I (to get out) my credit card when two gangsters (to rush) into the store.
9. Brian (to cross) the zebra crossing when a Ford (to run) into a Mini.
10. I (to go) through the red traffic lights when a bomb (to explode).

THE POSSESSIVE PRONOUNS – Die (substantivischen) Possessivpronomen

The possessive adjectives			The possessive pronouns		
This is	**my**	CD player.	This is	**mine**.	(der/die/das/meine)
This is	**your**	CD player.	This is	**yours**.	(der/die/das/deine)
This is	**his**	CD player.	This is	**his**.	(der/die/das/seine)
This is	**her**	CD player.	This is	**hers**.	(der/die/das/ihrige)
This is	**its**	CD player (ball).	This is	**its**.	(der/die/das/seinige)
These are	**our**	CD players.	These are	**ours**.	(die unseren)
These are	**your**	CD players.	These are	**yours**.	(die euren/Ihrigen)
These are	**their**	CD players.	These are	**theirs**.	(die ihren)

This is **his** motorbike. That's **mine**. His was more expensive than **mine**. Alan showed Judith **his** slides (Dias). She showed him **hers**.

Die **adjektivischen Possessivpronomen** stehen vor einem **Substantiv**. Die **substantivischen** stehen **allein** und **ohne Artikel**. Dem **substantivischen Possessivpronomen** muss ein **Substantiv** als Stützwort **vorausgehen**.

Joyce lifted **her** hand.
Joyce hob die Hand.
Arthur pressed **his** trousers.
Arthur bügelte die Hosen.
He lost **his** life in an earthquake.
Er kam bei einem Erdbeben um.

Die **adjektivischen Possessivpronomen** werden im Gegensatz zum Deutschen bei allem gebraucht, was zu einer **Person gehört: Körperteile, Kleidungsstücke** sowie bei den Wörtern **life**, **death** und **mind**.

10 Fill in: mine, yours, his, hers, its, ours, yours, theirs

PATTERN
Is this your wallet?
No, it is... .
No, it is **his (hers)**.

1. I have lost my telephone card. Would you give me ... ?
2. Is this your bunch of keys? No, it is ... .
3. Do you have any matches? No. Take ... .
4. Are these your records? No, these are ... .
5. I have forgotten my umbrella. Would you give me ... ?
6. We introduced our friends to Ted. He introduced ... .
7. Is that your chess computer? No, it is ... .
8. Whose electric shaver is this? It is ... .
9. Whose gas lighters are these? These are ... .
10. Simon settled his bill. I settled ... .
11. They gave us their e-mail addresses. We gave them ... .
12. Irene sent me her Internet address. Mark and Sheila sent me ... .

8 Always trouble with the boss and the parents

Stephen	This is Tanja, a friend of mine from Germany. This is Bob.
Bob	Hello, Tanja. Pleased to meet you.
Tanja	Hello, Bob. Thanks for inviting me to the party.
Bob	Thanks for coming. Stephen told me that you stayed in Brighton for a fortnight.
Tanja	Yes, I did.
Bob	Where do you live in Germany?
Tanja	In Hamburg.
Bob	Do you live with your parents?
Tanja	No, I don't. I have a small flat of my own.
Bob	That's rather expensive, isn't it? In London rents are very high.
Tanja	Yes, but I want to be independent. Too much trouble with my parents, who do nothing else but criticize. I couldn't stand it anymore.
Harry	Everywhere the same. It's the generation gap.
Tanja	Since I have left home, we are on better terms with each other. And what do you do, Bob?
Bob	I'm a bank clerk. I work at the counter where people pay money into their accounts or withdraw it.
Tanja	Do you like your job?
Bob	It isn't too bad. Sometimes problems with the boss. He is a bit difficult. He often grumbles.
Harry	Would you like to dance, Tanja?
Tanja	Yes, I would.
Harry	Are you enjoying your stay in Britain?
Tanja	Yes, I am. Have you ever been to Germany?
Harry	No, I haven't. Would you like a cigarette?
Tanja	Yes, please. What do you do, Harry?
Harry	I'm unemployed at the moment. I worked as a designer in a textile factory which went bankrupt last month.

Tanja   *Oh, what a pity. Is there any chance of finding a new job?*

Harry   *I hope so. Otherwise I'll attend a computer course. There is a big demand for computer specialists.*

Tanja   *I'll keep my fingers crossed for you.*

Harry   *Thanks.*

As Tanja intended to set off for the Lake District with its wonderful mountains and valleys the next morning, she left the party early. She said goodbye to everyone and thanked Bob for the nice party.

The Lake District

COMPREHENSION TESTS

1 Have a look at the dialogue text and answer the following questions:

1. Who gave the party?
2. Where does Bob work?
3. What does he do there?
4. Why does Tanja have a small flat of her own?
5. What did Harry ask Tanja?
6. What's Harry's job?
7. What does he intend to do if he doesn't find a job?
8. What did Tanja want to do the next morning?

2 Complete the following sentences:

1. Have you .... been to Germany?
2. I'll keep my fingers .... for you.
3. Yesterday Harry .... £100 into his account.
4. Bob .... £50 from his account.
5. Did you enjoy your .... in Britain?
6. Tanja said goodbye to .... and thanked Bob for the .... party.
7.
8.
5. When going to town, Jimmy ... a ride on a doubledecker bus.
6. Would you please ... me the telephone directory? Here you are.
7. First, you must ... the area code for Sheffield and then the telephone number.
8. You have forgotten to ... coins into the slot.

3 Rewrite the words adding the missing letter(s):

invit . tion, to withdr . w money from the a . ount, in a f . rtnight, unemplo . ed, mount . n, v . lley, gr . mble, ne . essary, cert . nly, immed . tely, to set o . for sth., wonderfu ., to criti . ize

4 WORD STUDY

Fill in the correct word:
to continue, to go, to give, to have, to book, to take part, to dial, to put

1. Yesterday Linda ... two tickets for Hamlet.
2. On Sunday Sheila ... her trip to Cornwall.
3. We ... in Oliver's moonlight party.
4. Tomorrow we'll ... to the Burger Brew and have a good steak there.

5 Find the verbs which correspond to the following nouns:

invitation ....
stay ....
inspection ....
enquiry ....
building ....
information ....
arrival ....
dance ....
offer ....
sale ....

6 DISCUSSION

What do you think? Are the problems with the parents and bosses discussed in the dialogue text universal?

49

7 A LETTER TO SALLY

Dear Sally,

We are glad to hear that you have got used so quickly to the American way of life. You complain of the winter there. Well, in the northwest of the States, as in Canada, winters are cold, but the summer is coming soon.

You ask how we have been getting on in the meantime. Well, we are worried about George. He has lost his job, drinks and probably takes drugs. We hope that he will find a job soon and quickly get over it.

Best wishes

Love Mum & Dad

1. Read the letter.
2. Translate it into German.
3. What does Mum write to Sally? Say it in your own words.

GRAMMAR AND EXERCISES

THE "OF"-GENITIVE – Der „of"-Genitiv

What's the maximum speed **of** your car?
110 miles an hour.
The quality **of** this Discman is excellent.

Der „**of**"-**Genitiv** steht in der Regel, um ein Merkmal einer **Sache** zu bezeichnen.

8 Make sentences according to the pattern. Use the "of"-genitive.

PATTERN
This is the entrance (the pub).
This is the entrance (Eingang) **of** the pub.

1. What's the name (the film)? "Mandy".
2. Do you know the address (this restaurant)? No, I don't.
3. What's the price (this magazine)? £1.50.
4. Do you know the phone number (the bank)? No, I don't.
5. Do you know the title (the book)? No.
6. Who is the author (this play)? Shakespeare.
7. Do you know the end (the story)? No.
8. Did you park your car in the car park (the store)? Yes.
9. The driver (the taxi) is in a hurry.
10. Did the telephonist (the hotel) give you a wake-up call? Yes, he did.

THE "S"-GENITIVE – Der „s"-Genitiv

How to form the "s"-genitive? – Die Bildung des „s"-Genitivs

Have you seen my sister**'s** bike? Yes, I have.
(**Wrong**: Have you seen the bike of my sister?)
Have you seen these girls**'** bikes ? No.
(**Wrong**: Have you seen the bikes of these girls?)
1. This lady**'s** perfume works wonders.
2. These women**'s** hats are old-fashioned (altmodisch).
3. Charles**'s** brother is an entertainer at this hotel.

Der „**s**"-Genitiv steht **vor** dem dazugehörigen Hauptwort. Er erhält in der **Einzahl die Endung -'s;** nach dem **Mehrzahl-„s" nur den Apostroph -s'**.

Ausnahmen:
1. Das „**y**" wird **nicht** in „**ie**" verwandelt.
2. Hauptwörter, die in der Mehrzahl **kein „s"** haben, erhalten **–'s**.
3. Hauptwörter, die in der Einzahl auf „**s**" enden, erhalten **-'s**.

The use of the "s"-genitive – Die Anwendung des „s"-Genitivs

1. Is this Alan's Walkman? Yes, it is.
   Is your dog's name Lord? Yes, it is.
2. I met Mary at the grocer's (shop). (Lebensmittelhändler)
   Yesterday we visited St Paul's (cathedral).

Der „**s**"-Genitiv wird angewendet:
1. bei **Besitzangaben** von Personen und Tieren.
2. bei **Läden** wie grocer's, butcher's (Fleischerei) und **Einrichtungen** wie shop, school, college, church, cathedral, etc.

MAN MERKE SICH FERNER

1. Man findet den „**s**"-Genitiv auch bei **Länder-, Städte-** und **Ortsangaben**.
   z. B. **London's** markets are well worth a visit.
2. Der „**s**"-Genitiv steht auch bei **Zeitangaben**.
   Do you like t**his year's** fashion (Mode)?
3. Er steht außerdem, wenn es sich aus dem **Sinnzusammenhang ergibt**.
   Is this your cheque card? No, it is **Jane's**.

9 Answer the following questions by using the "s"-genitive and the following words:

PATTERN
Whose umbrella is this? – **mother**
This is **mother's** umbrella.

Whose passport is this?	Whose cars are these?	Where is Alice going to?
This is …	These are …	She is going to …
Answer with: my father, my daughter, Jimmy, Mr Smith	**Answer with:** my friends, our teachers, my colleagues, my sisters	**Answer with:** the grocer, the stag party (James), the fiancée (Roger), the meeting (these women)

THE DEMONSTRATIVE ADJECTIVES/PRONOUNS
(Die adjektivischen/substantivischen Demonstrativpronomen)

1. this – that / these – those

Singular	Plural
this boy / *dieser Junge*	**these** boys / *diese Jungen*
that boy / *jener Junge*	**those** boys / *jene Jungen*
this letter / *dieser Brief*	**these** letters / *diese Briefe*
that letter / *jener Brief*	**those** letters / *jene Briefe*

Singular: **this** – **that**
Plural: **these** – **those**

Die Demonstrativpronomen beziehen sich auf **Personen** und **Sachen**.

Der Engländer gebraucht **this** und **these**, wenn sich Personen oder Sachen am **Standort** oder in **unmittelbarer Nähe** befinden. **That** und **those**, wenn sie **weiter entfernt** sind.

2. The use of the adjective/demonstrative pronouns
(Die Anwendung der adjektivischen/substantivischen Demonstrativpronomen)

ADJEKTIVISCHER GEBRAUCH	SUBSTANTIVISCHER GEBRAUCH
Singular	**Singular**
This "bobby" was polite.	**That** one was impolite.
This story was interesting.	**That** (one) was boring.
Plural	**Plural**
These policemen were polite.	**Those** were impolite.
These stories were interesting.	**Those** were boring.

MAN MERKE SICH

Die Demonstrativpronomen können **adjektivisch** und **substantivisch** gebraucht werden.

a) Bei **adjektivischem** Gebrauch stehen sie **vor dem Substantiv**. Adjektivisch gebrauchte Demonstrativpronomen werden auch Demonstrativbegleiter genannt.

b) Bei **substantivischem** Gebrauch stehen sie **allein** als Subjekt oder Objekt.

c) Das Stützwort „**one**" muss gebraucht werden, wenn sich das Demonstrativpronomen auf bereits **zuvor genannte Personen im Singular** (nicht im Plural) bezieht. Bei **Sachen kann** „one" hinzutreten.

These are inquiries[1], **those** are offers.

Das **substantivische Demonstrativpronomen** richtet sich in der **Zahl** nach dem **Substantiv**, auf das es sich bezieht.

10 Fill in: this - that / these - those

PATTERN

... video recorder costs £300; ... one £370.
This video recorder costs £300; **that** one £370.
... cost more than £350; ... cost less.
These cost more than £350; **those** cost less.

1. .... watch is fast; .... one is slow.
   .... clocks are fast; .... are slow.
2. .... overcoat is expensive;
   .... one is quite reasonable in price.
   .... overcoats are of first-class quality;
   .... are of average quality.
3. .... bag costs £18; .... one £22.
   .... bags are rather heavy;
   .... one is light.
4. .... film is a western;
   .... one is a detective film.
   .... films are very interesting;
   .... are rather boring.
5. .... gentlemen come from Belgium;
   .... one comes from Denmark.
6. ....tourists can speak French;
   .... Italian.
7. .... student attends a technical college; .... one a university.
8. Sheila bought .... diary; I bought .... one.
9. .... cars do about 80 miles per hour;
   .... about 100 miles.
10. .... train comes from Liverpool;
    .... one from Manchester.
11. .... ticket costs £15; .... cost £18.
12. .... suitcase weighs 18 kilos; .... weigh more.

11 Translate into English:

1. Dies ist mein Taschenrechner; das ist seiner.
2. Dies sind unsere Fahrräder; das sind ihre.
3. Ist das ihre Kamera? Nein, das ist seine.
4. Gefällt dir dieses Kleid?
   Mir gefällt jenes besser. (to prefer)
5. Diese Touristen kommen aus Schottland, jene aus Wales.
6. Ich rief dieses Reisebüro an, Vivian jene.

---
[1] auch: enquiries

9 Let's go to Harrods*

Mr and Mrs Brown go shopping at Harrods.

In the stationery department
- Can I help you?
- Yes. I'd like some picture postcards of London, please.
- Here they are.
- How much are these?
- The smaller ones are 18 pence and the larger ones 25 pence.
- I'll take these six.
- All right. That's £1.60, please.

In the toy department
- Excuse me, can this doll speak?
- Yes, it can. Listen.
- Lovely, how much is it?
- £32.50
- Have you got cowboys and Red Indians?
- Yes, look here! A whole range.
- I'll take these twenty. How much are they?
- £12.50
- That's £45 altogether, please. Here you are.
- Thank you.

In the ladies' wear department
- I'm looking for a kilt.
- Here are some.
- Do you have this in size 14?
- I'll have a look. Just a minute, please. Yes, I do have one.
- How much is it?
- £55.
- May I try it on?
- Of course. Go into the changing room over there, please.
- It fits. I'll take it.
- Good.
  Do you have any change?
- I'm afraid I haven't.
- That's all right.

At the hairdresser's
- What can I do for you, sir?
- A haircut, please.
- How would you like it? Short back and sides?
- Oh no! Don't cut too much off.
- Do you want it shampooed?
- Yes, please.
- Would you like to have a shave, too?
- Yes, mind my skin, please. It's very sensitive.
- Well, that's it.
- That's okay, thank you. Goodbye.
- Goodbye, sir.

* There is something funny in the text. Try to find it out.

54

424654

COMPREHENSION TESTS

1 Have a look at the dialogue texts. Are the following statements right? If not, correct them.

1. Mr and Mrs Brown did their shopping at Selfridges.
2. The smaller picture postcards are 18 pence, the larger ones 23 pence.
3. Mrs Brown bought a pair of jeans size 16 in the ladies' wear department.
4. She had no change when she wanted to pay.
5. The doll, which she bought in the toy department, could cry.

2 Explain in your own words:

A **department store** is a place where ...

A **shop assistant** is someone who ...

A **changing room** is a room where ...

A **cowboy** is someone who ...

3 Make complete sentences:

1. Oliver / his friend / a drink / bar / to invite for
2. Arthur / his girlfriend / to pick up / at eight o'clock / in the evening
3. Janet / disco / to go to / last night
4. She / a student / to meet / there
5. Arthur / her / to a dance / to invite

4 Replace the words in bold type by one which is indicated below:

chat   to tour around
to tell   to be prepared
to drop   to increase

1. James **said to** me that he would go to Anne's party tonight.
2. I had a nice **talk** with Sandra there.
3. Last week we **went on a tour of** Wales.
4. Prices **have risen** considerably in the last few months.
5. Prices **fell** last month.
6. Roger **was ready** to pay in cash.

5 Reproduce the contents of the text "Let's go to Harrods" in a few sentences and in your own words.

6 Here you can buy everything – from a pin to an elephant

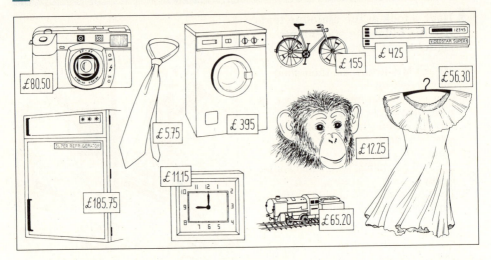

Do you agree with these prices?
What articles are those? What do they cost?

VOCABULARY AIDS
video recorder, tie – Schlips, alarm clock – Wecker, monkey – Affe, refrigerator – Kühlschrank, railway engine – Lokomotive

7 Picture story

VOCABULARY AIDS
to enter sth, counter, to pinch sth – etw. stehlen, to stand before sth, to seize sb – jmdn. fassen, thief – Dieb, cheap goods table – Grabbeltisch, store detective, to watch sb – jmdn. beobachten, to keep sth hidden – etw. versteckt halten, wall – hier: Wand

Interpret the individual pictures.
Find a suitable title for the story.

GRAMMAR AND EXERCISES

INTERROGATIVE AND NEGATIVE SENTENCES (Fragesätze und verneinte Sätze)

To be

George **is not/was not** at the fitness centre.
Is/was George at the fitness centre?
No, he **isn't/wasn't**.

„**to be**" ist ein **Hilfsverb** und wird in **Fragesätzen** und mit „**not**" verneinten Sätzen <u>nicht</u> mit „**to do**" umschrieben.

To have

Susan **does not have** (Vollverb) a baby.
Do you have (Vollverb) a mobile phone?
No, I **don't**.
Does Helen **have** (Vollverb) a mobile phone?
No, **she doesn't**.

Did you have (Vollverb) a date with Alice?
Yes, I did.
Did you have (Vollverb) a lot of fun?
Yes, **we did**.

Henry **does not** play soccer.
I **do not go** to pop concerts.
Henry **did not play** soccer.
I **did not go** to the pop concert.

Does Henry **play** soccer?
No, **he doesn't**.
Do you go to pop concerts?
No, **I don't**.
Did Henry **play** soccer?
No, **he didn't**.
Did you go to the pop concert?
No, **I didn't**.

„**to have**" kann „**Hilfsverb**" und „**Vollverb**" sein. Ist es ein **Vollverb**, so wird es in **Fragesätzen** und mit „**not**" verneinten Sätzen mit „**to do**" umschrieben.

Steht „**to have**" in Verbindung mit einem **anderen Verb** (z. B. in den zusammengesetzten Zeiten wie future, present perfect, etc.), so ist es **Hilfsverb** und wird **nicht** mit „**to do**" umschrieben.

Beispiel: <u>I haven't</u> (Hilfsverb) <u>got/ bought</u> (Vollverb) a mobile phone.

Fragesätze und mit „**not**" verneinte **Sätze** werden mit „**to do**" umschrieben, wenn das Verb ein **Vollverb** (hier: play) ist.
(Im „present" mit „**do**" und „**does**" im „past" mit „**did**".)

Die Antwort auf eine Frage erfolgt meist durch die **Kurzform**:

Yes, I do (did). Yes, I have (had).
Yes, he is (was).
No, I don't (didn't).
No, I haven't (hadn't).
No, he isn't (wasn't).

HOW TO TRANSLATE "NICHT WAHR" INTO ENGLISH (1):

Robert is a good footballer, **isn't he**? (nicht wahr)? Yes, **he is**.
Mike **has** got a Discman, **hasn't he**? (nicht wahr)? Yes, **he has**.
Alice **is** going to a yoga course, **isn't she**? (nicht wahr)? Yes, **she is**.

Wenn das Verb im Satz **ein Hilfsverb** ist, wird dieses bei der Übersetzung von „**nicht wahr**" wiederholt, und zwar zusammen mit „**not**".

8 Complete the sentences according to the pattern:

PATTERN
Harry is German, ... ? Yes, ...
Harry is German, **isn't he?** Yes, **he is.**

1. Bob is in a hurry, ... ? Yes, ...
2. Henry is engaged to Mary, ... ? Yes, ...
3. Sarah and Jack are married, ... ? No, ...
4. Anne is good at playing golf, ...? Yes, ...
5. Liz is playing squash with Thomas, ...? No, ...
6. Richard is an exporter, ... ? Yes, ...
7. He has got a nice family, ... ? Yes, ...
8. Marilyn, his wife, is a wonderful woman ... ? Yes, ...
9. They have got a son and a daughter, ... ? Yes, ...
10. They are going to have another child ... ? Yes. ... .

9 Transform the following sentences into negative and interrogative ones. Do it according to the pattern and use the present tense:

PATTERN
Jimmy has a snack in a cafeteria. (pub)
Does he have a snack in a cafeteria?
Jimmy **does not have** it in a cafeteria but in a pub.

1. Father goes to his office by underground. (bus)
2. He changes at Oxford Circus. (Bond Street)
3. He gets out at Charing Cross. (Westminster)
4. His office is three minutes' (ten minutes') walk from the underground station.
5. Dorothy and Andrew usually rent a car from the Starlight agency (Sunshine) when going on holiday.
6. This time they are spending their holidays in Florida. (California)
7. Most motels are full up in autumn. (summer)
8. Dorothy buys a guide to San Francisco. (a map of California)
9. They are enjoying their tour around Yosemite Park. (Grand Canyon)
10. When they arrive in San Francisco, they immediately see Tower Bridge. (...?)
11. They visit Fisherman's Wharf (Chinatown) in the evening.
12. The next day they drive to Dallas. (Seattle).

10 Make sentences according to the pattern. Use the past tense.

PATTERN
Sarah went to Harrods by bus.
She didn't go to Harrods by bus.
Did she go to Harrods by bus?
Yes, **she did.** No, **she didn't.**

1. Yesterday Harold went shopping in Oxford Street.
2. He bought a pair of jeans at Selfridges.
3. He tried them on in the changing room.
4. Anne bought a puzzle for Eileen in the toy department.
5. She paid in cash.
6. After that she went to the hairdresser's.
7. She had her hair shampooed and dyed.
8. Ronald lost his wallet in the store.
9. He went to the Lost Property Office at once.
10. He was lucky. He got it back.
11. Harry made a date with Nora.
12. They had a delicious meal at Baker's club.

10 An exciting football match

"What are you doing tomorrow, Henry?" "I'm going to the stadium to watch the Cup Final between Liverpool and Tottenham. Do you want to come with me?" "All right."

No Cup Final started more dramatically than this one. In the first minute Liverpool took the lead when the captain of the team scored from a penalty; but Tottenham equalized 10 minutes later. The match was often rough. Early in the second half, Liverpool's captain was severely lectured because he had kicked someone. Two Tottenham players were shown the yellow card. The match was watched by millions of TV viewers because Cup Finals are always a big event.

The last twenty minutes of the match were very exciting. Liverpool launched one attack after another. With a little more luck, Tottenham might have taken the game into extra time. But the winning goal was also scored by Liverpool's captain who blasted the ball into the net in the 89th minute.

There was a great atmosphere in the stadium; some of the fans went mad when he scored the winning goal.

After the winners had been handed the trophy, the band played the national anthem.

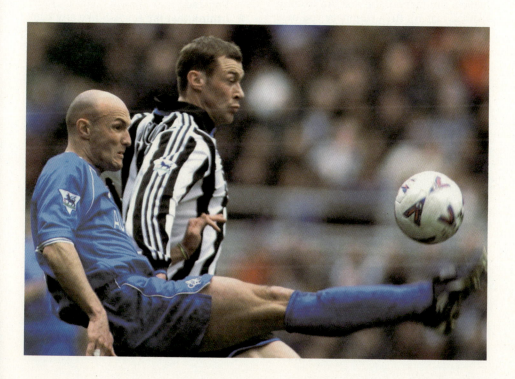

COMPREHENSION TESTS

There is a mistake in the picture.
Try to find it out!

1 Making a summary

Make a summary of the text "An exciting football match". (In a summary you only write down what is really important.)

Start the summary like this:

Henry went to the football stadium to watch the Cup Final between Tottenham and Liverpool. In the first minute Liverpool took the lead. The captain of Liverpool scored from a penalty.

Continue the summary.

2 Rewrite the words adding the missing letter(s):

dr . m . tic . l, to . o . row, the te . m,
to equ . l . ze, to be roug ., sev . rely,
v . wer, e . ent, to l . nch sth,
atm . sph . re, a . ack, tr . phy, anth . m

3 What's the opposite of:

to be lucky ... to be right ...
to be easy ... to be boring ...
to be small ... to be cheap ...

4 Replace the words in bold type by one of the following:

predominant (vorherrschend)
**to tell, to believe, to meet, nearly,
to regret** (bedauern)

1. Sports play a **very important** role in England.
2. I **think** that the English like any kind of sport.
3. Harry **said to** me that the English don't miss big sporting events.
4. The team from Birmingham had **almost** won the match.
5. We **got to know** many people at the Epsom Derby.
6. We **are sorry** to hear that a jockey has lost his life.

5 BIG SPORTING EVENTS IN BRITAIN

polite, race, dresses, famous, to watch, people, event, universities, miles

A football match between England and Scotland is a unique sporting ... (1) in Britain. The British are known as reserved and ... (2) people. But when watching such a match, they sometimes forget their good manners.

Ascot is the most fashionable of all horse ... (3) meetings. This meeting, which is always opened by the Queen, is an important social event. People say that visitors are much more interested in the hats and the ... (4) of the women than in the race itself.

Wimbledon is ... (5) for its tennis championships. Thousands of visitors ... (6) the Finals in the Centre Court and millions of ... (7) from all over the world on TV.

Another well-known sporting event is the boat race between Oxford and Cambridge ... (8). The distance of the race, which begins at Putney, is about four ... (9). Oxford won 68 times, Cambridge 72 times so far.

1. Look up the unknown words in a dictionary.
2. Fill in the gaps by using the words above.
3. Translate the text into German.
4. Your friend wants to know something about famous sporting events in Britain. What would you tell him?

GRAMMAR AND EXERCISES

THE INTERROGATIVE PRONOUNS – Die Fragepronomen

1. Who – wer

1. **Who** called the police?
   Wer rief die Polizei?
   Who sent the e-mail?
2. **Whose** wallet is this?
   Wessen Brieftasche ist dies?
   Whose parents are these?
3. **Who**(m) did you send the fax **to**?
   Wem schicktest du das Fax.
   Who(m) did you lend the money **to**?
4. **Who**(m) did you meet in the cinema?
   Who(m) did you phone last night?

1. „who" (wer) wird nur **substantivisch** gebraucht und fragt **nach Personen.**
2. „whose" – wessen?
3. „who(m) .... to" – wem?
   Im Dativ (wem?) wird das „to" in der Umgangssprache nachgestellt.
4. „**Whom**" – wen? wird in der Umgangssprache durch „**who**" wiedergegeben. („Whom" ist sehr förmlich ausgedrückt.)

2. Which – welcher (-e, -es)?

a) adjektivisch
Which boy asked the question?
Welcher Junge hat die Frage gestellt?
Which car had an accident?
Welcher Wagen hatte einen Unfall?
b) substantivisch
Which of the boys asked the question?
Welcher der Jungen hat die Frage gestellt?
Which of the cars had an accident?
Welcher der Wagen hatte einen Unfall?

„which" (welcher, -e, -es) wird **adjektivisch** und **substantivisch** gebraucht. Es bezieht sich auf **Personen** und **Sachen** und wird angewendet, wenn „welcher, -e, -es" **aus einer bestimmten Anzahl gemeint ist.**

→ „**Which**" im Sinne von „welcher, -e, -es" hat **Auswahlfunktion**.

3. What — was?

a) substantivisch
What are you doing?
Was tust du?
What is in this suitcase?
Was ist in diesem Koffer?
b) adjektivisch
What books do you prefer?
Welche (was für) Bücher bevorzugst du?
What sort of people came to the party?
Welche (was für) Leute kamen zu der Party?

„What" wird **substantivisch** und **adjektivisch** gebraucht.
a) „what" (was) fragt **beim substantivischen Gebrauch** nach **Sachen** und **steht allein**.

b) „what" (was für, welche) bezieht sich **beim adjektivischen Gebrauch auf Personen und Sachen.**
→ „**What**" im Sinne von „welche" hat **Bezeichnungsfunktion.**

6 Fill in: who, whose, which or what

1. ... does Kevin enquire about?
2. ... is that man?
3. ... car is this?
4. ... bus do you take?
5. ... of you has missed the train?
6. ... suggestion is the best?
7. ... apartment does Alice live in?
8. ... year did Charles get married (in)?
9. ... parents were against this marriage?
10. ... does your girlfriend look like?
11. ... did Ronald complain about?
12. ... have you given your word to?
13. ... proposal of marriage did Irene accept?
14. ... rang you up yesterday?
15. ... phone number do I have to dial?
16. ... is the area code for Brighton?
17. ... day of the week is it today?

INTERROGATIVE SENTENCES WITH INTERROGATIVE PRONOUNS
(Fragesätze mit Fragepronomen)

Who **knows** Sarah's address?
Which of you **drives** a MINI?
What **happened** at the airport?
aber:
Who **doesn't know** Sarah's address?
Which of you **doesn't have** a credit card?

Ist das Fragepronomen selbst **Subjekt** (hier: who, what) oder Teil des Subjekts, so wird der Fragesatz **nicht** mit „to do" umschrieben. Ist der Fragesatz jedoch **verneint**, so umschreibt man ihn mit „to do".

7 Make interrogative sentences according to the pattern:

PATTERN
Roy saw a thriller at the cinema **(who, what)**.
Who saw a thriller at the cinema?
What did Roy see?

1. Harry plays golf at weekends. **(who, when)**
2. Yesterday we saw the Tennis Finals at Wimbledon. **(where, when)**
3. Millions of people watch the Epsom Derby on TV. **(who, what)**
4. Maureen's brother won the trophy. **(who, what)**
5. Many youngsters tried to get an autograph from the pop star. **(who, what)**
6. A lot of people saw the football match. **(who, what)**
7. A terrible catastrophe happened in the football stadium yesterday. **(where, what)**
8. Many people were seriously hurt, one of them died. **(how many)**
9. Last year the Oxford boat won the boat race. **(when)**
10. They drank a toast to the health of the winners. **(what)**

THE ORDINAL NUMBERS (2)

the eleventh	(11th)	the eighteenth	(18th)	the fiftieth	(50th)
the twelfth	(12th)	the nineteenth	(19th)	the sixtieth	(60th)
the thirteenth	(13th)	the twentieth	(20th)	the seventieth	(70th)
the fourteenth	(14th)	the twenty-first	(21st)	the eightieth	(80th)
the fifteenth	(15th)	the twenty-second	(22nd)	the ninetieth	(90th)
the sixteenth	(16th)	the thirtieth	(30th)	the hundredth	(100th)
the seventeenth	(17th)	the fortieth	(40th)	the hundred and first	(101st

FRACTIONS (Brüche)

$1/4$	– a quarter
$1/3$	– a third
$1/2$	– a half
$2/5$	– two-fifths
$3\,4/7$	– **three** and **four-sevenths**

Außer $1/2$ (a half) und $1/4$ (a quarter) werden beim Nenner von Brüchen die **Ordnungszahlen** gebraucht. Im Plural erhalten sie ein „**s**".

8 Read:

This is the 2, 11, 7, 4, 1, 3, 5, 8, 16, 18, 40, 20, 12, 14, 60, 100 edition of this book.

THE DATE

	He was born on /He died on:
2000-02-03 or:	**the third of February two thousand.** **February the third, two thousand.** 3 February 2000 3rd February 2000 February 3, 2000
Informell:	3/2/00 (brit.) 2/3/00 (amerik.) Die Monatsangabe steht im Amerikanischen am Anfang.

9 Jimmy was born on:

02.05.43	31.08.74
22.06.68	04.12.95
15.01.77	07.01.00
14.11.82	14.04.00

10 Read:

$1/2$, $1/4$, $2/7$, $3/8$, $4\,2/5$, $8\,7/9$, $6\,5/6$

11 Going on a tour of South England

After the plane had landed at Heathrow, Jörg and Tanja looked for a car-rental office where they rented a "Golf". They wanted to go on a tour of the south coast which attracts millions of tourists every year. As you know, traffic drives on the left in Britain, which is a problem for many foreigners. But Jörg quickly got used to it.

First, they saw Windsor Castle, the summer residence of the Royal Family, which is about 20 miles away from London. As Eton is on the other side of the Thames, they visited the well-known Eton College. Most students from Eton later study at Oxford or Cambridge.

After a visit to Eastbourne, a lovely seaside resort on the south coast, they had a look at Beachy Head. From the "White Cliffs" you have a wonderful view of the sea and the lighthouse.

From there they drove to Bournemouth. There they enjoyed the wonderful beach with its golden sands and the marvellous shopping street, which invites you to stroll, to have a drink or to go shopping.

When they were driving through a village, they had a shocking experience. Suddenly a MINI turned into the main street; the driver was zigzagging. He must be as drunk as a Lord, thought Tanja. Fortunately, Jörg was able to stop in time.

Cornwall was the last destination on their tour. With its beautiful coastline, its mild climate and even tropical vegetation, Cornwall is another tourist attraction for the English as well as for foreign tourists.

As they had to go back to Hamburg the next day, they took the motorway from Bristol to London where this wonderful tour ended.

COMPREHENSION TESTS

1 Making a summary

Make a summary of the text:
"Going on a tour of South England".

2 Rewrite the following sentences in one sentence:

PATTERN
We had got the car - we set off for Cornwall. **(after)**
After we had got the car, we set off for Cornwall.

1. I had arrived at Eastbourne – I wrote Sarah a postcard. **(after)**
2. We went to Beachy Head – we wanted to see the White Cliffs and the lighthouse. **(because)**
3. Last week we drove to Oxford and Cambridge – we wanted to visit the two university towns. **(because)**
4. Harry took part in the excursion – he had caught a bad cold. **(though)**
5. We had dinner at a Chinese restaurant – it is well-known for its delicious Peking duck. **(which)**

3 Fill in the correct prepositions:

1. When I had arrived ... London Airport, I first went ... the Information Office.
2. I went ... bus ... the Regent Hotel.
3. The telephonist gave me a wake-up call ... 6 a.m.
4. I had a look ... the TV TIMES.
5. Tonight I'll watch a thriller ... BBC2.
6. Linda phoned me ... Sunday.
7. I had to interrupt the call because someone was knocking ... the door.
8. She said ... me that she would certainly fly ... the moon when it becomes possible.

4 What's correct?

1. Michael usually *wash/washes* his car himself.
2. Susan does the cooking. Don't disturb *her/them*.
3. *Had Thomas/did Thomas have* a drink with Janet? Yes.
4. This is the umbrella of my *father/my father's umbrella*.
5. Is this your suitcase? No, it is *her/hers*.

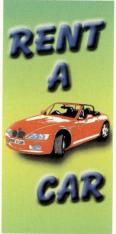

5 A MINI, PLEASE!

Listen to the cassette and answer the following questions:
Actors: Mr Hopkins, clerk

1. Where does Mr Hopkins rent a car?
2. Why does he rent a car?
3. What type of car does he rent?
4. How old are the cars of the car-rental office?
5. What does the charge include?
6. What's the charge for full insurance?
7. What did the clerk want to see?
8. What's the leaflet good for?

VOCABULARY AIDS	
car-rental office	– Autovermietung
to book in advance	– im Voraus buchen
charge	– hier: Gebühr
the mileage	– die Meilenleistung
is restricted	ist begrenzt
full insurance	– Vollkasko
driving licence	– Führerschein
contract	– Vertrag
leaflet	– Prospekt
accident	– Unfall

6 WHAT DO THE FOLLOWING ROAD SIGNS MEAN?

1. Stop and give way
2. maximum speed
3. no right turn
4. no left turn
5. give way to traffic on major road
6. ahead only
7. end of minimum speed
8. no vehicles
9. no motor vehicles
10. no stopping
11. no cycling
12. no pedestrians
13. no entry for vehicular traffic
14. minimum speed

GRAMMAR AND EXERCISES

THE "WILL"-FUTURE – Das Futur mit „will"; die Zukunft mit „will"

to be	to have	to ask	to see
I will[1] be ich werde sein you will be he she } will be it	I will[1] have ich werde haben you will have he she } will have it	I will[1] ask ich werde fragen you will ask he she } will ask it	I will[1] see ich werde sehen you will see he she } will see it
we will[1] be you will be they will be	we will[1] have you will have they will have	we will[1] ask you will ask they will ask	we will[1] see you will see they will see

I will ask Jane.
Bob will go to the party.
We will do the same.

Das Futur mit „WILL" wird gebildet mit:

| WILL | + | INFINITIV DES VERBS (ohne „to") |

1. **I'll go** on a tour of Wales in June.
   I'll do that for you.
2. In Scotland **it will be** cloudy (bewölkt) tomorrow.
   Maureen **will** certainly **follow** your advice (Rat).
   I'll help you if you need my help.

I suppose that **they will come** to see me tomorrow.

I think that he **will find** the mistake.

We are sure that **he won't do** it again.

Der Engländer verwendet das Futur mit „will":
1. bei einer **spontanen Absichts-/ Willenserklärung** oder wenn man von künftigen Handlungen oder Dingen spricht, über die man **jetzt** eine Entscheidung treffen will.
2. wenn man eine **Vorhersage** machen oder ein **Versprechen** geben will.
3. nach Verben, die in die Zukunft weisen:
   z. B. **to hope, to expect** (erwarten), **to suppose** (vermuten), **to think, to believe** (glauben), **to be afraid, to fear** (fürchten), **to be sure**, etc.

7 You and your colleagues wanted to attend a conference at the weekend, but it has been cancelled.

1. What will you do now?
2. What will Henry do now?
3. What will Bob and Sheila do now?

---

1 1. Person Singular und Plural auch I (we) shall statt I (we) will.

PATTERN

What will you (Henry/Bob and Sheila) do at the weekend?
— to go fishing
I (Henry/Bob and Sheila) will go fishing.
— to go surfing
— to take part in the excursion to Stratford-on-Avon
— to go on a tour of the Lake District
— to spend the weekend camping in Torquay
— to watch the tennis championships at Wimbledon
— to go to a party
— to relax at home

8 Translate the following sentences into English:

1. Ich werde morgen mit Jennifer zur Bank gehen.
2. Ich werde £125 auf das Konto von Mr Cowley überweisen.
3. Danach werden wir zur Post gehen.
4. Ich werde zehn Six-pence-Briefmarken kaufen.
5. Jennifer wird ein Päckchen an ihre deutsche Schreibfreundin schicken.
6. Ich werde außerdem ein Einschreiben an Mr Pillow schicken.
7. Wo ist die nächste Telefonzelle? Ich werde sie Ihnen zeigen.
8. Sie müssen zuerst Münzen in den Einwurf stecken.(to have to – future)
9. Ich werde auch an Mr Morgan faxen.
10. Ich hoffe, dass er schnell antwortet.

THE ADJECTIVE (1) – Das Adjektiv, das Eigenschaftswort

The comparison with "er" and "est" – Die Steigerung mit „er" und „est"

small – small**er** – small**est**
sincere – sincer**er** – sincer**est**
precise – precis**er** – precis**est**
clever – clever**er** – clever**est**
noble – nobl**er** – nobl**est**
narrow – narrow**er** – narrow**est**
busy – bus**ier** – bus**iest**

Mit „**er**" und „**est**" werden Adjektive gesteigert, die
a) **einsilbig sind,**
b) **zweisilbig sind** und auf der **zweiten Silbe** betont werden,
c) auf „**er**", „**le**", „**ow**" und „**y**" enden.

The comparison with "more" and "most" – Die Steigerung mit „more" und „most"

wonderful
more wonderful – **most** wonderful
important
more important – **most** important
hopeful
more hopeful – **most** hopeful
expensive
more expensive – **most** expensive
grateful
more grateful – **most** grateful

Mit „**more**" and „**most**" werden Adjektive gesteigert, die **drei- und mehrsilbig** sind, und **zweisilbige**, die auf der **ersten Silbe** betont werden.

Man merke sich:

Das deutsche „**als**" nach der ersten Steigerungsstufe heißt „**than**".

424669

9 Compare the following adjectives:

1. short
2. fine
3. large
4. important
5. hot
6. expensive
7. cheap
8. pleasant
9. easy
10. interesting
11. exciting
12. beautiful
13. thin
14. famous

10 Fill in the comparative or (and) superlative of the adjectives in brackets:

PATTERN

Maureen's suitcase weighs 12 kilos, Susan's 20 kilos and Anne's 30 kilos. Whose suitcase is ... **(light, heavy)**?

Maureen's suitcase is ... than Susan's, Anne's is ... than Maureen's.

Whose suitcase is **the lightest**, whose is **the heaviest**?

Maureen's suitcase is **lighter** than Susan's, Anne's is **heavier** than Maureen's.

1. Derek's book is ... than Mary's; Edgar's is the ... . **(interesting)**

2. This film was ... than the one we saw yesterday; the film we saw last week was the ... . **(exciting)**

3. In February it is usually ... than in March; January is often the ... month. **(cold)**

4. My stay in the Bristol Hotel was ... than that in the Eden Hotel; my stay in the Sunshine Hotel was the ... . **(pleasant)**

5. The steak which I had in the Block House was ... than that in the Burger Brew; the steaks in the Country Club are said to be the ... . **(delicious)**

6. Sheila is 21 years old, Jimmy 24 and Sarah 19. **(old, young)**

   Sarah is ... than Sheila; Jimmy is ... than Sheila, Jimmy is the ...; Sarah the ... .

7. The brown suit costs £80; the blue one £100 and the black one £115. **(cheap, expensive)**

   The brown suit is ... than the blue one; the black suit is ... than the blue one; the black one is the ...; the brown one is the ... .

8. The maximum speed of Snooky's car is 90 miles per hour; that of Helen's car is 85 miles and that of Irene's car is 110 miles per hour. **(slow, fast)**

   Snooky's car is ... than Helen's; Helen's is ... than Irene's; Irene's is the ... ; Helen's is the ... .

9. I was in New York, Dallas and Chicago last year. What do you know about the size of these cities? **(large, small)**

   New York is ... than Dallas; Dallas is ... than Chicago; Dallas is the ...; New York is the ... .

10. The distance from London to Oxford is 58 miles, that from London to Manchester 202 miles and that from London to Edinburgh 390 miles. **(long, short)**

    The distance from London to Oxford is ... than that from London to Manchester; the distance from London to Manchester is ... than that from London to Oxford. The distance from London to Edinburgh is the ... .

12 Having an accident

On the last day of her stay in Scotland, Anja had bad luck. While she was returning to Edinburgh, she had an accident.

(At the scene of the accident)

Anja	Good Heavens! You're bleeding. Do you feel any pain?
Driver	I think I've broken my leg. It hurts a lot.
Anja	I'll call an ambulance and the police. I'll be back in a minute or two.
	(On the phone)
Anja	This is Anja Hauser speaking. There has been an accident on the A 57 about two miles from Cheddam.
Voice	Is anyone injured?
Anja	Yes, the driver of the other car.
Voice	We'll call an ambulance and get there as quickly as possible.
Anja	All right.
	(At the scene of the accident)
Constable	Good morning. Was it you who called the police?
Anja	Yes.
Constable	How did it happen?
Anja	Well, the man in the Jaguar ran into my car while overtaking me.
Constable	Are you injured?
Anja	No, but I have a bad headache.

Constable	*You should consult a doctor. There's one in the next village.*
Anja	*It isn't too bad, but perhaps I'll do so.*
Constable	*May I see your passport and your driving licence?*
Anja	*Here you are.*
Constable	*Are there any witnesses?*
Anja	*No, there aren't, I'm afraid.*
Constable	*What's the registration number of the Jaguar? Oh, I can read it. It's OEF 235. Well, Miss Hauser, when the man in the Jaguar has been questioned, you'll hear from us. It seems quite clear who is to blame. Is your car okay?*
Anja	*Yes, it is. In any case, I can continue my trip.*
Constable	*Well, I think we can leave now. Goodbye.*
Anja	*Goodbye.*

COMPREHENSION TESTS

1 Have a look at the text. Answer the following questions:

1. What happened on the last day?
2. Where did it happen?
3. How did it happen?
4. Who(m) did Anja telephone?
5. Was she injured?
6. What did the policeman examine?

2 Are these statements right or wrong?

1. The driver of the Jaguar had broken his left arm.
2. There were two witnesses who saw the accident.
3. The Jaguar had an American registration number.
4. After ten minutes a doctor appeared on the scene.
5. The constable questioned the driver of the Jaguar.

3 Rewrite the words adding the missing letter(s):

to bl . d, to have a bad heada . e,
to contin . e one's trip, the w . ther (das Wetter), w . ther (ob), driving li . ence, to bl . me sb for, it s . ms qu . te cl . r

4 Fill in the correct preposition(s):

1. ... the last day ... her stay Anja had bad luck.
2. The accident was two miles ... Cheddam.
3. The constable was looking ... a witness.
4. I told him everything I could remember ... the accident.
5. A Jaguar ran ... a Ford.
6. Five miles ... the village a policeman stopped us.
7. ... ten minutes the ambulance appeared ... the scene.
8. Is there a doctor ... the next village?

5 Finding opposites:

Find the word with the opposite meaning:

1. rich ....
2. quick ....
3. possible ....
4. slow ....
5. to be interesting ....
6. to begin ....

6 WHERE DOES IT HURT?

Listen to the cassette and answer the following questions:

Actor: the doctor   **Actress:** Jane

1. Why does Jane consult a doctor?
2. Where does it hurt?
3. What does the doctor prescribe?
4. Where is the nearest chemist's?
5. What does she have to pay for the treatment?

VOCABULARY AIDS

headache – Kopfschmerzen
dizzy – schwindlig
couch – Sofa
pain – Schmerz
to prescribe – verschreiben
chemist – Apotheker
to owe sth – etw. schulden
treatment – Behandlung

7 Translate into English:

1. Wo tut es weh?
2. Tut es hier weh?
3. Ich habe hier Schmerzen.
4. Ich habe Kopf-/Halsschmerzen.
5. Ich habe Fieber.
6. Ich fühle mich sehr schlecht.
7. Mir ist schwindlig.
8. Ich glaube, ich habe die Grippe.
9. Ich bin gestürzt.
10. Muss ich in die Klinik?

GRAMMAR AND EXERCISES

THE "GOING TO"-FUTURE – Das „going to"-Futur

Sandra **is going to** write the letter after lunch.
We **are going to** take part in the open-air concert.
Mike **is going to** attend evening classes next month.
It **is going to** rain.

Das **„going to"-Future** wird gebildet mit:

| TO BE | + | GOING TO | + | INFINITIV DES VERBS |

Es wird im Gegensatz zum „will-future" verwendet, wenn **bereits zuvor** etwas **geplant war.**

Es wird ebenfalls bei **Vorhersagen** verwendet, die auch mit größter Wahrscheinlichkeit eintreten.

THE "PRESENT CONTINUOUS" – Die Verlaufsform im Präsens

I'm **leaving** for Nottingham tomorrow.
I'm **going** to Cardiff by train next week.

When **are you flying** to San Francisco?
I'm **flying** on Sunday.
I'm **meeting** Billy after the performance (Vorstellung).

Man drückt eine zukünftige Handlung durch das **„present continuous"** aus, wenn man über Dinge oder Handlungen spricht, für die man sich **bereits fest entschieden hat** oder die **bereits fest vereinbart** waren.

Um **Verwechslungen** mit **gegenwärtigen Handlungen** auszuschließen, wird meist eine **Zeitangabe** wie tomorrow, next week usw. benutzt.

Weitere Möglichkeiten, eine zukünftige Handlung auszudrücken, sind:

to be about to do sth   im Begriff sein etwas zu tun (etwas gleich tun)
(Norman **is about** to set off for Plymouth.)

das „present simple"   bei **feststehenden Terminen** wie Fahrplänen.
(The next train to Aberdeen **leaves** at 8.35 p.m.)

→ „WILL"-FUTURE UND „GOING TO"-FUTURE WERDEN IM ENGLISCHEN AM HÄUFIGSTEN VERWENDET!

8 Make sentences according to the pattern. Use the "going to"-future and if appropriate (geeignet) the "**present continuous**":

> **PATTERN**
> What **are you going to do (are you doing)** this afternoon? (I)
> – to attend evening classes at the College of Further Education in Leeds.
> **I am going to attend (I'm attending)** evening classes at the College of Further Education in Leeds this afternoon.

1. – to drop a line to Sarah (I)
2. – to show Jane the slides of my holiday in Spain (I)
3. – to watch the talk show on ITV (we)
4. – to do the gardening if weather permits (I)
5. – to listen to the pop concert (we)
6. – to play monopoly with Fred (I)
7. – to go jogging this morning (we)
8. – to go skating in Hyde Park in the afternoon (we)
9. – to make the necessary preparations for the exam (I)
10. – to swot up my maths (I)

9 Translate the following sentences into English. Put the verbs into that future tense which would be correct:

1. Morgen werde ich Kevin vom Bahnhof abholen. (bereits zuvor geplant)
2. Ich werde ihn heute Abend anrufen, um zu hören, ob alles okay ist. (spontan, nicht zuvor geplant)
3. Ich hoffe, dass er ein paar Tage bleibt.
4. Am Samstag werden wir uns das Musical „Phantom der Oper" ansehen. (bereits zuvor geplant)
5. Am Sonntag wird Carol Kevins Lieblingsgericht machen, einen Gänsebraten. (spontan, nicht zuvor geplant)
6. Montag und Dienstag werden wir Linda und Michael in ihrem Cottage in Ramsgate besuchen. (bereits zuvor geplant)
7. Ich hoffe, dass das Wetter gut ist.
8. Am Mittwoch werden wir unsere Freunde zu einer Party einladen. (spontan, nicht zuvor geplant)
9. Morgen werden wir mit unseren Kindern in den Zoo gehen. (Es ist bereits fest entschieden.)
10. Ich glaube, dass sie viel Spaß haben werden.
11. Michael ist im Begriff, zum Flugplatz zu fahren.
12. Die Maschine fliegt um 9.45 a.m. (planmäßig)

THE ADJECTIVE (2)

Irregular comparison – Unregelmäßige Steigerung

good (gut)	better	best	little (klein)	smaller	smallest
much (viel)	} more	most	bad (schlecht)		
many (viele)			evil (böse, übel)	} worse	worst
little (wenig)	less	least	ill (krank)		

older – oldest/elder – eldest

Eric is **older** than Mike. *prädikativ* My **elder** brother lives in Bristol. *attributiv* My **eldest** sister studied at London University.	„older – oldest" wird als **attributives** und **prädikatives** Adjektiv angewendet. „elder – eldest" steht nur bei **Verwandtschaftsbezeichnungen** und wird **nur attributiv** angewendet.

next – nearest

How far is the **nearest** petrol station? There is a petrol station in the **next** village.	next	– der, die, das Nächste in der **Reihenfolge**
	nearest	– der, die, das Nächste in der **Entfernung**

last – latest

You are lucky. This is the **last** catalogue. Is this the **latest** catalogue? Yes, it is.	last	– der (die, das) Letzte in der **Reihenfolge** und **zeitlich**.
	latest	– der (die, das) Letzte, Neueste **zeitlich gesehen**.

10 Fill in the adjectives in brackets according to the pattern:

PATTERN

Ann's translation is … than Joan's. **(good)** Eva's translation is … .	Ann's translation is **better** than Joan's. Eva's translation is **the best**.

1. Jennifer has made … mistakes in the test than Susan. Tommy has made … mistakes. **(many)**
2. On Wednesday the weather was … than yesterday, the day before yesterday was the … day of the week. **(bad)**
3. This matter is of … importance. I haven't the … doubt that he will manage it. **(little)**
4. Ann has saved … money than I thought. **(much/little)**
5. This overcoat is of … quality than that. I usually buy … quality. **(good)**
6. The … you have to do with him, the … it will be for you. **(little/good)**
7. Sales of this year were … than those of last year. Those of two years ago were … . **(good/bad)**
8. Do you know my … brother Jack? He is … than Mary. **(old/elder, etc.)**
9. I refer to the advertisement in the … issue of the GUARDIAN. **(last/latest)**
10. Is this the … edition of the TIMES? Yes, sir. **(last/latest)**
11. He was the … to leave the room. **(last/latest)**
12. Can you tell me the way to the … bank? Yes, I can. **(next/nearest)**
13. Where is the … bus stop? **(next/nearest)**
14. What's the … thing to do? **(next/nearest)**
15. Mr Shriver said that his … novel would be the … . **(last/latest/next)**
16. Harry's fiancée is … than his … sister. His … sister Maureen is 21 years old. **(old/eldest, etc.)**

13 Some aspects of modern British life

As in many other European countries, more and more men and women are living together without being married. Households are getting smaller and smaller because families often have only one child and because rents for flats are high. There is a strong trend to buy old houses, which are sometimes 50 and more years old and which are to be had at low prices today. On the other hand, people don't mind living 70 and more miles from their workplace in London because they can't or don't want to spend so much money on rents, which are enormously high there. Today it is unusual to find three generations living in one house. This is due to the generation gap.

Is that really possible? In Britain, people who want to drive a car take the driving test without attending a driving school? Indeed, it is. You just need someone in the car who has got a driving licence and shows you how to drive. In addition, you only need "L" plates on the front and on the back of the car. That's all.

The time of the hippies, who were against their parents' materialistic lifestyle, and also that of the punks who disliked work, is over. The young people of today want to be successful when they find a job. Money, cars, travelling and going out have again become fashionable.

COMPREHENSION TESTS

1 Have a look at the text and answer the following questions:

1. How do men and women often live today?
2. Why are households getting smaller and smaller today?
3. Why do people buy old houses today?
4. Why do people live 70 and more miles from their workplace today?
5. Name one of the consequences of the generation gap.

— — — — —

1. What were the hippies against?
2. What do you know about the punks?
3. What can you tell us about the young people of today.

2 Explain the words in bold type in your own words:

A **rent** is the price which ...
A **workplace** is a place where ...
A **driving school** is a school where ...
Generation gap means that ...

3 Complete the following sentences:

1. In Britain many men and women are living ... without being ... .
2. There is a strong ... to buy old houses.
3. Old houses are to be had at ... prices today.
4. ... are enormously high in London.
5. This is ... to the generation ... .
6. The hippies were ... their parents' ... lifestyle.
7. The punks ... work.
8. Young people want to be ... .
9. Money, cars and travelling have again become ... .
10. In Britain you can take the ... test without ... a driving school.

4 Fill in the corresponding words:

Noun	Verb	Adjective
luck	–	....
....	....	attractive
importance	–	....
....	to invite	–
decision	....	–
fashion	–	....
....	to arrive	–

5 CHANGING EATING HABITS

service   less   beer   to change   fashionable   foreign   place
boring   beef   to have

As in many other countries, a lot has ... (1) in the eating and drinking habits of the British as well. In Britain many people today prefer coffee to tea and wine to ... (2). Buying food which is frozen or in tins has become very popular because meals can quickly be prepared and are ... (3) expensive. The number of self-... (4) restaurants has risen enormously because there are more and more people who ... (5) breakfast or a snack in their lunch break or a light meal in the evening.

Since there have been Chinese, Indian, Italian and other ... (6) restaurants, which offer meals and specialities of their country at reasonable prices, going out to eat has become ... (7) in Britain, too. English food and cooking were always found a bit ... (8) and not very tasty. It is better to a have a pizza, spaghetti or lasagne, a good steak, Peking duck or an exotic meal. The traditional roast ... (9) and Yorkshire pudding, however, will always have their ... (10) among English meals, likewise turkey at Christmas.

1. Fill in one of the words given above.
2. Read the text.
3. Translate it into German.
4. Are these changes also true for Germany?

GRAMMAR AND EXERCISES

THE CONDITIONAL[1] – Das Konditional

I	would	be[2]	I	would	have	I	would	ask
ich	*würde*	*sein*	*ich*	*würde*	*haben*	*ich*	*würde*	*fragen*
you	would	be	you	would	have	you	would	ask
he			he			he		
she }	would	be	she }	would	have	she }	would	ask
it			it			it		
we	would	be[2]	we	would	have	we	would	ask
you	would	be	you	would	have	you	would	ask
they	would	be	they	would	ask	they	would	ask

I would ask him.
I would phone her.
She wouldn't do that.

Das „**Conditional**" wird gebildet mit:

WOULD + **INFINITIV DES VERBS**

▶ Die Kurzform von „I would" ist „I'd"

6 Make sentences with "I would like to ..." (I'd like to ...)
and the following verb:

I'd like to spend ...
I'd like to have ...
I'd like to go ...
I'd like to watch ...

Make sentences with "would you please ..." and the following verb:
Would you please help ...
Would you please telephone ...

Would you please try ...
Would you please answer ...

Make sentences with "would you be kind enough" and the following verb:
Would you be kind enough to show ...
Would you be kind enough to tell ...
Would you be kind enough to lend ...
Would you be kind enough to wait ...

7 Complete the following sentences so that they make sense:

PATTERN

Would you do that?	Yes, ...	No, ...
	Yes, **I would**.	No, **I wouldn't**.
Shall I bring you the menu?	If	
	If **you would**.	

1. Would you help him if he needed help? — Yes, ...
2. Shall I phone you as soon as I have heard from him? — If, ...
3. Would you start a family? — Yes, ...
4. Would you fall in love with Charly? — No, ...
5. Shall I say hello to him from you? — If, ...
6. Would Ronald help Liz out of a fix? — Yes, ...
7. Would you say it to her? — No, ...
8. Shall I explain it to you? — If, ...
9. Would Alice allow Bob to do this? — No, ...
10. Would Robert dare to do it? — Yes, ...

---

1 Auch „future in the past"
2 In der Schriftsprache findet man auch I (we) should statt I (we) would.

ADJECTIVES IN COMPARISON

Jack looks **like** his father.
Jack sieht wie sein Vater aus.
aber: He is a computer freak **as** you will know.

„**like**" im Sinne von „**wie**" steht beim **Vergleich** immer **vor** dem Substantiv oder einem Pronomen.
(**as** – „**wie**" leitet einen **Nebensatz** ein.)

This book is **as** good **as** that.
Dieses Buch ist so gut wie jenes.

as ... as – so ... wie

This book is **not as** good **as** that.
Dieses Buch ist nicht so gut wie jenes.

not as ... as – nicht so ... wie

This computer is more expensive **than** that.
Dieser Computer ist teurer als jener.

„**als**" nach der **1. Steigerungsstufe** heißt „**than**". (then – dann)

The more money you have, **the** more friends you have.
Je mehr Geld, desto mehr Freunde.

the ... **the** ... – je ... desto ...

He is getting **richer** and **richer**.
Er wird immer reicher.
He is growing **taller** and **taller**.
Er wird immer größer.

Das deutsche Wort „**immer**" vor einem gesteigerten Adjektiv wird durch **Wiederholung des gesteigerten Adjektivs** wiedergegeben.

The less you have to do with him, **the better** it will be.
Je weniger du mit ihm zu tun hast, desto besser wird es sein.

the less ... the better ...
je weniger ... desto besser

8 Fill in: than, as ... as, not as ... as, like or the ... the

1. The film we saw yesterday was ... exciting ... the one we saw last week. It was more exciting ... the one we saw on Monday.
2. Jane is older ... Catherine. She looks ... her mother.
3. Is the Guardian ... good ... the Times? People say that the Times is better ... the Guardian.
4. It's always ... that; ... more people have, ... more they want.
5. Is French wine better ... Italian? I think Italian wine is not ... good ... French wine.
6. ... more you know, ... more you will be respected.
7. Is this offer more favourable ... the first? I think it isn't ... favourable ... the first one.
8. Is this beer of better quality ... that? I think so. It tastes ... Guinness.
9. The price of this Walkman is lower ... the price of that one. This Walkman is not ... expensive ... that one.
10. Does Kevin drink more ... you? He drinks ... a fish.

MANY/MUCH

Many – viele

Do **many** people like TV?
Yes, a lot.
Peter has **a lot of** friends.
Peter hat viele Freunde.
We received **a large number** of phone calls.
Wir erhielten viele Telefonanrufe.

„**Many**" wird sowohl **substantivisch** als auch **adjektivisch** gebraucht und wird im Gegensatz zu „much" mit **Substantiven** im „**Plural**" verbunden.

„**Many**" steht in allen Satztypen. Es wird in **Aussagesätzen** auch ersetzt durch:
a lot of / lots of / a large number of / plenty of

Much – viel

How **much** time have we got?
Not **very much**.
*Wie viel Zeit haben wir?
Nicht sehr viel.*
Do you have **much** trouble with him?
A lot.
Hast du viel Ärger mit ihm? Viel.
There will be **plenty of** people at the party.
Es wird auf der Party viele Leute geben.

„**Much**" wird ebenfalls **substantivisch** und **adjektivisch** gebraucht. Es wird mit Substantiven im „**Singular**" verbunden.

„**Much**" steht in **Fragen** und **verneinten** Sätzen.

„**Much**" wird in **Aussagesätzen** ersetzt durch: *a lot of / a great deal of / plenty of*

9 Fill in: much, many, a lot of, etc.

1. Did you meet ... friends on the beach? Yes, ...
2. Does Sheila spend ... money on books? Yes, she does.
3. Were there ... people at the horse race? Yes, ...
4. Has he caused you ... trouble? Yes, he has.
5. Are there ... pictures in this catalogue? Yes, ...
6. Does he earn ... money? Yes, ...
7. Have you received ... replies to your advertisement? Yes, ...
8. Did you have ... difficulty in finding the street? Yes, I did.
9. Did you have ... fun at the party? Yes, we did.
10. Were there ... visitors at the exhibition? Yes, ...

14 A visit to an English school

John Mackinson is a teacher of German at a Grammar School in Bournemouth. As he is up to date in his teaching methods, he often invites Germans to his German lessons. Here is the talk between his pupils and a German friend.

John	This is Dörte from Germany. You are welcome to ask her any questions of general interest. If you have any trouble with your German, you may say it in English.
Pupil	Where do you live in Germany?
Dörte	In Hamburg.
Pupil	What's your job?
Dörte	I'm a trainee in a shipping company.
Pupil	Is there vocational training at German schools?
Dörte	Yes, there is. I attend a commercial school twice a week, the rest of the week I have practical training with the shipping company.
Pupil	Do you have to take an examination?
Dörte	Yes, I do. In Germany these examinations are held by the Chamber of Commerce. Do you have trainees and commercial schools in Britain, too?
Pupil	In Britain we have no vocational training as you have in Germany. Pupils who want to get a job in commerce, trade or industry attend a college of further education or a technical college, full-time. On the other hand, there are a lot of evening courses available which prepare people for a job.

Dörte	In Germany we have evening courses, too.
Pupil	Are there any unions or organisations in Germany which represent the pupils' interests?
Dörte	No, there aren't.
Pupil	By the way, your English is very good.
Dörte	Oh, no. It's rather bad.
Pupil	Now you are fishing for compliments. (Laughter) (The bell rings.)
Dörte	Thanks for your kind invitation. I really enjoyed the conversation with you.
John	Thanks for coming. It was very nice to have you here.

COMPREHENSION TESTS

1 Have a look at the text and answer the following questions: (Use a dictionary if necessary.)

1. Where and what does John Mackinson teach?
2. Where does Dörte come from?
3. What's her job?
4. What are Dörte and the pupils talking about?
5. What can you tell us about vocational training and examinations in Germany?
6. What do you know about vocational training in Britain?

to be important ....
to like sth ....
to be lucky ....
to be complete ....
to be possible ....
to be popular ....
to be necessary ....

2 Rewrite the following words adding the missing letter(s):

comm . rce and tr .de, tw . ce a week, pr . ctic . l tr . ning, evening c . rses, t . ping, t . ching meth . ds, train., to be av . lable, shi . ing c . mpan . s, l . ghter

3 Finding opposites:

Find the words with the opposite meaning by putting "in", "im", "un" or "dis" before the following words:

4 Choose the right answer:

to run the whole show
– to watch a circus show
– to manage everything
– to go halves (halbe, halbe machen)

to hit the nail (Nagel) **on the head**
– to kill someone
– This book is a real hit.
– to say exactly what is meant

to kill two birds with one stone
– to do two things at the same time
– to kill two birds (Vogel) with one stone
– to be cruel (grausam)

5 SOME OTHER ASPECTS OF ENGLISH SCHOOLS

quality   to start   famous   age   to attend   to take   to enter   to pay

In England children ... (1) school when they are five. From five to eleven they go to primary school. There are also middle schools whose pupils are between eight and fourteen.

Secondary education begins at the ... (2) of eleven. Pupils ... (3) comprehensive schools or grammar schools. There are two examinations which can be ... (4) by secondary pupils at the age of 16-18. The first leads to the GCSE (General Certificate of Secondary Education), which corresponds to our "Mittlere Reife". The second leads to A-levels, which are necessary ... (5) universities.

Public schools are attended by about 7% of English pupils. In contrast to the situation at state schools, at public schools parents have ... (6) school fees. Classes at public schools are smaller, and the ... (7) of public schools is said to be better than that of state schools. Eton College is the most ... (8) of the public schools.

1. **Fill the gaps with one of the words given above. Use a dictionary if necessary.**
2. **Read the text.**
3. **Translate it into German.**
4. **Try to compare the German school system with the English one.**

6 TALKING ABOUT EXAMS

The question of whether school exams should be abolished or not was dealt with at a round-table discussion. The following arguments were brought forward by teachers, psychologists and students. Mark the arguments **for** with (+), the arguments **against** with (-) and if you don't know with (o).

- [ ] people must work harder
- [ ] exams motivate people
- [ ] youngsters even commit suicide
- [ ] people can't show their real talents
- [ ] necessary for applications (qualifications)
- [ ] success depends on good luck
- [ ] people easily get nervous
- [ ] success satisfies
- [ ] good preparation for life
- [ ] you can't compare yourself with other people

Are you for or against exams? Give your arguments.

GRAMMAR AND EXERCISES

THE PRESENT PERFECT SIMPLE – Das einfache Perfekt

to be		to have		to ask		to go	
I	have been	I	have had	I	have asked	I	have gone
ich	*bin gewesen*	*ich*	*habe gehabt*	*ich*	*habe gefragt*	*ich*	*bin gegangen*
you	have been	you	have had	you	have asked	you	have gone
he she it	} has been	he she it	} has had	he she it	} has asked	he she it	} has gone
we	have been	we	have had	we	have asked	we	have gone
you	have been	you	have had	you	have asked	you	have gone
they	have been	they	have had	they	have asked	they	have gone

I have been.
He has had.
You have asked.
She has answered.
They have learnt.
I have written.
You have caught.

Das „**present perfect simple**" wird gebildet mit:

HAVE/HAS + **PAST PARTICIPLE (2. Partizip)**

Das „**past participle**" der regelmäßigen Verben wird durch Anhängen der Endung „**ed**" an das Verb gebildet (ask**ed**, answer**ed**). Das „**past participle**" der unregelmäßigen Verben ist die **3. Form** der Stammformen (z. B. written).

I **have** gone
  - *ich **bin** gegangen*
she **has** arrived
  - *sie **ist** angekommen*

Das „**present perfect simple**" der Verben der Bewegung **(to go, to run, to drive, to jump, to arrive u. a.)** wird im Gegensatz zum Deutschen (sein) ebenfalls mit „**to have**" gebildet.

Linda **has programmed** the computer.
Linda hat den Computer programmiert.
Look, Steve **has finished the** puzzle.
Schau, Steve ist mit dem Puzzle(spiel) fertig.
Have you seen this film?
No, I haven't.
Hast du (schon) diesen Film gesehen? Nein.

Man verwendet das „**present perfect simple**", wenn eine Handlung oder ein Vorgang/Zustand **bis jetzt/bis zum gegenwärtigen Zeitpunkt andauert** oder **gerade beendet ist.**
(Man denkt hierbei an die jetzige Auswirkung einer Handlung/eines Vorgangs oder an das Ergebnis.)
Man verwendet das „**present perfect simple**", um festzustellen, ob etwas Erfragtes **bereits (einmal) geschehen ist.**

MAN MERKE SICH

1. Man verwendet das „**present perfect simple**" in Verbindung mit folgenden **Ausdrücken/Zeitbestimmungen:**
for	seit (Zeitspanne)	**just**	gerade
since	seit (Zeitpunkt)	**never**	nie, niemals
up to now	bis jetzt	**ever**	je, jemals
not yet	noch nicht		u. a.

   (z. B. I have**n't** been to Ireland **yet**.)

2. Man verwendet es ebenfalls, wenn ein Vorgang oder ein Ereignis bereits in der **Vergangenheit** zu Ende gegangen ist, **das Ergebnis oder dessen Auswirkung** aber noch bis in die **Gegenwart** reicht (andauert).
   (z. B. Anne **has bought** a computer. Now she can do things more quickly.)

THE PRESENT PERFECT CONTINUOUS – Die Verlaufsform des Perfekts

I	have been studying law since ...	
Ich	studiere Jura seit ...	
you	have been studying ...	
he she it }	has been studying ...	
we	have been studying ...	
you	have been studying ...	
they	have been studying ..	

Ann **has been programming** the computer for five hours.
Ann programmiert den Computer (bereits) seit fünf Stunden.
Mark **has been attending** the j(i)u-jitsu course since Easter.
Mark besucht den Jiu-Jitsu-Kurs (bereits) seit Ostern.

Dennis, **I have been waiting** for you for more than half an hour!
Dennis, ich warte auf dich (schon) über eine halbe Stunde!

Das „**present perfect continuous**" wird gebildet mit:

HAVE/HAS BEEN + **ING-FORM des Verbs**

Man gebraucht das „**present perfect continuous**", wenn:
– eine Handlung oder ein Vorgang in der **Vergangenheit begann** und **bis zum gegenwärtigen Zeitpunkt** oder aber auch **darüber hinaus dauert**. (Hier wird **der Ablauf der Handlung betont**.)

– eine Handlung, Tätigkeit oder ein Geschehen als „**unendlich**" lang empfunden wird, wodurch oft eine Missbilligung, Verärgerung usw. ausgedrückt wird.

7 Make sentences according to the pattern.
a) Use the present perfect simple.

PATTERN
What has Sarah done?
– to pack her suitcase
Sarah **has packed** her suitcase.

What has Alice done?

1. to go on a tour of Majorca
2. to buy a road map of the island
3. to fill up the tank
4. to check the oil
5. to put water into the radiator
6. to cause an accident
7. to run into a Ford
8. to hitchhike back to the caravan site

b) Use the present perfect continuous.

Start the answer with the words in brackets.

PATTERN
What has Patrick been doing? (he)
– to teach French at a grammar school for several years
He **has been teaching** French at a grammar school for several years.

What has Ronald (have they/we, etc.) been doing?

1. to study chemistry at London University since February 20... (Ronald)
2. to live in Canada for twenty years (the Crofts)
3. to play ping-pong for half an hour (we)
4. to queue up for tickets for the ice revue for two hours. (they)
5. to listen to the transmission of the Olympic Games for hours. (we)
6. to watch the Football Cup Final on TV since 4 p.m. (the Mills)

8 Explain the sense of the following sentences:

1. I lost my umbrella.
   I have lost my umbrella.
2. I lent him $20.
   I have lent him $20.
3. The cat caught the mouse.
   The cat has caught the mouse.
4. Prices rose.
   Prices have risen.

9 Put the verbs in brackets into the "past", "present perfect simple" or "present perfect continuous":

1. Yesterday I (to have) lunch at McDonald's.
2. Edgar (to book) not the flight yet.
3. I (to receive) just the telegram.
4. We (to see) the musical "Hello Dolly" two weeks ago.
5. He (to be) in the States since May.
6. You already (to cash) the traveller's cheque?
7. She (to hear) not from him so far.
8. It (to happen) last week.
9. The film (to begin) already.
10. The film (to begin) five minutes ago.
11. Sally (to watch) the tennis championships on TV since 10 o'clock.
12. I (to wait) for you since 8 o'clock.
13. Andrew (to study) economics at London University since 20...
14. His friend (to take) the Bachelor of Arts degree last year.
15. Sandra (to look) for a job since January.

SINCE – FOR

„Since" kennzeichnet einen **Zeitpunkt**, „for" eine **Zeitspanne**.

10 Fill in: since or for

1. Sally has been in hospital ... ten days.
2. David has attended the holiday course ... July 1.
3. Trevor has lived in Birmingham ... half a year.
4. Trevor has been living in Birmingham ... Christmas.
5. Clifford has been listening to the concert ... 9 o' clock.
6. Clifford has been listening to the concert ... an hour.
7. He has been staying in this hotel ... two days.
8. Mr Jones has been working in Britain ... May.
9. I have known him ... two years.
10. I haven't seen him ... ages.

AGO – BEFORE

ago — vor (ein Zeitpunkt ist vorüber, liegt zurück)
before — vor (ein bestimmter Zeitpunkt **steht/liegt noch bevor**)

11 Fill in: ago or before

1. I met him at the exhibition two months ... .
2. We won't see each other ... July.
3. How long ... is it since you last saw him.
4. Linda was born two days ... Christmas.
5. I have never seen him ... .
6. I'll drop you a line ... my departure.
7. This film was shown two weeks ... .
8. That happened long ... .
9. You should have told me so ... .
10. Her father died three years ... .

15 What to do after school?

At the age of 16, young people have to decide whether they want to stay on at school or to find a job. This is a difficult decision because most of them do not know what kind of job would be the best for them. Moreover, it is difficult for them, above all for unskilled young people, to find a job because the youth unemployment rate is still rather high in Britain.

In order to help young people to have a better start in life, the Government introduced "Modern Apprenticeships", a new reform of the training system in England and Wales. "Modern Apprenticeships" offers a new opportunity for young people who leave school or college at 16 or 17 and want to get the skills and qualifications which are required to become one of the managers or technicians of tomorrow. Young people who are going to do vocational training under "Modern Apprenticeships" can choose among a lot of jobs such as banking, international trade, telecommunications, hairdressing, floristry and so on. If they decide in favour of

this new training system, there will be a training agreement between the apprentice and his or her employer. Under this new training system, apprentices get wages while they are learning. After their vocational training they get a certificate which shows employers that they can do the job to the high standard which their industry requires.

As these apprentices earn money, and as the chances of getting a job with this certificate are very good, many young people take advantage of this opportunity.

"Modern Apprenticeships" is a real chance for those who want to have a good start in working life.

COMPREHENSION TESTS

1 Making a summary

Make a summary of the text: "What to do after school?"

2 Explain in your own words:

Unskilled people are people who …
Vocational training means that someone …
The **unemployment rate** says how many …
A **manager** is a woman or a man who …

3 Rewrite the following sentences in one. Do it according to the pattern:

PATTERN

Mr Smith draws a good salary.
– he is highly qualified. **(because)**
Mr Smith draws a good salary because he is highly qualified.

1. Mr Crofts is a very popular teacher – he is very good and liberal as well. **(because)**
2. Linda goes to a foreign language school – she wants to learn English commercial correspondence. **(in order to)**
3. She works hard – it is difficult to get a good job. **(as)**
4. Sarah attends evening classes at the College of Further Education in Leeds – she wants to remain up to date. **(because)**
5. She has a full-time job – she has a family. **(although)**

4 Find the mistakes in the following sentences:

1. Last year I **have attended**/*attended* a computer course.
2. Joan learns foreign languages easier **then/than** Bob.
3. Nora has been studying economics at this university **for/since** two years.
4. Ronald **applied/has applied** for this job three days ago.
5. I think **he gets/will get** it.

COURSES

WHICH CAREER SUITS BEST?
Professional Guidance and Assessment for all ages.
15-24 yrs: Courses, Careers
25-34 yrs: Progress, Changes
35-54 yrs: Review, 2nd Careers
Full details in free brochure:–
CAREER ANALYSTS
90 Gloucester Place, W.1.
01-935 5452 (24 hrs)

TOP SECRETARIES TRAIN AT ST. ALDATES
Secretaries are in constant demand at top salaries.
St. Aldates training provides:
■ RSA and Pitmans qualifications
■ Training on the latest equipment
■ Unique training office
■ Help in finding employment
■ Supervised accommodation.
Send for details in our Prospectus.
Tel (0865) 240963
ST. ALDATES SECRETARIAL & BUSINESS COLLEGE
Rose Place (Dept. 46C) OXFORD

5 JOBS/ACTIVITIES

Find the correct combination. Answer in complete sentences:

1. a bank
2. a housewife
3. an insurance company
4. an electrician
5. an engineer
6. a computer programmer
7. an optician
8. a camera shop
9. a hairdresser
10. an exporter
11. an importer
12. a shipping company

a) – to sell cameras
b) – to produce software
c) – to construct machines
d) – to install electrical equipment
e) – to receive and pay out money
f) – to make offers to importers
g) – to import goods
h) – to ship goods
i) – to sell glasses
k) – to do the housework
l) – to insure risks
m) – to cut hair

6 STILL A MAN'S WORLD?

A German student and an English one are talking about the question of whether this world is a man's world. Here is the conversation.

pay   same   to qualify   show   jobs   work   reason   to do   lower

"What do you think, Maggie, is this world a man's world?" "It is, Inge. As statistics... (1), more than 75% of employed women do the low-level ... (2), only some get top positions." "There is also the question of equal .... (3) for men and women". "It is true that a lot has been .... (4) to achieve equal opportunities for men and women. There is a law in Great Britain under which men and women have to get equal pay for the same ... (5). As it is pretended, however, that women do not do the same work as men, women's pay is often more than 50% lower than men's pay, above all in the ... (6) -paid jobs"."That's the ... (7) in Germany. Men say that women are less ... (8)." "What a shame! The fact that women often have a family and thus have to look after their babies is the real .... (9) for discrimination." "That's the point, Maggie."

1. Look up the unknown words in a dictionary.
2. Complete the sentences with one of the words given above.
3. Read the text.
4. Translate it into German.
5. What do you think? Is our world a man's world?

GRAMMAR AND EXERCISES

THE PAST PERFECT – das Plusquamperfekt, die vollendete Vergangenheit

to be	to have	to ask
I had been *ich war gewesen* you had been he ⎫ she ⎬ had been it ⎭ we had been you had been they had been	I had had *ich hatte gehabt* you had had he ⎫ she ⎬ had had it ⎭ we had had you had had they had had	I had asked *ich hatte gefragt* you had asked he ⎫ she ⎬ had asked it ⎭ we had asked you had asked they had asked

Bildung:
Man bildet das „past perfect"
mit:

had + 2. Partizip

After Mike **had done** his shopping, he went to the hairdresser's.
The film **had** already **begun** when he arrived.
Alice **had forgotten** to phone Richard.

Man verwendet das „**past perfect**", wenn:

— ein Vorgang **bereits vor einem anderen** zu einem bestimmten Zeitpunkt in der Vergangenheit **begann oder stattgefunden** hat. (Kein Unterschied zum Deutschen.)

— Das „**past perfect**" steht häufig in Verbindung mit den Konjunktionen „**after**" und „**when**".

7 Fill in the "past perfect" or the "past".

PATTERN

to leave	After Harold .... the office, he went swimming.
to go	After Harold **had left** the office, he **went** swimming.

1. to finish, to phone — As soon as Joyce .... her work, she .... Arthur.
2. to drive off, to pick up — After Susan .... Henry, they .... .
3. to do, to go — After Marilyn .... the gardening, she .... to the solarium.
4. to read, to take — After I .... my dog for walkies, I .... a detective story.
5. to watch, to visit — I .... Alice after I .... the thriller on TV.
6. to seize, to put — The police .... Jimmy after he .... a few drinks away.
7. to have, to cause — Jack .... to pay a fine because he .... an accident.
8. to become, to order — As Dorothy .... suspicious, she .... a private detective to shadow her husband.
9. to fire, to have — She .... him because he .... an affair with her friend.
10. to happen, to hear, to feel — When I .... what ...., I .... sorry for her.

THE ADVERB (1) – Das Adverb, das Umstandswort (1)

Adjective	Adverb
quick	quick**ly**
certain	certain**ly**
beautiful	beautiful**ly**
easy	easi**ly**
possib**le**	possib**ly**
happy	happi**ly**

He translated the letter **precisely**.

– Wenn ein Adverb von einem Adjektiv abgeleitet ist, so hängt man an das Adjektiv die Endung „**ly**".
– (Endung „y" - ily)
– (Endung „le" - ly)
– „well" ist das **Adverb** von „good".
– Das Adverb antwortet auf die Frage „**wie**"; es bezieht sich meist auf ein **Vollverb**.

8 Transform the adjective which is in brackets into the adverb:

PATTERN

He did it (correct).
He did it **correctly**.

1. He works very (quick).
2. She does her work very (careful).
3. She did it quite (nice).
4. Speak more (distinct), please.
5. Walk more (slow), please.
6. He can speak English (good) .
7. Write more (clear), please.
8. He did it (prompt).
9. The train will arrive (punctual).
10. You will (certain) miss it if you don't hurry up.
11. I am (deep) interested in this book.
12. Alice will (probable) celebrate passing her exam.

9 DURING - WHILE

„**During**" ist eine **Präposition** (Verhältniswort).
„**While**" ist eine **Konjunktion** (Bindewort).

Fill in: during or while

1. ... my holidays in Scotland I often went fishing.
2. ... my vacation I went surfing as well.
3. ... I was playing cricket, Sally was playing squash.
4. ... the break I had a talk with Peter about yesterday's football match.
5. In Britain people are allowed to smoke ... the film.
6. ... the break many people have a refreshment.
7. ... I was pressing my trousers, Sarah was ironing her shirts.
8. We are open from 9.30 a.m. until 7.30 p.m. ... the week.

16 Communicating in business

Mr Newman, who works for a big import-export firm, was showing some students from the Technical College in Leeds round the firm. First, they passed Mrs Baxter's workplace. "This is Mrs Baxter. She is just faxing Fowler & Co in Dover. In a few seconds the fax will arrive there, and some minutes later Fowler & Co will answer." One of the students wanted to know what it costs to send a fax. Mr Newman said that this depended on the distance between the two fax users, and how long it took to transmit the information.

After that they came to Mr Barner, the head of the import-export department. Mr Barner was just studying the homepage of Hailey & Co on the screen. Mr Barner wanted to see whether the company had already launched their new cordless telephone on the market. As they had, Mr Newman asked him to print out the whole text about this new telephone. He wanted to see what it was like and to show it to the students. As they wanted to be the first to offer this new cordless telephone on the market, Mr Barner immediately sent an order to Hailey & Co by e-mail.

After that Mr Newman went with his visitors to the guest room in order to show them a video on the latest innovations, which had been demonstrated at the CeBIT.

COMPREHENSION TESTS

1 Have a look at the text and answer the following questions:

1. What was Mr Newman doing?
2. What was Mrs Baxter doing?
3. How long does it take for a fax to reach the addressee?
4. What did Mr Barner want to see on the homepage?
5. Why did he immediately order the new cordless telephone?
6. What was demonstrated at the CeBIT?

2 Fill in the correct preposition:

1. Mr Seller communicated ... Rover Limited by e-mail.
2. What did Jack pay ... the fax?
3. Jackson & Co sent a sales letter ... Shriver & Co.
4. Have they launched a new telephone ... the market? Yes, they have.
5. What's there ... the screen? Mr Fowler's homepage.
6. Were they interested ... this information? Yes, they were.

3 Give an alternative expression for those in bold type:

These words may be of help:
to fax, to launch, to order, to depend on

1. Mr Calder **is employed** by an insurance company.
2. He **is sending a fax to** Burns Ltd.
3. **How much is it** to send an e-mail to this company?
4. That **is dependent on** the distance and time.
5. Witney & Co **have introduced** a new Discman on the market.
6. The German importer **placed an order for** this new Discman.

VOCABULARY AIDS
advertisement – Anzeige, Inserat
perfume – Parfum
exciting scent – berauschender Duft
temptation – Versuchung
seductive – verführerisch
irresistible – unwiderstehlich
try – Versuch

4 What's correct?

1. They **have ordered/ordered** a fax machine last week.
2. Mr Finch **looks/is looking** at the homepage of Barley & Co.
3. He studies it **carefully/careful**.
4. Sarah, **which/who** is single, is a good programmer.
5. Is sending a letter by e-mail **faster/more fast** than sending one by fax?

5 ADVERTISEMENT

Oh là là

This perfume with its **exciting scent** is like **temptation, very feminine, seductive** and **irresistible**. **One try** and you will for ever say

Oh là là

Write to PERFUMA & CO
5 Main Street, Birmingham B4S 5RT
Fax: 0121-245 798
e-mail: perfu-wvd@impact.uk

6 MAKING AN ENQUIRY BY E-MAIL

Cosmetica & Co have seen an advertisement by Perfuma & Co in the magazine COSMETICS in which this company is offering its new perfume "Oh là là". As they are interested in this new perfume, they are sending the following e-mail:

Message

To: perfu-wvd@impact.uk
From: cosmetica-wvd@net.uk
Subject: Your new perfume "Oh là là"
Date: 5 April 20..   16:45
Attachments: —

Dear Sir/Madam

We have seen your advertisement in the April issue of the magazine COSMETICS in which you are offering your new perfume "Oh là là".

We are very interested in it and would be grateful if you would send us further information about it and a sample.

Yours faithfully

Alan Hurd

COSMETICA & CO
2–6 Marlow Street
London RE2P 4KL
Tel.: 0171-238 79852
Fax: 0171-238 61234
e-mail: cosmetica-wvd@net.uk

---

1. Read the text.
2. Translate it into German.
3. Ask questions on the text and answer them.

7 SUBMITTING A QUOTATION BY FAX

From: Photo Optika GmbH
        Lange Reihe 5
        20099 Hamburg
        Fax: 040-356 7591
        Date: 12 July 20   11:13
        Subject: Your enquiry of 11 July

To: Barner & Co
    12 Cockney Street
    Plymouth PL3G 3EL
    Fax: 01752-236 741

Number of pages: 1 including cover

Dear Mr Barner

We thank you for your interest shown in our products and have much pleasure in sending you our illustrated catalogue and current price list.

May we specially call your attention to our new instant camera "PINKY" on page 9 of our catalogue. This camera really makes instant photography dead easy. You simply load, shoot and you have a clean dry picture in marvellous colours, which develops before your eyes. This camera is the hit of the year.

We would be very pleased to welcome you among our customers and assure you that your order will receive our prompt and careful attention.

Yours sincerely
Photo Optika GmbH

Susanne Meister
Sales manager

1. **Read the text.**
2. **Translate it into German.**
3. **Ask questions on the text and answer them.**

GRAMMAR AND EXERCISES

THE RELATIVE PRONOUNS – Die Relativpronomen, die bezüglichen Fürwörter

Die Relativpronomen heißen im Englischen: „who", „which" und „that" (der, die, das, welcher, welche, welches) und leiten Relativsätze ein.

Who bei Personen	Which bei Sachen und Tieren	That bei Personen und Sachen	
who	which	that	der, die, das/welcher (-e, -es)
whose, of whom	whose, of which	–	dessen
to whom who(m) … to	to which which … to	–	dem/welchem
who/whom	which	that	den, die das/welchen (-e, -es)

MAN MERKE SICH

„Whom" ist die **förmliche**, „who" die **allgemein gebräuchliche** Ausdrucksweise.

Who

1. My friend, **who** lives in London, is a shop assistant.
   Mein Freund, der in London wohnt, ist Verkäufer.
2. Jimmy, **whose** dog is called Rex, likes animals.
   Jimmy, dessen Hund Rex heißt, liebt Tiere.
3. Is it Henry **who**(m) you have lent the money **to**? Yes.
   Ist es Henry, dem du das Geld geliehen hast? Ja.
4. The man **who**(m) I met in the bar is an actor.

– Der Engländer gebraucht das Relativpronomen „**who**", wenn es sich auf **Personen** bezieht. (Satz 1 – 4)
– Die „**Non-defining**"-Sätze sind eingeschobene Relativsätze, ohne die der Satz auch verständlich wäre. Sie werden in **Kommata eingeschlossen.** (Satz 1/2)
– „**Defining**"-Sätze sind **notwendig**, um den Sinn des Satzes zu erklären. Bei diesen Sätzen steht **kein Komma.** (Satz 3/4)
– Die Präposition „**to**" bei „**to whom**" tritt in der Umgangssprache an das **Ende** des Satzes. (Satz 3)

Which

He made a suggestion (Vorschlag) **which** was acceptable.

The horse **which** you bought last year won the race.

The car **whose** owner was drunk had an accident.

– Der Engländer gebraucht das Relativpronomen „**which**", wenn es sich auf **Sachen** und **Tiere** bezieht.
– Wenn sich das Relativpronomen „**which**" im **Genitiv** auf **Sachen** bezieht, verwendet man vorzugsweise **whose** statt **of which**.

That

We caught the train **that** left at 8 a.m.
This is the most beautiful love story **that** I know.
This was the first phone call **that** I received this morning.
He is the only man here **that** I know.
Everyone **that** had seen the film was fascinated (begeistert) by it.
It's always the same swear words (Kraftausdruck) **that** he uses.

— Der Engländer gebraucht das Relativpronomen „**that**", wenn es sich auf **Sachen/ Personen** bezieht. Bei Personen **bevorzugt** er jedoch das Relativpronomen „**who**" und bei Sachen „**which**".

— Das Relativpronomen „**that**" steht meistens nach:
1. **Superlativen** oder **superlativen Ausdrücken** wie: *the first, the last, the only.*
2. *all, everything, same, something, anything, much, little, nothing.*

RELATIVE CLAUSES WITHOUT A RELATIVE PRONOUN
(Relativsätze ohne Relativpronomen)

The man I got to know in a bar is an actor.

The horse you bought last year won the race.

This is the first phone call I received this morning.

Das Relativpronomen kann **fortfallen**, wenn es ein **direktes Objekt** (Akkusativ) ist und es sich um einen „**Defining**"-Satz handelt.

8 Fill in the correct relative pronoun. Decide if the relative pronoun can be left out.

1. Do you know Oliver, ... works for Harris & Co? No, I don't.
2. Joan, ... girlfriend is a nurse, is on duty.
3. Does Harry, ... you met in Bath last week, speak a lot of slang? Yes.
4. Can Sarah, ... is a stewardess at British Airways, speak several languages? Yes, she can.
5. The tourist office, ... boss you know, organised the safari, didn't it? Yes, it did.
6. Is Irene, ... is engaged to Mike, a foreign correspondent? Yes, she is.
7. All ... glitters is not gold. That's really true.
8. Is Steve, ... you had invited for a drink, a good actor? Yes, he is.
9. Claire, ... died three years ago, was a talented actress.
10. The musical ... we saw last night was excellent.
11. Have you received the parcel ... I sent you last Friday. Yes, I have.
12. You may be sure that I will do everything ... is in my power.

SOME – ANY
Some

some	– irgendein, etwas, einige	**someone**	– jemand
somebody	– jemand	**something**	– etwas

Would you give me **some** sugar, please?
Some like dark-haired women, others like blondes.
I think **somebody** has knocked (klopfen) at the door.

– „Some" wird **adjektivisch** und **substantivisch** gebraucht, die Zusammensetzungen von „some" werden nur **substantivisch** gebraucht.

– „Some" und seine Zusammensetzungen stehen meistens in **bejahenden Sätzen/Aussagesätzen.**

Any

any	– irgendein, etwas	**anyone**	– irgendeine(r), irgendjemand, jeder Beliebige
not ... any	– kein		
anybody	– irgendeine(r), irgendjemand, jeder Beliebige	**anything**	– irgendetwas, (alles) Beliebige

Do you know **any** of these youngsters? No, I don't (know **any** of them).
If you have **any** problems with Fred, please let me know.
Has **anyone** seen this film? No.

– „Any" wird **adjektivisch** und **substantivisch** gebraucht.

– „Any" und seine Zusammensetzungen stehen meistens in:

Fragesätzen
Verneinungssätzen
Bedingungssätzen (if-Sätzen)

Do you have **some** sugar, Ann? Yes, darling.

Wird auf eine Frage eine **bejahende Antwort** erwartet, so gebraucht man „some" statt „any".

9 Fill in: some, any, something, anyone, etc.

1. Are there ... tickets for Macbeth for tonight?
   You are lucky, there are still ... seats in the stalls.
2. Do you have ... photos of him? Look, here are ... .
3. Do you have ... trouble with Jimmy? If you have ..., I'll talk to him.
4. I'm looking for ... picture postcards of the Docklands. Do you have ... good ones?
5. Do you have ... change? I'm afraid, I haven't.
6. I have found ... that will certainly interest you. Really?
7. Harry has made ... good suggestions. Bob hasn't made ... . If he had made ..., we would have welcomed them.
8. Do you have ... records of Elvis Presley? Yes. Here you are.
9. Can you lend me ... money? Sorry, I can't. If I had ... , I would do so.
10. Is there ... among you who saw the accident? No, there isn't.
11. There must be ... wrong with your car. Definitely.
12. Have you had ... news from him? No, if I had had ..., I would have told you.
13. Have you got ... rooms free? I'm sorry, we haven't.
14. Has ... asked for me? Yes, Mr Smith.
15. Are there ... letters for me ? I'm afraid, there aren't ... .

 17 The Media

THE TIMES, PLEASE!

Britain is one of the classical countries for newspapers. People say that newspapers are the bread and butter of the English. It is true that the English are very fond of reading newspapers, but since prices – a copy of the TIMES costs 90 pence, the SUN 30 pence – have risen so enormously, the circulation of newspapers has sharply fallen.

When you have a look at the "quality" newspapers such as the DAILY TELEGRAPH or at the "popular" ones such as the DAILY MAIL, you will find that all of them deal with politics, sport, economics and current affairs such as catastrophes, murder, bank robbery, hijacking, drugs, etc. They also publish letters to the editor and print advertisements. This is also true for the many regional newspapers, which inform people of all that has happened in their local area. The RADIO TIMES and the TV TIMES as well as THE ECONOMIST are well-known "periodicals".

As most newspaper companies were losing money or making very small profits, a lot of them were forced to sell their companies. In order to reduce costs, the newspaper companies have modernized their plants. They have also reduced staff, which has led to sharp conflicts with the trade unions. Print workers, who once set the pages of articles, have been replaced by computers. Newspaper articles, etc. are now directly typed into computer systems.

COMPREHENSION TESTS

1 Have a look at the text and answer the following questions:

1. Name some well-known English newspapers.
2. What are newspapers for the English?
3. What does a copy of the TIMES cost?
4. What do English newspapers usually deal with?
5. Why has the circulation of newspapers sharply fallen?
6. Why were a lot of newspaper companies forced to sell their companies?
7. What can a company do to reduce costs?
8. What has led to sharp conflicts with the trade unions?

2 Rewrite the words adding the missing letter(s):

enorm . sly, circ . lation, economi . s, c . rrent aff . rs, m . rder, ro . ery, h . jacking, dr . gs, periodic . ls, region . l ar . a, to moderni . e, to p . blish, advertis . ment, edit . r

3 Replace the words which are in bold type by one given below:

to happen, to like, to increase, reputable, to have to

1. The English **are fond of** reading newspapers.
2. Prices have **risen** enormously.
3. Regional newspapers inform people of all that has **occurred** in their region.
4. The ECONOMIST is a **well-known** periodical.
5. A lot of newspaper companies were **compelled to** sell their companies.

4 Rewrite the following sentences in one sentence:

PATTERN

The circulation of newspapers has declined – Prices have risen. (as)

The circulation of newspapers has declined as prices have risen.

1. Mr Stephenson reads newspapers every morning – He is a politician. **(who)**
2. I had read the latest issue of the TV TIMES – to go out. **(when)**
3. A businessman advertises in newspapers – He wants to find new customers. **(in order to)**
4. All those people are silly – They believe in horoscopes. **(who)**
5. Newspaper readers often write letters to the editor – They want to discuss problems of common interest. **(because)**
6. Print workers were replaced by computers – The newspaper companies wanted to reduce costs. **(as)**

5 HOROSCOPE

VIRGO (Aug. 22 – Sept. 22):

The chance to make a change to your social life shouldn't be missed. Grab any such opportunity now, for you may not have the chance to do so again. Friends, relations or neighbours will be urging you to join them in doing something pleasant. Just say Yes!

What should all people born under "Virgo" do this week?

6 ASTROLOGY

Aquarius

People born under Aquarius are energetic, ambitious and creative. They want to dominate and to be successful in life. They like to have friends, but can be without company, too. They are sensitive and need romance.

1. What sign of the zodiac were you born under?
2. Does the description of the star sign match your personality?

7 WATCHING TV IN GREAT BRITAIN

For most people life without a television set is almost unthinkable. In fact, the British are just as enthusiastic about watching TV as people anywhere else.

Which of the following major TV channels would you choose when in Britain?

 *Lighter entertainment:* plays, films, humour, sport, children's programmes

 *More serious entertainment:* documentaries, discussions, operas, concerts, more serious plays

Every kind of entertainment: Current affairs, advertising, light and serious programmes

There is an even wider choice now because there is satellite and cable television. And those who dislike the current TV programme watch videos. If you want to be currently informed about the weather, traffic jams, football results, last minute flights and the like, switch on video text.

8 BBC 1 (Extracts from the programme)

9.00 a.m.	News and weather
9.30 a.m.	Inside the House (A debate in the House of Commons)
10.30 a.m.	The Muppet Show Their guest is James Coco, but what does Muppet genius (Genie) need guests for?
2.00 p.m	Tennis (Highlights from the morning's match)
3.15 p.m.	On safari in Kenya
5.50 p.m.	Sports news
8.15 p.m.	African Queen Humphrey Bogart Katherine Hepburn
1.15 a.m.	Close National anthem (Hymne)

9 LISTENING TO THE RADIO

People who prefer to listen to the radio have a wide choice. Most choose one of the four main BBC channels, each of which specializes in specific subjects.

RADIO 1	RADIO 2	RADIO 3	RADIO 4
Rock and pop music	Light entertainment Comedy Sport	Classical music Serious plays Talk on serious subjects	The main news reports Talks and discussions Documentaries Radio plays

1. What would be your favourite TV channel(s)?
2. Which TV programme(s) would you like to watch?
3. What would be your favourite radio programme(s)?

GRAMMAR AND EXERCISES

THE DEFINITE ARTICLE (2) – Der bestimmte Artikel (2)

Der Artikel fällt fort:	Der Artikel steht:
1. On **Sundays** we usually go on a trip.	**The** Sunday I got to know him was my birthday.
2. We have **breakfast** at 8 o'clock.	I prefer **the** English breakfast to the German one.
3. **Asia** is the largest continent.	**The** Asia of the 21st century will considerably differ from that of the 20th.
4. Most English kings are buried in **Westminster Abbey.**	
5. **Tea** comes from Sri Lanka.	**The** tea from Sri Lanka tastes good.
6. He led the football team to **victory**.	**The** victory **of** the football team was celebrated.
7. Bills are passed by **Parliament**.	**The** English Parliament has an old tradition.
8. **School** is over.	He is waiting in front of **the** school.
9. **Queen Elizabeth II** was crowned on June 2, 1953.	

MAN MERKE SICH

> **Der bestimmte Artikel fällt fort:**
>
> 1. bei **Wochentagen, Monaten, Jahreszeiten,** sofern diese nicht **näher bestimmt** oder **hervorgehoben** sind;
>
> 2. bei **Mahlzeiten** (supper, dinner, breakfast), sofern diese nicht **näher bestimmt** sind;
>
> 3. bei **Erdteilen, Ländern** und **Inseln**, sofern sie nicht im **Plural** stehen oder in Verbindung mit dem **of-Genitiv**;
>
> 4. bei **Straßennamen, Brücken, Plätzen, Bahnhöfen** und **Parkanlagen**;
>
> 5. bei **Stoffnamen**, sofern diese nicht **näher bestimmt** oder **hervorgehoben** sind;
>
> 6. bei **abstrakten Hauptwörtern**, sofern diese nicht **besonders hervorgehoben** werden oder mit dem **of-Genitiv** verbunden sind;
>
> 7. bei **Parliament** oder **Congress**, wenn nicht ein **bestimmtes** Parlament usw. gemeint ist;
>
> 8. bei „**school**" und „**church**", wenn man an den **Unterricht** oder den **Gottesdienst** und **nicht** an das Gebäude denkt;
>
> 9. bei **Personennamen, Titeln** und **Verwandtschaftsbezeichnungen**.

10 Decide whether the definite article must be used or not:

PATTERN
(Summer) is the most wonderful season of the year.
Summer is the most wonderful season of the year.

1. When do you play tennis? Usually on (Saturday).
2. (Monday) I was in Stratford was a bank holiday.
3. When do you have (dinner)? At about one o'clock.
4. I enjoyed (dinner) I had in the Chinese restaurant last week.
5. The train arrived at (Victoria Station) at 9.30 a.m.
6. Tomorrow I'll go to (Hyde Park), which is near (Oxford Street).
7. (Wine) is imported from France and Italy. I prefer (wine) that comes from France.
8. (School) is over.
9. Do you know (school) that had a bomb alarm last week?
10. What time does (church) begin? At 10 a.m.
11. I like (church) in your village.
12. (Health) is better than (wealth).
13. (Crime) and (violence) have above all increased in cities.
14. (Prince Philip) is the husband of (Queen) Elizabeth.
15. Have you seen (English Parliament)? Yes, I have.
16. Are the Members of (Parliament) members of a political party? On the whole, yes.
17. (Gibraltar) is still claimed by (Spanish).
18. (Europe) of the 21st century will greatly differ from that of (20th century).
19. Poland and other countries will become members of (European Union).
20. (Europe) is expected to play an important role in the 21st century.

THE INDEFINITE ARTICLE (2) – Der unbestimmte Artikel (2)

1. Mr Jones is **a** manufacturer of textiles.
   Mr Jones ist Hersteller von Textilien.

   Mr Smith is **an** Englishman.
   Mr Smith ist Engländer.

   Luther was **a** Protestant.
   Luther war Protestant.

Der unbestimmte Artikel steht im Gegensatz zum Deutschen:

1. bei Angaben über den **Beruf**, eine **Mitgliedschaft**, die **Nationalität** oder die **Konfession**;

2. This cloth costs £2 **a (per)** yard. (je oder das Yard)

   Sugar costs 45 pence **a** pound. (je oder das Pfund)

   I attend evening classes twice **a** week. (die oder pro Woche)

2. **als Zahlbegriff** bei Maß-, Gewichts- und Zeitangaben:

   je, per, pro = „a"

11 Decide whether the words in brackets require the indefinite article or not:

PATTERN

What do you do?   I'm (pilot) at Singapore Airlines.
                  I'm **a** pilot at Singapore Airlines.

1. Who is this? This is Mr Pitt.   He is (American).
2. What's your job?   I'm (reporter).
3. What's your nationality?   I'm (Italian).
4. Are you (Baptist)?   No, I'm (Catholic).
5. How many performances are there every day?   There are three (day).
6. What is Jack doing?   He is going for (walk).
7. How often do you go bowling?   Twice (week).
8. Would you say you are (European) or (Englishman)?   It is difficult to say.
9. What does this coffee cost?   £2.50 (pound)
10. What does that material cost?   £18.50 (yard)

EVERY

every – jeder, jede, jedes (adjektivisch)

everybody – jeder ⎫
everyone – jeder ⎬ substantivisch
everything – alles ⎭

Every question will be answered.
Jede Frage (jede ohne Ausnahme) wird beantwortet.

Everybody will do his very best.
Jeder (jeder ohne Ausnahme) wird sein Allerbestes tun.

Der Engländer gebraucht „**every**" und seine Zusammensetzungen, wenn

„**jeder ohne Ausnahme**"

gemeint ist. Bei „**every**" sieht man die Anzahl/Menge von Personen/Sachen in ihrer **Gesamtheit**. (Die Anzahl/Menge ist meist **unbegrenzt**.)

EACH – jeder

Each question will be answered.
*Jede (einzelne) Frage wird beantwortet.
(Die Anzahl liegt meist fest.)*

Each of these questions will be answered.
Jede dieser Fragen wird beantwortet.

Each boy wanted to try his luck.
Jeder (einzelne) Junge wollte sein Glück auf die Probe stellen.

Each of the boys wanted to try his luck.

– Der Engländer verwendet „**each**", wenn bei einer Anzahl von Personen oder bei einer Menge **jeder(-e, -es) Einzelne herausgehoben werden soll.** (Meist ist die Anzahl/Menge begrenzt.)

– „**Each**" **muss** stehen, wenn „**of**" darauf folgt. (substantivischer Gebrauch)

– „**Every**" und „**each**" sind oft austauschbar.

These stockings cost £2.60 **each** (a pair).
Diese Strümpfe kosten (je) £2,60 (das Paar).

„**Each**" wird im Sinn von „**je**" nachgestellt.

---

12 Fill in: each, every, everybody, everyone or everything

1. Did you spend your last holidays in California? Yes, I did. I enjoyed ... minute of it.
2. Twenty people have come to Catherine's party. ... of them is single.
3. What does Mr Mills sell? He sells ... needed for cars.
4. Was there an accident at the crossing? Yes. There are accidents almost ... day.
5. Did he give you some good advice? Yes, he did. He had good advice for ... of us.
6. Do you know these books? Yes. I have read ... book on that shelf. He spends ... penny on books.
7. What do these postcards cost? 20 pence ... .
8. Do you know Mr Crofts? Yes, I do. In a small village ... knows ... else.
9. Have you won in the lottery? Yes, I have. Such things don't happen ... day.
10. What can you buy in that shop over there? You can buy ... needed for camping.

18 How Great Britain is governed

The Monarchy

The monarch's role is more representative than political. She reigns but does not govern. She receives heads of government and diplomatic representatives from other countries and makes state visits abroad. She appoints and dismisses ministers on the advice of the Prime Minister. She is Commander-in-Chief of the Navy, Army and Air Force and signs Bills which have been passed by Parliament.

The Houses of Parliament and "Big Ben"

The House of Commons

The head of the House of Commons is the Speaker. The House consists of members of the political parties such as the Labour Party, the Conservatives, the Liberal Democrats, the Green Party and the Scottish Nationalists; sometimes one or two of them are independent. Its members must be at least 21 years old and are elected in general elections. The main functions of MPs are to represent the opinion of the people, to discuss political, economic, social and public affairs, to pass Bills and to control the Government's work.

The House of Lords

The House of Lords is in a state of change. For centuries the House has consisted of Lords who automatically became members. In the course of time the power of the House of Lords has been restricted more and more whereas that of the House of Commons has been increased immensely. Many people regard the House of Lords as a pure "debating" club which costs a lot of money. At the moment, the House of Lords is in a transitional phase. There is even talk that it is going to be

The Prime Minister

The Prime Minister is the political head of the country and governs it. He is the head of the Cabinet, which consists of ministers such as the Chancellor of the Exchequer, Home Secretary, Foreign Secretary, etc. He and his Cabinet are responsible for the growth and prosperity of the nation. As a rule, the leader of that political party which has won the most votes becomes Prime Minister.

COMPREHENSION TESTS

1 Have a look at the text and answer the following questions:

1. What are the main functions of the British monarch?
2. What do the Members of the House of Commons have to do?
3. What is the House of Lords regarded as by many people?
4. Name the official titles of some ministers.

2 Are these statements right? If not, correct them.

1. The British monarch is the political head of the United Kingdom.
2. The Prime Minister appoints and dismisses ministers.
3. The Members of the House of Commons are people coming from all social classes.
4. The Labour Party is in power now.

3 Rewrite the words adding the missing letter(s):

repres . nt . tive, to r . gn, to g . vern, to make a sp . ch, to app . nt sb, to di . miss sb, to di . olve, Parl . ment, the Chance . or of the Exche . er, to contro . sb, in practi . e, Secret . ry

4 Rewrite the following sentences in one:

1. The Prime Minister had made a brilliant speech in Parliament – he returned to No 10 Downing Street. **(after)**
2. The Money Bill was passed by the House of Commons – it helped to fight inflation. **(because)**
3. People are allowed to listen to debates from the Strangers' Gallery – it is in the House of Commons. **(which)**
4. Sir Winston Churchill was a great politician – he was Prime Minister in Word War II **(who)**
5. Lord Nelson was a famous admiral – he defeated his enemies in many battles. **(because)**

5 Say in a few sentences whether you would like to have a monarchy.

6 ELECTION CAMPAIGN

At an election meeting, the following arguments and counterarguments were brought forward by the political party in government and by those parties in opposition.

1. Our economy is prospering again. Exports are increasing, unemployment is declining and the pound sterling is becoming stronger and stronger.

2. Unemployment, above all youth unemployment, is much too high.

3. Schools and the National Health Service are in a bad way. There must be equal opportunities for everybody and the social services must be improved.

4. We need a good police force to protect the population against crime and violence.

5. The crime rate has risen considerably.

6. Pollution is a real danger for all of us. We are spending a lot of money to fight pollution.

7. Schools and the National Health Service have continuously been developed.

8. More or less nothing has been done to fight pollution.

1. Look up the words you don't know in a dictionary.
2. Read the individual parts.
3. Translate them into German.
4. Find out the arguments brought forward by the political party in government and the counterarguments brought forward by the parties in opposition.
5. Ask questions on the text and answer them.
6. Do we have to face the same problems in Germany?

GRAMMAR AND EXERCISES

THE PASSIVE VOICE (1) – das Passiv, die Leideform

Present Tense	Past Tense	Future Tense
I am asked *ich werde gefragt* you are asked he } she } is asked it } we are asked you are asked they are asked	I was asked *ich wurde gefragt* you were asked he } she } was asked it } we were asked you were asked they were asked	I will be asked* *ich werde gefragt werden* you will be asked he } she } will be asked it } we will be asked* you will be asked they will be asked

Conditional	Present Perfect	Past Perfect
I would be asked* *ich würde gefragt werden* you would be asked he } she } would be asked it } we would be asked* you would be asked they would be asked	I have been asked *ich bin gefragt worden* you have been asked he } she } has been asked it } we have been asked you have been asked they have been asked	I had been asked *ich war gefragt worden* you had been asked he } she } had been asked it } we had been asked you had been asked they had been asked

* In der Schriftsprache gebraucht man in der 1. Person Singular und Plural auch I (we) shall … bzw. I (we) should …

He was called by his mother.
Er wurde von seiner Mutter gerufen.
He will be called by his mother.
He has been called by his mother.
He had been called by his mother.

Der Engländer bildet das Passiv mit dem Hilfszeitwort „to be" und dem 2. Partizip.

to be + 2. Partizip

Die Präposition **„von"** beim Passiv wird im Englischen durch **„by"** wiedergegeben.

7 Put the verbs in brackets into the "present", "will-future", "conditional", "present perfect" and "past perfect":

1. I was phoned by Janet.
2. Mark was invited to Paul's birthday party.
3. Rose was given a wake-up call by Telecom.
4. Roger was interviewed by Mr Perkins.

8 Put the verbs in brackets into the tense indicated:

1. The flight to New York (to be cancelled). **(past)**
2. Cars (to be leased) by this company. **(present)**
3. The crossword puzzle (to be solved) by Irene. **(present perfect)**
4. The shirts (to be ironed) by Joan. **(future)**
5. The trousers (to be pressed) by Janet. **(past perfect)**
6. Sally (to be offered) a good post. **(present perfect)**
7. Thomas (to be introduced) to the TV reporter by Mr Fowler. **(past)**
8. The prices (to be reduced) considerably. **(past perfect)**
9. These conditions (not to be accepted) by us. **(conditional)**
10. The contract (to be signed) by Newman & Co. **(past)**
11. The offer (to be submitted) by Hurt Ltd. **(present perfect)**
12. The order (to be placed) by the English import firm. **(past perfect)**

Ich auch

Rose is a teacher, **so am I.**
Rose ist Lehrerin, ich auch.
Roy likes to flirt, **so do I.**
Roy flirtet gern, ich auch.
They went to the theatre last night, **so did we. (Wir auch.)**

Bei der Übersetzung von „ich auch" ins Englische wird das **Hilfsverb** wiederholt; das **Vollverb** wird durch „to do" ersetzt.

„Ich auch" wird durch „so" eingeleitet.

9 Fill in: "ich (er, sie, ...) auch"

PATTERN

You were at the cinema last night, ... ? Yes, ... /... .
You were at the cinema last night, **weren't you?**
Yes, **I was / So was I** (he, Anne, etc.).

1. Henry spent his summer holidays in Cornwall, ... ? Yes, .../... .
2. He took a lot of photos, ... ? Yes, .../... .
3. Vivian is going to attend a holiday course in Brighton, ... ? Yes, .../... .
4. She will live with an English family, ... ? Yes, .../... .
5. You have stayed at the Bristol Hotel in London, ... ? Yes, .../... .
6. You had part board, ... ? No, I had full board. ... .
7. You have married, ... ? Yes, .../... .
8. Your wife is going to have a baby, ... ? Yes, .../... .
9. You are invited to Harry's party, ... ? Yes, .../... .

Ich auch nicht

> Mike is not interested in this offer.
> **Nor am I.**
> *Mike ist an diesem Angebot nicht interessiert. Ich auch nicht.*
> I haven't seen him for ages.
> **Nor has Liz.**
> *Ich habe ihn seit Jahr und Tag nicht gesehen. Liz auch nicht.*
> You didn't go to the pop concert? No.
> **Nor did I.**

Bei der Übersetzung von „**ich auch nicht**" wird das **Hilfsverb** bzw. „**to do**" **wiederholt**.

Das „**nicht**" bei „**ich auch nicht**" wird durch „**nor**" wiedergegeben.

10 Fill in: "ich (er, sie, Ronald and Mary) auch nicht"

PATTERN
I can't understand him.
... .
I can't understand him.
Nor can I (he, she, Ronald and Mary).

1. I haven't been to England yet. ... .
2. I don't know Mr Blackshaw. ... .
3. She hasn't had any news from Arthur so far. ... .
4. I'm sorry, but I have no cigarettes. ... .
5. I can't believe that. ... .
6. We don't take it seriously. ... .
7. I have not (got) the foggiest idea. ... .
8. I don't care. ... .
9. He wouldn't do that. ... .
10. I wouldn't tell her the truth. ... .

19 A bloody day

A bomb exploded in a supermarket in the City of London last week. The explosion was heard five miles away. Two men and one woman died, 24 other people were seriously injured and taken to hospital. Many of them were children. The terrorist had placed the bomb behind a curtain. There was no warning before the explosion for which the IRA is held responsible.

A taxi driver who had seen the explosion said, "It all went black. I could hear people crying and screaming. First, I couldn't see anything. There was a big hole in the floor on one side of the supermarket. There was blood everywhere, a woman with her leg cut off, kids with their clothes torn."

The Home Secretary, speaking in the House of Commons, expressed his sympathy for the victims. A man, who was interviewed by a reporter after the explosion, had a short, sharp answer to bomb outrages. "There must be rigid inspections, the death penalty must be reintroduced. This will frighten them off. This is the only way to beat bombers, who are all cowards at heart".

COMPREHENSION TESTS

1 Make a summary of the text.
(Do it in your exercise book.)

2 Explain in your own words the words which are underlined:

1. An <u>exhibition</u> is a place where .....
2. A <u>guard</u> is a man who .....
3. A <u>terrorist</u> is a man who .....
4. <u>Death penalty</u> means that someone .....

3 Find the nouns which correspond to the following words:

to succeed	...	to explode	...
important	...	to advertise	...
to inspect	...	to produce	...
to improve	...	to express	...
to fascinate	...	to exhibit	...

How to translate "groß" into English:

great	– above average (Durchschnitt) in size (Größe), quantity, quality, to be famous
big	– of great size or importance (volume)
large	– considerable size or number, taking up much space (Raum, Platz)
huge	– very large, to be enormous
tall	– of persons – of more than average height (Höhe, Größe)

4 Fill in: big, great, large, huge or tall.

1. Ann has a ... family.
2. Eric is the ... man I have ever seen.
3. Ralph has ... ideas.
4. That's ... .
5. It was a ... success.
6. We had a ... meal at the Chinese restaurant.
7. London is very ... .
8. New York is ... .
9. Nelson's column is very ... .
10. Churchill was a ... politician.

5 Which is correct?

Dublin is
the capital of Ulster
the capital of the Irish Republic
a county in England

Northern Ireland (Ulster)
is independent
belongs to the United Kingdom
belongs to the Irish Republic

The capital of Northern Ireland is
Belfast
Dublin
Londonderry

112

6 NO LONGER WAR IN NORTHERN IRELAND?

bloody, to accept, success, thousands, to want, to govern, majority

It is difficult to believe that war in Northern Ireland, also called Ulster, where ... (1) of people have been killed, has come to an end.

The main reason for this ... (2) conflict between the Protestants and Catholics in Ulster was that in 1921 the island was divided into the independent Free State (the Irish Republic) with a vast ... (3) of Catholics, and Northern Ireland with a Protestant majority of 66%.

The Catholics in Ulster, who lived in misery and poverty, refused to ... (4) the partition and wanted Northern Ireland to be reunited with the Irish Republic, whereas the Protestants in Ulster, who are said to be more British than the British, ... (5) everything to stay as it is.

In the past, there have been many attempts to solve the so-called "Irish problem", but without ... (6). The attempts made by Tony Blair in 1999 seemed to have been successful. Sinn Fein, the representative of the IRA (Irish Republican Army), the Ulster Protestants, the British and Irish Governments finally came to an agreement which provided that Northern Ireland should be ... (7) by the Protestants and Catholics. Since there have been new bomb attacks, it is doubtful whether there will be peace in Northern Ireland.

1. Look up the unknown words in the dictionary.
2. Fill the gaps by using one of the words given above.
3. Read the text.
4. Translate the text into German.
5. Ask questions on the text and answer them.

GRAMMAR AND EXERCISES
THE PASSIVE VOICE (2)

Changing the active voice into the passive voice
(Verwandeln eines Aktivsatzes in einen Passivsatz)

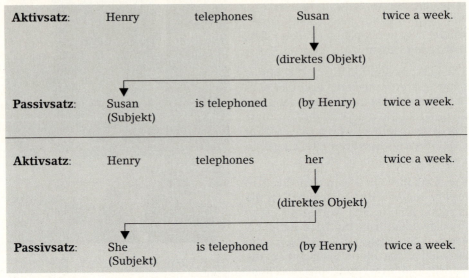

Der Engländer verwandelt einen Aktivsatz mit direktem Objekt (Akkusativ) in einen Passivsatz, indem er das **direkte Objekt** des Aktivsatzes zum **Subjekt** des Passivsatzes macht. Die Zeit des Verbs wird dabei **nicht** verändert. Das Subjekt des Aktivsatzes kann im Passivsatz mithilfe von „**by**" angefügt werden. Dies geschieht, wenn der Handelnde **ausdrücklich** genannt werden soll.

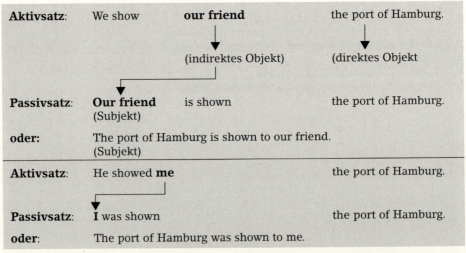

Der Engländer verwandelt einen Aktivsatz mit direktem und indirektem Objekt in einen Passivsatz, indem er das **indirekte Objekt** (ohne to) oder das **direkte Objekt** des Aktivsatzes zum **Subjekt** des Passivsatzes macht. Die Zeit des Verbs wird **nicht** verändert.

7 **Put the following sentences into the passive voice:**

1. Mr Taylor introduced me to his wife.
2. The Taylors have invited us to dinner.
3. The fans have rapturously welcomed the pop singer.
4. He also sang a lot of "evergreens".
5. He most readily gives autographs.
6. The police had stopped Mr Anderson because he was obviously drunk.
7. They arrested him.
8. A robber had stolen Mrs Jenkin's jewellery.
9. An inspector will question Mrs Jenkins.
10. He has also interrogated other hotel guests.
11. Mr Jones is sending a fax to Hopkins & Co.
12. Hopkins & Co answer it at once.
13. Bradley Bros have ordered 20 pairs of football boots from Parker Ltd.
14. The company will deliver the boots promptly.
15. They settled the invoice by cheque.

HOW TO TRANSLATE THE GERMAN "MAN" INTO ENGLISH
(Die Übersetzungsarten von „man")

One should always be tolerant.
Man sollte immer tolerant sein.

We should always be tolerant.
Man sollte immer tolerant sein.

People should always be tolerant.
Man sollte immer tolerant sein.

They maintain that he is a liar.
Man behauptet, dass er ein Lügner ist.

He was given a good position.
Man gab ihm eine gute Stellung.

one – man (sehr unpersönlich)
we – man (der Sprechende schließt sich ein)
people – man ⎫
you – man ⎬ (der Sprechende schließt sich nicht ein)
they – man ⎭

Wiedergabe durch das Passiv
(Das Objekt des deutschen Satzes wird meistens zum Subjekt des englischen Satzes.)

8 **Translate into German / English:**

1. You should think it over again.
2. We should help him out of his difficulties.
3. He is supposed to settle the matter himself.
4. It is to be hoped that everything will change for the better.
5. People say that everything has changed for the worse.
6. He is said to have cancer.
7. The doctor was sent for.
8. Man hätte es ihm sagen sollen.
9. Man vermutet, dass Steve es getan hat.
10. Man versuchte ihm zu helfen.
11. Man sagt, dass Sheila einen Unfall gehabt hat.
12. Man hätte sich um sie kümmern sollen.
13. Man hofft, dass er die Angelegenheit zu unserer vollen Zufriedenheit regelt.
14. Man kann niemals wissen.
15. Man sollte nichts unversucht lassen.

20 Great Britain and its ethnic minorities

When in Britain, above all in London, you will find that there are a lot of coloured people and foreigners there. Where do they come from? Most of them come from the Commonwealth countries such as India, Pakistan, the West Indies, etc., others from various European countries where the unemployment rate is very high and the standard of living very low.

Masses of Commonwealth citizens flooded into Great Britain in the 1960s and 70s when the economic situation in their countries was getting worse and worse, and when it was rather easier to emigrate to Britain. These immigrants, who wanted to try their luck in Britain, quickly realized, however, that it was very difficult for them to find work and accommodation there, and that coloured people are discriminated against. This is certainly true, but, on the other hand, it should not be forgotten that this is not only due to their colour, but also to the fact that different customs, traditions, religions and finally the language barrier have made it difficult for them to be fully accepted.

As they have to take the lowest paid jobs, social unrest and bitterness have been growing among them. If the British Government fails to introduce effective laws to protect them and does not create new jobs, above all for coloured youngsters, crime and violence will continue to increase.

COMPREHENSION TESTS

1 Have a look at the text and answer the following questions:

1. Why have a lot of coloured people and foreigners emigrated to Britain?
2. Where do these people come from?
3. Why did masses of coloured people leave their countries in the 1960s and 70s?
4. What did the immigrants realize very quickly?
5. What makes it difficult for coloured people to be fully accepted?
6. When will crime and violence continue to increase?

2 Rewrite the words adding the missing letter(s):

for . gner, v . rious, stand . rd of li . ing, citi . en, to e . igrate, to i . igrate, to real . ze, a . o . odation, . ertainly, cust . ms, lang . age ba . ier, to introd . ce l . ws, viol . nce, to incr . se

3 Test your vocabulary by filling in appropriate (passend) words:

1. Henry Singh, who ... from India, emigrated to Britain in 1970.
2. When he ... in London, the difficulties started.
3. After some time he managed to get a ... as a dustman.
4. He worked hard, for he wanted to ... a little shop, to meet a ... and to have children one day.
5. He opened a tobacconist's shop in a ... of London where coloured people ... .
6. He sent his children to a good school in order to give them better ... .
7. He realized very ... that there is some discrimination against ... people.
8. Crime and violence will continue to ... unless the Government ... laws to protect them.

4 Fill in: **hard** (schwer) or **hardly** (kaum)

1. I need ... say that I dislike his behaviour.
2. Jimmy has worked ... all his life.
3. He is a ... worker.
4. He tried ... to be successful.
5. You can ... expect me to lend you money again.
6. I am so tired, I can ... walk.
7. That's ...-earned money.
8. I ... know him.

117

Sydney

5 A GLANCE AT THE COMMONWEALTH OF NATIONS

century, head, language, to obtain, to call, independent

The Commonwealth of Nations is a free association of sovereign independent states, which recognize the British monarch as their ... (1). In the 17th ... (2) the British began to found colonies in Canada, Australia, India, Ceylon[1], New Zealand, Nigeria, etc. and thus established the British Empire, which is now ... (3) the "Commonwealth of Nations".

In the 19th century the colonies wanted to become free, that is to say to become politically and economically ... (4) of Britain. Since more or less all the Commonwealth countries have meanwhile ... (5) their political and economic independence – Hong Kong was returned to China in 1997 – and Britain has been a member of the EC, now EU, the ties between them have become looser and looser. One thing that still links them together is the English ... (6), which is an official language in almost all the member countries.

1. Complete the sentences by using one of the words given above. Use a dictionary if necessary.
2. Read the text.
3. Translate the text into German.
4. Ask questions on the text and answer them.
5. Reproduce the most important facts in the text: "A glance at the Commonwealth of Nations".

---

[1] now Sri Lanka

GRAMMAR AND EXERCISES
REVISION OF THE MOST IMPORTANT TENSES

	Diese Zeiten werden, kurz gesagt, gebraucht, wenn:
Present simple	etwas **immer/ständig/regelmäßig** so ist.
Present continuous	etwas **gerade in diesem Augenblick** geschieht.
Past simple	eine Handlung in der **Vergangenheit abgeschlossen** war.
Past continuous	eine Handlung **gerade lief,** als eine **neue begann**. (Bei der neuen Handlung steht das **past tense**.)
"Will"-future	man etwas **spontan** zu machen gedenkt, also etwas **nicht bereits zuvor** geplant war. Nach Verben wie: to think, to hope, to suppose, etc.
"Going to"-future	man etwas zu tun gedenkt, was **bereits zuvor geplant** war.
Present perfect simple	eine Handlung bereits **in der Vergangenheit begann** und **bis jetzt** andauert. (Dauert die Handlung noch weiter an, so verwendet man das „**Present perfect continuous**".)

6 What do the individual (einzelnen) **sentences express?**

1. Roger plays chess.
2. Roger is playing chess with Henry.
3. Roger was playing chess with Henry when I arrived.
4. Roger will play chess with Henry.
5. Roger is going to play chess with Henry.
6. Roger has played chess with Henry.

7 Translate the following sentences into English:

1. Die Katze fing die Maus.
2. Katzen fangen Mäuse.
3. Schau, die Katze hat die Maus gefangen.
4. Ich bin sicher, die Katze wird die Maus fangen.
5. Schau, die Katze fängt die Maus.
6. Der Reporter interviewt Mr Hicks.
7. Der Reporter hat Mr H. interviewt.
8. Der Reporter wird Mr H. interviewen.
9. Der Reporter hatte Mr H. interviewt.
10. Reporter interviewen Leute.

IRREGULAR VERBS (page 191)

8 Fill the gaps.

...	taught	...	...	sold	...
...	...	built	...	...	spent
to go	...	...	to know	...	...
...	chose	...	...	told	...
...	...	fled	...	...	taken
to write	...	...	to write	...	...
...	bought	...	...	drew	...
...	...	caught	...	...	begun
to come	...	...	to eat	...	...
...	led	...	...	fought	...
...	...	lost	...	...	laid
to drive	...	...	to give	...	...

9 Fill in the appropriate tense or form of the verbs in line with the pattern:

PATTERN

to be, to spend

Hello Irene! Have you ... to Britain yet?
No, I haven't. I ... in France last year.
Next year I'll ... my holidays in England.

Hello Irene! Have you **been** to Britain yet?
No, I haven't. I **was** in France last year.
Next year I'll **spend** my holidays in England.

1. **to know, to meet, to make**
   Do you ... Mr Calder? Yes, I do. Where did you ... him? I ... him at an exhibition in London last year. Did you ... friends there. Yes, I did.

2. **to go, to buy, to pay**
   Yesterday I ... shopping at Selfridges. What did you ... ? I ... a lot of things. Did you ... in cash or by cheque? I ... by credit card.

3. **to be, to do, to see**
   What did you ... last night? I ... at the cinema. What did you ... ? I ... "Ladykillers".

4. **to fly, to think, to hear, to send**
   How did Alice go to Edinburgh? She ... . When did she ... ? I ... last week. Have you ... from her yet? Yes, she ... me a picture postcard.

5. **to leave, to tell, to think, to be**
   Why have you ... your wife? Who on earth has ... you that? Alice. She must ... out of her mind. I have never ... of leaving her.

6. **to take, to lose, to see, to get**
   My goodness! I have ... my key. When did you ... it last? I remember, the bar was the last place where I ... it out. Perhaps, you will ... it back.

7. **to sell, to buy, to take**
   Why did you ... your car? I wanted to ... a new one. As Jack offered a good price, I ... the opportunity to sell it.

8. **to forget, to begin, to drive, to get**
   My goodness. I have ... the tickets. That can't be true. When does the horse race ...? At ten o'clock. Well, time enough to ... back and to ... them.

9. **to give, to drink, to think**
   What's wrong with you? My boss ... me the sack. He ... I ... too much and too often. Are you often ... ?

10. **to fall, to hurt, to break**
    What has happened to you? Did you ... down? Have you ... yourself? Yes, I have. I think I have ... my arm.

21 Let's have a look at the British economy

As a member of the "Group of Seven", Great Britain is one of the most important economic countries in the world.

In the last thirty years there has been a great change in the structures of the British economy. While the North of England was the centre of British industry until the 1960s, it is now Greater London and the South of England, especially the South-East. A great number of automobile, aerospace, electronic companies, etc. which enjoy a worldwide reputation have settled above all near the M4 motorway.

There has been another big change. As in other industrial countries, especially the heavy, shipbuilding and textile industries have greatly lost in importance. Ships, textiles and other products, mainly those from the Far East, are produced there at much lower cost. In contrast to this, expansion has been particularly rapid in the chemical, engineering and electronics industries. Telecommunications, Internet and other new technologies are going to revolutionize our life.

As competition has become stiffer on the world market, the trend towards merging with other big international companies or swallowing them up is getting stronger and stronger. The takeovers of British companies such as Jaguar, for instance, are sufficient evidence of this development. Globalization is now the new challenge. Thanks to high standards in technology, reduced production costs, the strong pound sterling and, last but not least, considerable foreign investments, Great Britain will certainly master this new challenge.

Nuclear power station

COMPREHENSION TESTS

Electrostatic accelerator

1 Have a look at the text and answer the following questions:

1. What "Group" does Great Britain belong to?
2. What changes have taken place in Great Britain's economy/industry?
3. Why have the British shipbuilding and textile industries greatly lost in importance?
4. What companies are to be found near the M4 motorway?
5. Why have big companies merged or even been swallowed up by others?
6. Why will Great Britain be able to master the new challenge "globalization"?

2 Explain in your own words:

1. <u>Heavy industries</u> are ...
2. A <u>motorway</u> is a road where ...
3. <u>To merge</u> means that ...
4. <u>To be swallowed up</u> means that ...

3 Rewrite the following sentences in one sentence:

1. The British shipbuilding industry is mainly located on the Clyde – it has greatly lost in importance. **(which)**
2. The Black Country has become a poor region – coal has largely been substituted by natural gas and oil. **(because)**
3. Mr Shriver moved to London – he became unemployed in Newcastle. **(as)**
4. Denis Hunter is the owner of an export firm – he lives in Birmingham. **(who)**
5. We went to London last week – we wanted to visit the trade fair. **(because)**

4 Choose the right answer: What is to be understood by:

1. **You are splitting hairs.**
   – to have one's hair cut
   – to be pedantic (pedantisch)
   – to be successful

2. **She is my cup of tea.**
   – I like her tea best.
   – She is just the woman who suits (gefallen) me.
   – She doesn't interest me at all.

3. **All that glitters is not gold.**
   – Such people are intolerant.
   – All metals (Metalle) that glitter (glitzern) are not gold.
   – Things are often quite different (anders) from what they seem.

4. **A bird in a hand is worth two in the bush.**
   – You would like to kill two birds with one stone.
   – It mostly pays to be modest. (bescheiden)
   – Things are often less interesting than they look.

5 VISITING A CAR COMPANY

interesting   **tour**   **working**   **shift** (Schicht)   **to install** (installieren)
showing   **to send**   **to produce**   **wheels** (Rad)   **to spray** (hier: spritzen)

A group of students, who study economics, are visiting a car company. A guide shows them round the plant and explains to them everything they want to know.

Guide: Good morning, ladies and gentlemen.
Students: Good morning.
Guide: I've the pleasure of .... (1) you round the plant. If you have any questions, you are welcome to ask.
First, we'll go to the press shop. Look, here the front and rear body sections of the car are fitted together by automation.
Student: Very ... (2). What's done over there?
Guide: There the front and rear body sections of the car are joined to the roof.
Student: What happens to the bare body now?
Guide: It is ... (3) to the paint shop.
Student: How long does it take to ... (4) the car?
Guide: About one hour.
Let's go to Hall 15 now. On a conveyer¹ belt, the interior equipment, bumpers and the electrical equipment are ... (5).
Student: When does the car become mobile?
Guide: It becomes mobile at the final assembly stage where the ... (6) are added to the chassis and the engine.
Student: What are the ... (7) hours at the factory?
Guide: People work for seven hours a day in two ... (8).
Student: When does the first shift begin?
Guide: It begins at 5.30 a.m.
Student: How many cars are ... (9) every day?
Guide: About 10,000.

After three hours' ... (10) round the plant, the visit was finished.

1. Fill the gaps with one of the words given above.
2. Read the text.
3. Translate it into German.
4. Ask questions on the text and answer them.

1 also: conveyor belt

GRAMMAR AND EXERCISES

THE ADVERB (2)

Adjective	Adverb	Predicative complement
This is a **precise** translation.	He translated the text **precisely**.	The translation is **precise**.
1. Das Adjektiv bezieht sich auf ein **Hauptwort**.	1. Das Adverb bezieht sich u. a. auf ein **Vollverb**.	1. Das Prädikatsnomen steht u. a. in Verbindung mit dem Hilfsverb „**to be**".
2. Es antwortet auf die Frage „**was für ein**".	2. Es antwortet auf die Frage „**wie**".	2. Obwohl es auf die Frage „**wie**" antwortet, wird es wie ein Adjektiv (**also ohne** „**ly**") behandelt.

MAN MERKE SICH

1. Verben, nach denen ebenfalls das Prädikatsnomen (predicative complement) steht, sind:

to look	aussehen	**to remain**	bleiben
to taste	schmecken	**to feel**	sich fühlen
to smell	riechen	**to seem**	scheinen
to turn	drehen, wenden	**to sound**	klingen, sich anhören
to keep	halten, bleiben		

   u. a.

2. **hardly** (Adverb) – kaum, **hard** (Adjektiv/Adverb) – schwer
   good (Adjektiv), **well** (Adverb)

6 Decide whether the words in brackets must be inserted as adjectives, adverbs or predicative complements:

PATTERN
That was an (easy) test.
That was an **easy** test.

1. That was a (correct) answer.
2. He can speak English (good).
3. They will (probable) win the match.
4. It was a (complete) surprise to me.
5. I'm quite (certain) that he will pass the exam.
6. Your watch is (slow).
7. The matter will be examined (careful).
8. We have (safe) arrived in Bristol.
9. The tea set must be (complete).
10. The coffee tastes (good).
11. She found it (hard) to tell him the truth.
12. I need (hard) mention that I dislike your behaviour.
13. He was (punctual) in his payments.
14. Sarah is pretty (good) at shorthand and typing.
15. The prices have risen (considerable).
16. Is the beach (safe) for bathing?
17. She looks (beautiful).
18. It's (nice) to see you.
19. He has a (good) knowledge of French.
20. That's a (considerable) amount of money.
21. That smells (bad).
22. It was (easy) to get there.

23. He did his work (satisfactory).
24. He was (complete) exhausted.
25. She will (certain) reach her goal.
26. You can (hard) expect me to lend you money again.
27. The train arrived (punctual).
28. Is it (true) that he has gone bankrupt?
29. My father was (serious) injured.
30. He had to pay a (heavy) fine.

The comparison of the adverb – Die Steigerung des Adverbs

promptly – **more** promptly – **most** promptly wonderfully – **mor**e wonderfully – **most** wonderfully soon – soon**er** – soon**est** late – lat**er** – lat**est**	Die **„ly" Adverbien** werden mit **„more"** und **„most"** gesteigert. Die **ursprünglichen Adverbien** werden mit **„er"** und **„est"** gesteigert.
well (gut) – better – best **much** (viel) – more – most	**little** (wenig) – less – least

THE WORD ORDER (3)

1. He answered **promptly**.
2. He **promptly** answered the letter.
3. He **answered** the letter **promptly**.
4. a) He has **promptly** answered the letter.
   b) The letter was **promptly** answered by him.
   c) The letter has been **promptly** answered.*
5. a) He is **remarkably** good at English.
   b) This is a **remarkably** good result.

* auch: The letter has promptly been answered.

Das **abgeleitete Adverb** steht:
1. unmittelbar **nach** dem Verb, **wenn kein anderer Satzteil vorhanden ist;**
2. **vor** dem konjugierten Verb;
3. **hinter** dem Objekt;
4. **zwischen** Hilfsverb und Partizip;
5. **vor** dem Adjektiv (Prädikatsnomen), wenn es dieses näher bestimmt.

Achtung!
Das abgeleitete Adverb steht **nicht** zwischen dem **Prädikat** und **Objekt**.

Falsch: He answered promptly the letter.

7 Where must the adverb be placed?

PATTERN
He will win the prize. (certainly)
He will **certainly** win the prize.

1. Please, walk (more slowly).
2. You must speak (more clearly).
3. He speaks English (very well).
4. The solution can be found. (easily)
5. You have overlooked it. (certainly)
6. It started to rain. (suddenly)
7. This film was exciting. (particularly)
8. The plane has landed. (smoothly)
9. The bus arrived at Newcastle. (punctually)
10. The pop singer was welcomed by his fans. (rapturously)
11. He was injured in the accident. (seriously)
12. The results are good. (remarkably)
13. The unemployment rate is high. (surprisingly)
14. The prices have risen in the last few months. (considerably)
15. The prices were increased last week. (enormously)

IRREGULAR PLURALS (2)

Folgende gebräuchlichen Hauptwörter werden im Gegensatz zum Deutschen nur im **Singular** gebraucht:		Folgende Hauptwörter werden im Gegensatz zum Deutschen nur im **Plural** gebraucht:	
food	– Lebensmittel	**goods**	– die Ware
progress	– Fortschritte	**clothes**	– die Kleidung
knowledge	– Kenntnisse	**glasses**	– die Brille
information	– Auskünfte	**scissors**	– die Schere
advice	– Ratschläge	**trousers**	– die Hose
furniture	– Möbel	**jeans**	– die Jeans
news	– die Nachrichten	**shorts**	– die Shorts
machinery	– die Maschinen	**spectacles**	– die Brille

Great Britain imports **food**.
He has made a lot of **progress**.

He wore black **jeans**.
Please, pass me the **scissors**.

MAN MERKE SICH

Bei Gegenständen, die aus **zwei symmetrischen Teilen** bestehen, gebraucht man beim **unbestimmten Artikel** und bei **Zahlwörtern**: „a pair of".

He bought **two pairs** of jeans. He bought **a pair** of trousers (scissors).

8 Translate into English:

1. Deine Englischkenntnisse sind gut.
2. Die Auskünfte (Informationen), die wir über diese Firma erhielten, waren gut.
3. Er gab mir einige gute Ratschläge.
4. Er kaufte sich eine weiße Hose.
5. Die Ware ist von guter Qualität.
6. Sind das deine Kleider?
7. Gefallen dir diese Möbel?
8. Ist das deine Brille?
9. Hier sind die Nachrichten von BBC 1.
10. Ich möchte diese Shorts.

22 Is the world facing an environmental catastrophe?

"Hello, Susan." "Hello Jack." "Nice to see you. How are you?" "Fine." "Have you read the TIME article "Is the world facing an environmental catastrophe?" "No, I haven't. Do you think it is?" "I'm afraid it is. The biggest danger for the environment and mankind is not pollution of the air and water, it is the ozone hole, global warming and deforestation." "That's true. Do you think that there will be an environmental catastrophe one day? The world has been sufficiently warned." "Well, the fact that it has been possible to bring about Earth Summits – the first took place in Rio in 1992 – shows that more or less all countries are aware of how necessary it is to take common action to save the earth." "Well, but where are the results?" "It is true that very little has been done so far. There are at least some steps that have been taken to reduce greenhouse gases such as carbon dioxide." "In the meantime, the ozone hole has extended in a way which is beginning to endanger our health." "Well, Susan. You are right. Sometimes I think that much more must happen before politicians and people are fully aware of this great danger for mankind. Let's hope that it will not be too late one day."

COMPREHENSION TESTS

1 Have a look at the text and answer the following questions:

1. What does the text deal with?
2. What's the great danger for the environment and mankind?
3. Why is the ozone hole so dangerous?
4. When and where did the first Earth Summit take place?
5. What were the results of these Summits?

2 Find the opposite of the words which are underlined:

1. The pollution danger is <u>decreasing</u>.
2. The prospects for a change are rather <u>unfavourable</u>.
3. The general situation is getting <u>worse and worse</u>.
4. The ozone hole has become <u>smaller and smaller</u>.
5. This environmental project is <u>good</u>.

3 Fill in an appropriate preposition:

1. Sellafield is known ... its nuclear power station.
2. It is located ... the North ... England.
3. Silicon Glen ... Scotland is comparable ... the high-tech area ... California.
4. The environment is highly polluted ... carbon-dioxide emissions.
5. The ozone hole is a great danger ... mankind.

4 WHAT CAN THE GOVERNMENT AND WE DO TO FIGHT POLLUTION?

Find the correct combination:

1. We can reduce
2. We can increase
3. We can severely punish (hart bestrafen)
4. We can introduce (einführen)
5. We can recycle
6. We can buy
7. We can save (sparen)

a) cans (Dosen), bottles and paper
b) environmentally safe (umweltfreundlich) products
c) energy
d) carbon-dioxide emissions
e) environmental polluters (Umweltsünder)
f) petrol prices
g) an energy tax (Energiesteuer)

5 ENERGY – important for all of us

to need	gas	important	technical	stations
to introduce	wind	to replace	clear	to reach

Energy is very ... (1) for industry and private use. Since the Industrial Revolution such economic and ... (2) changes would have been impossible without natural resources and energy. The traditional sources of energy are coal, oil and natural ... (3). The massive price increases of oil in the 1970s and pollution problems made it necessary to find other sources of energy. To solve this problem, nuclear power ... (4) were built. However, there has been general talk that nuclear power should be ... (5) by other sources of energy, especially since the Tchernobyl catastrophe. The German coalition government under Mr Schröder has made efforts in this direction and recently ... (6) an agreement with the nuclear industry. Solar and wind energy have meanwhile been ... (7). Though these sources of energy do not cause any pollution problems, it is quite ... (8) that this kind of energy can only be produced in regions where plenty of sunshine or ... (9) is available. On the other hand, everybody knows that these sources of energy are unable to produce all the energy that is ... (10). It remains to be seen whether the new energy policy of the government will prove to be an advantage for Germany.

1. Look up the words you don't know in a dictionary.
2. Fill the gaps with the words given above.
3. Translate the text into German.
4. What do you think about this problem?

GRAMMAR AND EXERCISES

THE REFLEXIVE PRONOUNS – Die rückbezüglichen Fürwörter

Singular		Plural	
I wash	**myself**	we wash	**ourselves**
you wash	**yourself**	you wash	**yourselves**
he washes	**himself**	they wash	**themselves**
she washes	**herself**	to wash	**oneself – sich** waschen (Infinitiv)
it washes	**itself**		

May **I** introduce **myself**?
My name is Hopkins.
*Darf ich **mich** vorstellen?*
Mein Name ist Hopkins.

He helped **himself** to some sandwiches.
*Er nahm **sich** einige belegte Brote.*

Das Reflexivpronomen steht, wenn **Subjekt** und **Objekt dieselbe** Person sind.

In the morning father **washes, shaves** and **dresses** quickly.
*Morgens wäscht, rasiert und zieht **sich** Vater schnell an.*

Der Engländer verwendet im Gegensatz zum Deutschen die Reflexivpronomen **nicht** häufig. Wenn klar ersichtlich ist, dass sich das Verb auf das Subjekt zurückbezieht, **entfällt** im Englischen das Reflexivpronomen.

I have found the mistake **myself**.
*Ich habe den Fehler **selbst** gefunden.*

Has father repaired the car **himself**?
*Hat Vater den Wagen **selbst** repariert?*

Wenn das Substantiv oder Pronomen **hervorgehoben** werden soll, verwendet man das Reflexivpronomen. In diesem Fall steht es meist **am Ende** des Satzes.

He recovered from the accident quickly.
*Er erholte **sich** schnell von dem Unfall.*

They met at the swimming pool.
*Sie trafen **sich** in der Badeanstalt.*

Die meisten Verben, die im Deutschen reflexiv gebraucht werden, können im Englischen nicht reflexiv gebraucht werden. Es sind z. B. die folgenden genannten Verben:

to meet	– sich treffen, sich kennen lernen	to refuse	– sich weigern
to remember	– sich erinnern	to be glad that	– sich freuen, dass
to happen	– sich ereignen	to decide	– sich entschließen
to apply for	– sich bewerben um	to refer to	– sich beziehen auf
to change	– sich ändern	to amount to	– sich belaufen auf
to complain of/about	– sich beschweren über	u. a.	

6 Translate the following sentences into English:

1. Tun Sie es bitte selbst!
2. Ich möchte mich vorstellen. Mein Name ist Brown.
3. Erinnern Sie sich an die Hunters? Ja.
4. Wir trafen uns letzte Woche.
5. Es ereignete sich gestern Abend.
6. Bedienen (help) Sie sich bitte selbst.
7. Das Wetter änderte sich.
8. Tom bereitete sich auf die Fahrprüfung vor.
9. Es freut mich, dass er sie bestanden hat.
10. Er weigerte sich, das zu tun.
11. Ich bezog mich auf das Inserat in der Times.
12. Die Rechnung beläuft sich auf 230£.

THE ADVERB (3)

Die **ursprünglichen Adverbien** haben im Gegensatz zu den abgeleiteten kein „ly".

Ursprüngliche Adverbien		Die ursprünglichen Adverbien stehen
des Ortes	**there, here**	am Anfang oder Ende des Satzes;
der Zeit (unbestimmt)	**always, ever, never, soon, at last, often**	vor dem konjugierten Verb, bisweilen am Ende des Satzes;
der Zeit (bestimmt)	**today, yesterday, tomorrow, last night**	am Ende, bisweilen auch am Anfang des Satzes;
der Art und Weise	**only, very, quite** (ganz), **rather** (ziemlich), **so, too** (zu), **almost** (fast)	vor Adjektiven, Hauptwörtern, Adverbien und Verben, je nachdem, worauf sie sich beziehen.

7 Where must the adverb be placed?

PATTERN

He has missed the train. (probably)
He has **probably** missed the train.

1. Are there any tickets for tonight (still)? Yes, there are.
2. Have you seen this film? (already). No, I haven't.
3. We'll see each other (tomorrow). All right.
4. Have you taken a decision (already)? No, I haven't taken it (yet).
5. I was in Brighton (last month). I felt happy there (quite).
6. Have you thought of her birthday (ever)? I have forgotten it (never).
7. You have made the same mistakes as Thomas has (almost). That's not true (quite).
8. That's an interesting story (quite). It is not bad (too).
9. Here are the tickets. I had forgotten them (almost).
10. This bike costs £70 (only)? Yes. It is reasonable in price (quite).

LITTLE – FEW / wenig – wenige

Little – wenig

I have (got) **little** money.
Ich habe wenig Geld.

I have understood **little** of his talk.
Ich habe wenig von seinem Vortrag verstanden.

Few – wenige

He is a man of **few** words.
Er ist ein Mann, der wenig Worte macht.

Only **a few** reached their goal.
Nur ein paar erreichten das Ziel.

I haven't seen him in the last **few** years.

„**Little**" wird **adjektivisch** und **substantivisch** gebraucht.

„**little**" steht im Gegensatz zu „few" vor Substantiven im **Singular**.
little **money** – wenig Geld
few **children** – wenige Kinder

„**Few**" und „**a few**" (ein paar) werden **adjektivisch** und **substantivisch** gebraucht.

„**Few**" steht im Gegensatz zu „little" vor Substantiven im **Plural**.

Bei **Zeitangaben** steht nach „**last**" ein unübersetzbares „**few**".

8 Fill in: little or few

1. I have very ... time for reading.
2. He is ... known.
3. She has only ... friends.
4. Do you know Spanish? Only a ... .
5. You have made ... mistakes in the translation.
6. Can you explain it in a ... words?
7. This week only a ... people won in the lottery.
8. He understood ... of his speech.
9. We received only a ... offers in the last ... days.
10. There is ... hope that we will get more next week.

23 Social aspects of Great Britain

A discussion about trade unions in Britain

A group of students of economics have come to Britain in order to discuss social problems with English politicians. They have been invited by Mr Fox, a Member of Parliament, to his house and have been warmly welcomed.

Mr Fox	Good afternoon, ladies and gentlemen.
Students	Good afternoon, Mr Fox.
Mr Fox	Did you have a pleasant flight?
Students	Yes, we really did.
Mr Fox	My wife and I are very glad to welcome you to our house.
Student	Many thanks for your kind invitation. (They make themselves comfortable beside the fire and have a glass of wine.)
Mr Fox	Well, you are interested in getting to know something about social life in our country. You are welcome to ask any questions.
Student	I have heard that the trade unions have greatly lost in influence during the last few years. Is that true?
Mr Fox	Yes, it is.
Student	How was it possible to restrict the power of the unions?
Mr Fox	In the past the British economy greatly suffered from the many and endless wildcat strikes.

Student	*Didn't the coal miners' strike in 1984 last longer than one year?*
Mr. Fox	*It did. As these strikes caused considerable damage to the economy, there was general agreement that something had to be done.*
Student	*A very big problem.*
Mr Fox	*Yes, but it was solved. The trade unions accepted that there should be a secret vote before a union could go on strike. The most effective step against wildcat strikes, however, was taken by the Government. Under the new Employment Act, people who work for a company or firm can no longer be forced to join a union if they don't want to.*
Student	*That means that an end was put to the "closed shop", or rather, compulsory membership of the trade unions.*
Mr Fox	*Yes. And wildcat strikes, too.*

After the conversation Mr Fox invites his guests to visit the House of Commons the next day and to listen to the debate on social security.

COMPREHENSION TESTS

1 **Have a look at the text and answer the following questions:**

1. Why had a group of students come to Britain?
2. Why was the power of the trade unions restricted?
3. What strike lasted longer than one year?
4. What was done in order to put an end to wildcat strikes?
5. What was on the students' programme the next day?

2 **Rewrite the following words adding the missing letter(s):**

ec.nomi.s, Parl.ment, pl.sant, to s.ffer, infl.nce, endle., to c.se dam.ge, to sol.e a problem, to be for.ed to do sth, comp.ls.ry, deba.e, they made themsel.es c.mfortable

3 **Make sentences of your own using the following expressions:**

– to be very glad that...
– to be interested in ...
– to take steps ...
– to be true that ...
– to join sth ...

4 **Explain in your own words the words which are underlined:**

1. A politician is a person who ...
2. To go on strike means ...
3. Trade unions are organisations which ...
4. Coal miners are people who ...

5 **Choose the right answer**

to seize the bull by the horns
to fight with a bull
to take an opportunity
to trick sb

to give sb the sack
to play with sb
to fire sb
to hang sb

to pull somebody's leg
to fall in love with sb
to flirt with sb
to make fun of a person in a playful way

6 SOCIAL SERVICES IN GREAT BRITAIN

There is Mrs Longman who is unable to work for some time.

There are Mr and Mrs Hunter who are going to have a baby.

There is Mr Brent who became unemployed three months ago.

There is Miss Jackson who is ill and must consult a doctor.

There are the Shrivers whose income has decreased and who can't pay the rent for their flat any longer.

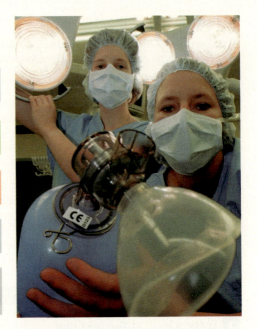

How does the State help Mrs Longman, Mr Brent, Miss Jackson, Mr and Mrs Hunter and the Shrivers? Use the following particulars:

- to get unemployment benefit (Arbeitslosenunterstützung)
- to receive family allowances (Kindergeld)
- to get sickness benefit (Krankengeld)
- to get medical treatment free of charge (medizinische Behandlung) (in Britain many people are privately insured.)
- to get housing benefit (Wohngeld)

7 TALKING ABOUT SHORTER WORKING HOURS

At a college, students discussed the question as to whether shorter working hours would create (schaffen) more jobs. Here are some arguments which were brought forward. If you think that an argument holds water (stichhaltig sein), mark with (+) if not, with (-), if you have no definite opinion, mark with (0).

If working hours are reduced,
- there will be more workplaces available.
- people have more free time.
- there will be more quality of life.
- people won't know what to do with their free time.
- people will become dissatisfied/aggressive.
- wages and salaries will be too low.
- there will be more disputes in families.
- there will be more divorces. (Scheidung)
- people won't have enough money for their hobbies.
- people will have more time for their family and other activities.
- unemployment will be reduced and there will be fewer social problems.

What's your opinion on this matter. Write this down and discuss the problem in class.

GRAMMAR AND EXERCISES

THE MODAL AUXILIARIES – die modalen Hilfsverben

	Past tense			Past tense	
can	could	– können	must[1]	–	– müssen
may	might	– können, mögen, dürfen	shall	should	– sollen
			will	would	– wollen

General rules

1. He speaks English.
   Er spricht Englisch.
2. He **can** speak English.
   Er kann Englisch.
3. **Can** I help you?
   Yes, you **can**.
4. He **doesn't** speak English but French now.
5. He **cannot** speak English.
6. You **must not** park here.
7. **May** I ask you a question?
8. I **cannot (could not)** do the crossword puzzle.
   Ich kann (konnte) das Kreuzworträtsel nicht lösen.
9. I **will not be able** to do the crossword puzzle.
   Ich werde das Kreuzworträtsel nicht lösen können.

– Die modalen Hilfsverben haben in der **3. Person Singular Präsens** (present tense) **kein „s"**. (Satz 2)

– Die modalen Hilfsverben haben ein Vollverb **nach** sich. Bei Kurzantworten aber: Yes, **I can**. (Satz 2/3)

– Die modalen Hilfsverben werden in der **Frage** und **Verneinung** nicht mit „to do" umschrieben. (Satz 5 – 8)

– **Cannot** wird zusammengeschrieben!

– Die modalen Hilfsverben schließen den Infinitiv des folgenden Verbs **ohne „to"** an.

– Die modalen Hilfsverben werden in der Regel nur im **„present"** und **„past tense"** verwendet.
Sie haben in der Regel in den zusammengesetzten Zeiten **„Ersatzformen"**. (Satz 9)

can	– to be able to
may	– to be allowed to u. a.
must	– to have to u. a.
will	– to want, to wish, to intend
shall	– to be to, to be said to, ought to

---

[1] Es gibt keine Vergangenheitsform von „must", sondern nur Ersatzformen.

CAN – to be able (in der Lage sein)

1. **Can** you work with a computer?
   Yes, I **can**.
   Can you carry this heavy suitcase?
   No, I **can't**.

2. This **can** happen.
   It is possible that it will happen.
   The train **can** be half an hour late.
   It is possible that the train will be half an hour late.

3. **Can** I come in? Yes, you **can**.
   Darf (kann) ich hereinkommen? Ja.
   Can I open the window?
   Yes, you **can**.
   Darf (kann) ich das Fenster öffnen? Ja.

4. **I will not be able** to do this.
   Ich werde dies nicht tun können.
   The firm **has not been able** to deliver the goods in time.
   Die Firma hat die Waren nicht rechtzeitig liefern können. (... war nicht in der Lage ...)
   The firm **is not able** to deliver the goods in time.
   Die Firma ist nicht in der Lage (kann nicht) ...

1. „**Can**" drückt eine **geistige** und **physische** Fähigkeit aus.

2. „**Can**" drückt eine **Möglichkeit** aus. In diesem Fall kann „can" auch mit **it is possible, it is impossible** umschrieben werden.

3. Statt „**can**" verwendet man bei der **Bitte um eine Erlaubnis** auch „**may**". (**May** I come in?)
   „**Can**" ist **nicht** unhöflich und wird in diesem Sinn häufig gebraucht.

4. In den **zusammengesetzten Zeiten**, wird „can" durch die Ersatzform „**to be able**" ersetzt.

   Bei **stärkerer Betonung** steht die Ersatzform „**to be able**" auch in den **einfachen Zeiten**.

8 Answer the following questions in line with the pattern:

PATTERN
Can I help you?
Yes, you can. I'm sorry, but you can't. No, you can't.

1. Can you speak French?
2. Can you understand me?
3. Can I do anything for you?
4. Can you explain it to me?
5. Can you help me with the translation?
6. Can you show me how to play squash?
7. Can I smoke here?
8. Can I go for a swim?
9. Can you tell me the way to the nearest telephone box?
10. Could he solve the crossword puzzle?

9 Make sentences in line with the pattern:

PATTERN
to find the mistake (he)
He cannot (can't) find the mistake.
He isn't able to find the mistake.
He could not (couldn't) find the mistake.
He wasn't able to find the mistake.
He will not (won't) be able to find the mistake.
He has not been able to find the mistake.
He had not been able to find the mistake.

1. to answer the questions (they)
2. to spell the word (he)
3. to explain it to him (she)

10 Put the sentences into the tense indicated. Use "can" or "to be able".

PATTERN
He (to answer) not the question. **(past)**
He could not answer the question.

1. I'm sorry, but I (to help) not you with the translation. **(present)**
2. He (to give) not the correct answer. **(past)**
3. Harry (to settle) not the matter. **(future)**
4. I'm sorry, but I (to do) not that for you. **(present)**
5. We (to agree) not to his proposal. **(present perfect)**
6. He (to trick) not the police. **(past perfect)**
7. Eric (to solve) not the crossword puzzle. **(past)**
8. They (to settle) not the dispute. **(present perfect)**
9. The exporter (to deliver) not the goods next week. **(future)**
10. The firm (to execute) not the order at once. **(past perfect)**

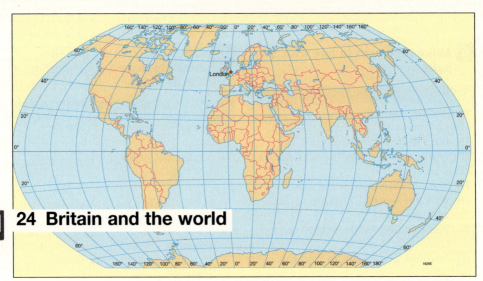

24 Britain and the world

Great Britain is one of the most important export countries in the world. It exports capital goods, electronic equipment, telecommunications products, chemicals, cars and other goods all over the world.

The markets in the Commonwealth of Nations and the sterling area were once the largest for British export goods. Since the 1960s, however, a lot has changed in British export trade. The reason for this is that the markets in highly industrialized countries such as the United States of America, those in Western Europe and in Japan have become more and more important for British exports while sales to the Commonwealth countries have declined.

When the British realized that it was necessary to create new markets for their goods, they joined the European Community in 1973. Since that time Western Europe has been the largest market for British goods.

Now globalization is a big challenge for Great Britain and other industrial countries. Since China, countries in the Far East and others have become keen competitors on the world market, Britain has made every effort to keep pace with all of these. As economic conditions such as economic growth, the situation on the labour market and the exchange rate of the pound sterling have improved considerably, especially at the end of the 1990s, Britain will certainly master this challenge.

COMPREHENSION TESTS

1 Have a look at the text and answer the following questions:

1. What does Great Britain mainly export?
2. Which were once the largest British export markets?
3. Which are the most important export markets now?
4. What did the British do when sales to the Commonwealth of Nations and the sterling area were declining?
5. What is a big challenge for Britain and other industrial countries today?

2 Complete the following sentences:

1. From the 1960s a lot has ... in British export trade.
2. China and other countries in the Far East have become stiff ... for British goods.
3. Britain ... the European Community in 1973.
4. The exchange rate of the pound sterling has ... considerably.
5. Britain will certainly ... the globalization challenge.

3 Find the nouns or verbs corresponding to the following words:

1. introduction   ....
2. to inform   ....
3. inspection   ....
4. to agree   ....
5. opposition   ....
6. expression   ....
7. to warn   ....
8. to explode   ....

4 Replace the words underlined by one given below:

to decline   major
to increase   to establish
to change for the better

1. In the 17th century the British <u>founded</u> colonies in North America.
2. Sales to the Commonwealth countries have <u>fallen</u> considerably.
3. Exports to the USA and the EU countries have <u>risen</u>.
4. Electronic equipment is one of Britain's <u>main</u> export articles.
5. The situation of the British economy has <u>improved</u>.

5 TOWARDS A UNITED EUROPE

to take	agricultural	creating
which	to establish	to join
to date back	Steel	entering

The idea to create a united Europe ... (1) to the beginning of the 19th century. The first effective step, however, was ... (2) by France, Germany, Italy, Belgium, the Netherlands and Luxemburg by setting up the Coal and ... (3) Community. This common market, which was first restricted to coal and steel, was extended to industrial and ... (4) products under the Rome treaty in 1957, by which the European Economic Community (EEC) was established. The reasons for creating a common market were political and economic ones: to avoid further wars in Europe and to remove customs barriers within the EEC. Britain ... (5) the EC[1] in 1973; the Republic of Ireland, Spain, Portugal, Greece and Denmark followed.

Further decisive steps towards ... (6) a united Europe were taken. First, a European Parliament was set up, then the Single Market was ... (7), which made it possible that persons, capital and services could move freely within the EC. Above all, however, there is the European Union now, ... (8) has the euro as its common monetary unit. The next step towards a united Europe will be taken by ... (9) into negotiations for membership of Poland, the Czech Republic and Hungary. If it should be possible to create a political Union, a united Europe would come true.

1. Complete the sentences by filling in the words given above.
2. Read the text.
3. Translate it into German.
4. Ask questions on the text.
5. Say in two or three sentences whether you are for a united Europe.

---
1 later EC

GRAMMAR AND EXERCISES

MAY – to be allowed, to be permitted (erlaubt sein)

1. **May** I open the window?
   Yes, you **may**.
   Darf (kann) ich das Fenster öffnen?
   Ja, du darfst (kannst).
   May I come in? Yes.

2. This remedy **may** help you.
   Diese Arznei wird dir vielleicht helfen.
   He **may** reach his goal.
   Er wird vielleicht sein Ziel erreichen.
   (He **will perhaps** reach his goal.
   It is possible that he will reach his goal.)

3. **May** I leave now?
   Darf ich jetzt gehen?
   No, you **may not.**
   No, you **must not!**
   (allgemeines Verbot)
   Nein, du darfst nicht.
   You **must not** park here.
   Sie dürfen hier nicht parken.

4. Jack **will not be allowed** to go on (a) safari.
   Jack wird nicht auf Safari gehen dürfen.
   Jack **has not been allowed** to go on (a) safari.
   Jack **isn't allowed** to go on (a) safari.

„May" drückt aus:

1. **eine Erlaubnis oder Bitte um eine Erlaubnis.** Es wird in diesem Sinn vorwiegend in **Frage** und **Antwort** verwendet.

   Statt „may" verwendet man häufig „**can**". Can I come in? (Siehe auch Seite 136)

2. **eine denkbare Möglichkeit.**
   Im Deutschen bietet sich im Sinne einer denkbaren Möglichkeit die Übersetzung „**wird vielleicht**" an.

   „May" kann man bei einer denkbaren Möglichkeit auch durch „**will perhaps**" oder „**it is possible**" ersetzen.
   Man verwendet „**might**" statt „may", wenn etwas **sehr ungewiss** ist.

3. „**may not**" – **nicht dürfen**
   (was man besser nicht tun sollte).

   Bei einem **strengen, allgemeinen** oder **offiziellen** Verbot wird „etwas nicht tun dürfen" durch „**must not**" wiedergegeben. **(nur in der Verneinung)**

4. Die Ersatzformen von „**may**" sind „**to be allowed to**", „**to be permitted to**". Die Ersatzformen von „may" verwendet man **nur**, wenn „may" im Sinn einer **Erlaubnis** gebraucht wird. In diesem Fall stehen die Ersatzformen **in allen Zeiten.**

6 Make sentences according to the pattern:

PATTERN

- to do this (he)
He **is** (not) **allowed** to do this.
He **was** (not) **allowed** to do this.
He **will** (not) **be allowed** to do this.
He **has** (not) **been allowed** to do this.
He **had** (not) **been allowed** to do this.

– to smoke in the compartment. (they)
– to make out cheques. (he)
– to sign the contract. (she)

7 Transform the following sentences according to the pattern. Use "may", "will perhaps" or "to be allowed to".

PATTERN

1. Derek will manage it.
   Derek **may** manage it.
   Derek **will perhaps** manage it.

   or:

2. Anne used the ICE with this ticket. **(to be allowed to)**
   Anne **was allowed to** use the ICE with this ticket.

1. Roger will join this golf club.
2. Susan will apply for this post.
3. She will get the job.
4. She will run the whole show.
5. The boss will raise her salary.
6. Mr Fowler will become manager of this firm.
7. Janet will get a job on the side.
8. Have you crossed the border without a visa? **(to be allowed to)**
9. The firm imported the goods duty-free. **(to be allowed to)**
10. The Potters overdrew their bank account. **(to be allowed to)**
11. Mr Perkins will sign the sales contract. **(to be allowed to)**
12. We cancelled the agreement. **(to be allowed to)**

BOTH / AS WELL AS – sowohl als auch

8 Transform the following sentences in line with the pattern:

PATTERN

Alan **as well as** Simon refused to do it.
Both Alan **and** Simon refused to do it.

1. Linda as well as Sarah is a member of this club.
2. Clifford as well as David went to the exhibition in Leeds.
3. Mr Rider as well as Mrs Rider took part in the excursion.
4. Tony as well as Liz enjoyed the sightseeing tour around London.
5. Bob as well as Joyce went out to eat last night.

Now the other way round:

1. Both Mr Douglas and Mrs Day are Americans.
2. Both Canada and Australia are members of the Commonwealth of Nations.
3. Both Spain and Portugal are members of the EU.
4. A lot of high-tech companies have settled both in Scotland's Silicon Glen and in California's Silicon Valley.
5. Computers are produced both in Great Britain and in Germany.

New York City – Aerial View

 ## 25 New York

Thorsten Schwarz, a sales manager, had decided to go on a tour of the USA with his family this year. In the plane – a jumbo – they met an American businessman, with whom they had a nice chat. As the plane had not yet received landing permission, it was circling over New York.

Jimmy	*Look, there is New York.*
Thorsten	*That's the Empire State Building over there, isn't it?*
Jimmy	*Yes. You should go there when it is getting dark. From the top you have a wonderful view of New York. At night, the lights of New York are marvellous.*
Thorsten	*That's the famous skyline with all its skyscrapers, isn't it?*
Jimmy	*Yes, it is.*
Thorsten	*That's Wall Street, the financial center and the Stock Exchange, isn't it?*
Jimmy	*Yes. The two rivers which meet there are the East River and the Hudson River. On the other side of the Hudson is New Jersey, one of the fifty States of the US.*

Thorsten	There is the Statue of Liberty. What a wonderful statue!
Jimmy	It certainly is. It was given to the American people by the French and commemorates the hundredth anniversary of the USA.
Thorsten	Where is 5th Avenue? Is it true that it begins in Harlem and ends at the southern tip of Manhattan?
Jimmy	Yes, it is. Look, there's Central Park with 5th Avenue.
Thorsten	What is that building?
Jimmy	That's the United Nations Building.
Thorsten	What other sights of New York are well worth a visit?
Jimmy	A visit to the Metropolitan Opera, to Chinatown, to the Rockefeller Center and to Broadway should also be on your program.
Thorsten	Do Blacks and Whites live on better terms with one another now?
Jimmy	I'd say that the situation has improved, especially in New York.
Thorsten	It is said that the Blacks have to do the "dirty" work.
Jimmy	Well, it's not always like that. When you go to a bank, a travel agency or to public authorities, you'll find that Blacks work there as well.

Twenty minutes later, the plane touched down and landed smoothly at Kennedy Airport.

Chinatown

COMPREHENSION TESTS

1 Have a look at the text and answer the following questions:

1. What do Thorsten Schwarz and his family want to do in the States?
2. Name some sights of New York.
3. Where should you go in order to have a wonderful view of New York?
4. What does the statue of Liberty commemorate?
5. What are the names of the rivers New York is situated on?
6. What is said about the color problem in the text?

2 Are the following statements right or wrong?

1. The Schwarzes met an American reporter on the plane.
2. The Empire State Building is in Chicago.
3. Wall Street is the amusement center of New York.
4. The United Nations have their headquarters in New York.
5. Harlem is the quarter where mainly Blacks live in New York.

3 Find the opposite of:

1. tall ....
2. to close ....
3. true ....
4. to decline ....
5. to import ....
6. to refuse ....

4 Rewrite the following sentences in one sentence:

1. Thorsten had arrived at Kennedy Airport. – He enquired about hotels at the tourist office. **(after)**
2. Alice was strolling along Broadway. – She wanted to see New York's amusement center. **(because)**
3. Michael and Helen spent the evening in Chinatown. – You can find colorful restaurants and buildings in the Chinese style there. **(where)**
4. Thomas bought two tickets for the Metropolitan Opera. – It is said to be the best Opera House in the world. **(because)**
5. Tomorrow we will go to Central Park. – It is the playground for the entire city. **(which)**

5 Would you like to live in the city or in the country?

Many people like to live in the city, others prefer to live in the country. Mark with (1) if the following statements are true for living in the city, mark with (2) if they are true for living in the country.

- ☐ life is more attractive (cinemas, theaters, stores, etc.)
- ☐ life is not so hectic
- ☐ all types of schools
- ☐ no crowded streets
- ☐ no rush hour
- ☐ no packed trains
- ☐ life is a bit boring

- ☐ better pay (wages and salaries)
- ☐ higher cost of living (rents for apartments)
- ☐ less crime and violence
- ☐ the air is cleaner (less pollution problems)
- ☐ always close to nature

Would you like to live in the city or would you prefer to live in the country? Write down your opinion and discuss it in class.

GRAMMAR AND EXERCISES
MUST – müssen

You **must** forget it. *Du musst es vergessen.*	„Must" wird nur im „**present tense**" gebraucht und besagt:
You **must** clear up the matter. *Du musst die Sache in Ordnung bringen.*	man verlangt, erwartet etwas von mir, etwas ist unerlässlich, notwendig.
You **must not** park here. *Du darfst hier nicht parken.*	„**Must not**" (nicht dürfen) drückt ein **allgemeines, offizielles Verbot** aus.
You **have to** keep your promise. *Du musst dein Versprechen halten.*	In der Umgangssprache umschreibt der Engländer „**must**" hauptsächlich mit
You **have got to** keep your promise. *Du musst dein Versprechen halten.*	„**to have to**", „**to have got to**".
Do we **have** to learn the poem? *Müssen wir das Gedicht lernen?*	In der **Frage** und **Verneinung** wird „**to have to**" meist mit „**to do**" umschrieben.

MAN MERKE SICH

1. Bei einem **Zwang** umschreibt der Engländer „**must**" durch „**to be compelled to/to be forced to**" (gezwungen sein), bei einer **Verpflichtung** durch „**to be obliged to**" verpflichtet sein.
   You **are obliged** to help him.
   The rain **compelled** us to stay indoors.

2. „Etwas nicht tun müssen" wird im Englischen durch „**need not**" wiedergegeben. (nicht „must not")
   You **need not** decide now whether you will come or not.
   Sie müssen jetzt nicht entscheiden, ob Sie kommen oder nicht.

6 Make sentences in line with the pattern:

PATTERN
He (to do) it again.
He **must** do it again.
He **has to** do it again.
He **had to** do it again.
He **will have to** do it again.

1. Helen (to repeat) it.
2. Sally (to answer) the fax at once.
3. Jimmy (to give back) the money to Ronald.
4. Mary (to show) her passport.
5. She (to open) her suitcase.

7 Put the verbs in brackets into the tense indicated. Use "must" or its substitute "to have to".

PATTERN
You (to repeat) it again. **(future)**

You will have to repeat it again.

1. You (to speak) more distinctly. **(present)**
2. Sheila (to take) it more seriously. **(present)**
3. Oliver (to settle) the matter at once. **(future)**
4. Alan (to have) to consult a doctor. **(future)**
5. He (to have) to give up taking drugs. **(future)**
6. Bob (to have) not to take this nasty soup. **(past)**
7. Alice (to return) the buggy Liz has lent her. **(future)**
8. Nicole did not obey the traffic rules. She (to have) to pay a fine. **(past)**
9. Hurds & Co (to ship) the goods by 5 March. **(future)**
10. The prices (to be reduced) by 5% at least. **(present)**

8 Fill in:
must not – nicht dürfen
need not – nicht brauchen, nicht müssen

1. You ... do that.
2. You ... worry about that.
3. You ... go yet.
4. We ... be late.
5. Cars ... be parked here.
6. You ... trick other people.
7. You ... tell lies.
8. You ... disobey the rules.
9. You ... be frightened of him.
10. You ... crib from your neighbour.

26 Impressions of the United States

Breakfast in New York, lunch in San Francisco – modern transportation has made it possible to cross the 2,565 miles from the Atlantic to the Pacific coast of the States within only a few hours; early settlers would have required several months for it.

The United States, which has about 240 million inhabitants, is a melting pot. Its population is composed of people from all continents and all races. The States, the capital of which is Washington, is about twenty-five times as large as the British Isles.

Let's now have a look at some areas in the States. Florida with its lovely seaside resorts Miami and Palm Beach is one of the tourist paradises of the States. Florida is also well-known for Cape Kennedy, which is the major testing and launching center of space rockets.

If you like wild, empty lands, you will love the deserts of Nevada and Arizona, the Rocky Mountains and Alaska with all its snow and ice. For those who want to see the many cattle ranches with their cowboys, Texas is the right place.

The North-East of the States with the great cities like New York, Boston and Washington is the most important center of culture, education and government. Every visitor to Washington will be fascinated by the fantastic Presidential Memorials such as the George Washington, Thomas Jefferson and Abraham Lincoln Memorials as well as by the classical architecture of the Congress, which the Americans are very proud of. Near Boston, an old historical city, is Harvard, the most famous university in the States.

COMPREHENSION TESTS

1 Have a look at the text and answer the following questions:

1. What's the distance between the Atlantic and the Pacific coast?
2. What can you tell us about Florida?
3. Where are the wild and empty lands in the States?
4. What attraction does Texas have to offer for tourists?
5. What's the North-East of the States known for?
6. Which is the most famous university in the States?

2 Complete the following sentences:

1. Early ... would have required several months to ... the 2,565 miles from the Atlantic to the Pacific.
2. The States is about twenty-five ... as large as the British Isles.
3. Cape Kennedy is the major ... and ... center of space rockets.
4. Texas is well-... for its many cattle ... .
5. Every ... to Washington will be ... by the Presidential Memorials.

3 Explain in your own words the words which are underlined:

1. The USA is called a <u>melting pot</u> because ...
2. A <u>desert</u> is a region where ...
3. A <u>space rocket</u> is something that ...
4. A <u>cowboy</u> is a man who ...

4 Make sentences with:

to have a look at, to be fascinated by, to be proud of, to be famous, as well as, to require

5 Which of the underlined words is correct?

1. We arrived <u>safely/safe</u> in Seattle yesterday.
2. Bob has been living in Vancouver <u>since/for</u> three years.
3. While I <u>was driving/drove</u> along the Highway, a police car followed me.
4. I <u>were stopped/stoped</u> by the police because I was zigzagging (Zickzack fahren) all over the road.
5. The policeman <u>examines/is examining</u> my driving license.

San Francisco, Golden Gate Bridge

Cable car

6 IMPRESSIONS OF THE UNITED STATES (cont.)

holiday-makers, to range, standard, area, to regard, experiences, purposes

The great Mississippi River Basin between the Appalachians and the Rocky Mountains is the most important agricultural ... (1) in the States. It is also rich in oil, coal and iron ore. Chicago and Detroit are very important industrial cities where automobiles and all other products for industrial and private ... (2) are produced.

California is ... (3) as the pearl of the States. It has developed into a prosperous commercial and tourist area with a high ... (4) of living. There are industries which ... (5) from the processing, packing and marketing of food to the manufacture of aircraft, cars and ships.

Silicon Valley has become the most important center of "high tech". The Pacific States in which the Indians have their "reservations" are also rich in gold, silver and copper.

When talking to ... (6) in the States, you will find that most of them will tell you that San Francisco with its famous Golden Gate Bridge and the visit to the Yellowstone Park, but above all the helicopter flight over the Grand Canyon, were the greatest ... (7) during their stay.

1. Fill in the gaps by using one of the words given above. Use a dictionary if necessary.
2. Read the text.
3. Translate the text into German.
4. Ask questions on the text and answer them.

Grand Canyon

GRAMMAR AND EXERCISES

WILL – wollen

1. Tony **wants** to polish up his knowledge of English.
   Tony will seine Englischkenntnisse aufpolieren.
2. Diana **intends** to go on a world tour.
   Diana will eine Weltreise machen.
3. The company is **prepared to** pay compensation.
   Die Gesellschaft will für den Schaden aufkommen.

„**Will**" drückt aus:

1. einen Wunsch
   Ersatzformen: **to want, to wish, I would like** (ich würde gern)
2. eine Absicht
   Ersatzformen: **to intend, to be going to do sth**
3. eine Bereitschaft
   Ersatzformen: **to be willing to, to be prepared to**

7 Transform the following sentences by using the substitutes of "Will".

PATTERN

Harry booked a charter flight to Miami.

Harry **wanted (intended, was going)** to book a charter flight to Miami.

1. The Shrivers went on a tour of Florida.
2. Susan and Henry hitchhiked through Florida.
3. The driver stopped at a self-service restaurant.
4. He had a snack there.
5. They had some refreshments at a motel.
6. Susan took some photos of Henry and the driver.
7. She phoned her boyfriend from the post office.
8. She told him that she was getting on well.
9. She also bought some stamps there.
10. She paid by credit card.

8 Translate into English:

1. Wie viel Euro wollen Sie in Dollar umtauschen?
2. Wollen Sie per Scheck, Kreditkarte oder bar bezahlen?
3. Henry will einen Kredit aufnehmen.
4. Er will ihn erst nach drei Jahren zurückzahlen.
5. Die Bank wollte ihm den Kredit gewähren.
6. Sarah will in einem Viersternehotel wohnen.
7. Der Empfangschef fragt sie: „Wollen Sie ein Einzel- oder Doppelzimmer?"
8. Wollen Sie geweckt werden?
9. Ich möchte um 7 Uhr geweckt werden.
10. Sarah wollte einen Wagen mieten.
11. Wollen Sie einen Mini oder Ford? Einen Mini bitte.
12. Mr Fox fragte sie: „Wollen Sie Vollkasko?"

How to translate "pflegen" into English

Eric **usually** goes jogging in the morning.
Eric pflegt morgens zu joggen.

Eric **used to** go jogging in the morning.
Eric pflegte morgens zu joggen.

Der Engländer gibt „**pflegen**" durch „**usually**" wieder, wenn das Verb im „**present tense**" steht.

Er gibt „**pflegen**" durch „**used to**" wieder, wenn das Verb im „**past**" steht.

9 Transform the following sentences according to the pattern:

PATTERN

Gerald rings me up on Friday.
Gerald **usually** rings me up on Friday.

Gerald rang me up on Friday.
Gerald **used to** ring me up on Friday.

1. My son-in-law plays squash once a week.
2. My father-in-law goes swimming every morning.
3. My sister-in-law goes out at the weekend.
4. My daughter-in-law eats out when on holiday.
5. My in-laws, who have retired, go bowling on Saturday.

NEED – DARE

You **need not** worry.
Du brauchst dir keine Sorgen zu machen.

I **dare not** contradict him.
Ich wage nicht ihm zu widersprechen.

Wenn „**need**" (brauchen) und „**dare**" (wagen) als **modales Hilfsverb** gebraucht werden, dann haben sie **keine Umschreibung mit „to do"** und **keinen anschließenden Infinitiv mit „to"**.

Die **3. Person Singular** „present tense" hat **kein „s"**.

Das modale Hilfsverb „need" kann **nur** im „**present**" gebraucht werden.

I **don't need** to work today.
Ich brauche heute nicht zu arbeiten.

I **didn't dare** to contradict him.
Ich wagte nicht ihm zu widersprechen.

Wenn „**need**" und „**dare**" als **Vollverben** gebraucht werden, dann werden sie mit „**to do**" **umschrieben** und haben **einen anschließenden Infinitiv mit „to"**.

Die **3. Person Singular** „present tense" hat **ein „s"**.

10 Fill in: **need** or **dare**

1. He ... not apologize for coming late.
2. I ... hardly mention that I dislike the way you treat him.
3. You ... not worry about that.
4. He did not ... to blackmail me.
5. You ... not bother.
6. I have never ... to ask him whether his wife has cancer.
7. Do you ... any support?
8. He wouldn't ... to be so rude.
9. It only ... good will from both sides.
10. I wonder how he ... to say such things.

 27 Some aspects of modern American life

Like British families, American families are small. Usually, you will not find more than two children in a family.

As in Britain, young people usually don't live with their families either. They want to be independent, too. If they can afford it, they share an apartment with a friend or a partner or rent a small one-room apartment. It is unusual today that three generations live together in one house.

As emancipation of women has made great progress in the States, the divorce rate is rather high here, too.

In general, American families have more money to spend than English families. An English family usually has a car, a color TV set and a washing machine whereas an American family often has two or three cars, a large modern kitchen and more.

The everyday life of the Americans and English is more or less the same. Like the British, the Americans watch television for many hours every week.

In their free time they go to the cinema, theater, a disco or a party, watch a football match or baseball, or attend courses for further education. To have lunch in one of the many thousands of fast-food restaurants or to go out eating in one of the many foreign restaurants, is fashionable in the States, too.

Tina Turner

Americans often change their homes. When young people or families earn more money, they look for a better home and, if possible, for a house with two or three garages and a swimming pool. If they can, they end their life in California, the Federal State with its everlasting spring, as people say.

In the United States young people are music fans as well. The music scene ranges from pop music over rock music and folk songs to country and western music.

Groups from Britain such as the Rolling Stones or ex-Beatle Paul McCartney are still on top. One of the biggest country and western stars is Dolly Parton, not to be forgotten Tina Turner, one of America's best pop stars.

COMPREHENSION TESTS

1 Find out and write down what is typical of American life.

2 Fill the gaps with words which are suitable (passen):

1. Sarah and Michael ... the evening in Chinatown where you can find colorful restaurants and buildings.
2. Tomorrow we will drive to Hollywood, which is ... for its film industry.
3. After the gamblers and playboys had ... in Las Vegas, they went to the "strip" of casinos, night-..., etc.
4. Many tourists travel to the west of the States because they want to ... the National Parks such as Grand ..., Yosemite, Yellowstone and others.
5. When in the States, Washington with its many Memorials to US Presidents is also worth a ... .

3 ENGLISH AND AMERICAN SPELLING

Some words which are different in English and American spelling. How are the English words spelt?

AMERICAN	ENGLISH
color	....
favorable	....
program	....
traveling	....
center	....

4 Translate into English:

also/too – auch
in **bejahenden** Sätzen

not ... either – auch nicht
in **verneinten** Sätzen

1. Kennen Sie Mr Huxley? Nein. Ich kenne ihn auch nicht.
2. Hast du an Claire geschrieben? Ja. Ich habe auch an sie geschrieben.
3. Hast du den Film „Airport" gesehen? Nein. Ich habe ihn auch nicht gesehen.
4. Hast du dieses Buch gelesen? Ja. Ich habe es auch gelesen.
5. Warst du am Wochenende in Eastbourne? Ja. Ich war auch dort.
6. Hast du Roger im Kino gesehen? Nein. Ich habe ihn auch nicht gesehen.
7. Würdest du das tun? Nein. Ich würde es auch nicht tun.

5 SCHOOLS AND SPORT IN THE USA

vocational, events, to start, to wear, popular, role, to repeat, medicine, mid-afternoon

In the States children ... (1) school when they are six. They spend six years at elementary school. After that they go to a high school for four or six years. As in Britain, children have lunch at school and come home by ... (2). At the end of every school year, they have to take a test. If they fail, they have to ... (3) the "grade". When they leave school, they receive a "high school" diploma.

Those who want to study ... (4), law or economics, for instance, go to a college or university. Those who want to get a job quickly attend technical institutes or other schools, which offer ... (5) training courses.

In America sport also plays an important ... (6). Baseball is the most ... (7) sport. There are two teams with nine players; the "pitcher" throws the ball and the "batter" hits it with his baseball bat. Tennis, hockey, basketball and most other international sports are also played in the States.

Football is also one of the biggest sporting ... (8). As you know, American football is played in a different way; even the ball is different. American footballers can run with the ball, touch and push each other. As the game can be dangerous, they ... (9) special clothes and helmets.

1. Look up the words you don't know in a dictionary.
2. Complete the sentences with one of the words given above.
3. Read the text.
4. Translate the text into German.
5. Ask questions on the text and answer them.

GRAMMAR AND EXERCISES

SHALL – sollen

Shall I ask Joyce?
Soll ich Joyce fragen?

Shall we meet tomorrow?
Sollen wir uns morgen treffen?

„Sollen" wird im „**present**" durch „**shall**" wiedergegeben, wenn **eine Person auf eine Frage eine Antwort oder Anweisung erwartet**.

6 Ask questions according to the pattern:

PATTERN:

– to ring you up tomorrow (I)
Shall I ring you up tomorrow?

1. to do it for you (he)?
2. to leave now (we)
3. to help you with the crossword puzzle (I)
4. to visit you in Cornwall next month (we)
5. to reserve a room for you (we)
6. to call a taxi for you (I)
7. to rent a car for our tour through the Grand Canyon (I)
8. to buy a road map of California (I)

TO BE SAID TO – to be supposed to

Dorothy **is said to** be pregnant.
Dorothy soll schwanger sein.
Michael **is said to** have done it.
She **is said to** have fallen head over heels in love with him.
Sie soll sich über beide Ohren in ihn verliebt haben.

Der Engländer umschreibt „**sollen**" im Sinne einer(s)
Vermutung, Annahme, Gerüchts
mit:
to be said to
to be supposed to

7 Make sentences in line with the pattern:

PATTERN

Is Percy popular?
He is said to be popular.

1. Is Mr Pitt an engineer?
2. Does he work for a car company?
3. Is he a computer freak?
4. Has Mrs Cook a part-time job?
5. Is she employed in a travel agency?
6. Is she married?
7. Does the firm enjoy a good reputation?
8. Has Henry attended a technical college?
9. Has he been successful?
10. Has he applied for this job?

TO BE TO

You **are to** come to the boss.
Du sollst zum Chef kommen.

Miriam **is to** make an appointment with Mr Shepard.
Miriam soll mit Mr Shepard einen Termin vereinbaren.

She **was** also **to** book a flight to San Francisco.
Sie sollte auch einen Flug nach San Francisco buchen.

8 Translate into English:

1. Mr Roberts soll ein guter Schauspieler sein.
2. Er soll sehr beliebt sein.
3. Mrs Sunshine soll eine Teilzeitbeschäftigung haben.
4. Sie soll sehr tüchtig sein.
5. Diese Firma soll Ersatzteile (spare parts) für Autos verkaufen.
6. Sie soll auf dem Markt sehr erfolgreich sein.
7. Das Angebot der Firma Newman & Co. soll günstig sein.
8. Die Firma soll einen guten Ruf genießen.
9. Die Firma soll die Waren rechtzeitig geliefert haben.
10. Der Exporteur soll den Auftrag sofort ausgeführt haben.

Der Engländer umschreibt „**sollen**" im „**present**" und „**past**" mit

„TO BE TO"

wenn es sich um eine **Anweisung, einen Auftrag oder eine Vereinbarung** handelt. (Oft wird in diesem Sinn auch „to have to" gebraucht.)

(siehe auch Seite 145)

9 Make sentences in line with the pattern:

PATTERN
Harry – to answer the fax at once
Harry **is to** answer the fax at once.

1. Susan   – to ring him up tomorrow
2. Mike   – to book tickets for the show
3. Maureen   – to take the money to the bank
4. Henry   – to pick up Mr Roberts from the station
5. Sarah   – to call a taxi
6. John   – to post the letters
7. Alan   – to be at the airport at 5.30 p.m.
8. Sheila   – to check in at the BA desk

SHOULD

You **should** follow his advice.
Du solltest seinen Rat befolgen.

You **should** keep your eyes open.
Sie sollten Ihre Augen offen halten.

OUGHT TO

You **ought** not **to** smoke so much.
Du solltest nicht so viel rauchen.

Such things **ought** not **to** be allowed.
Solche Dinge sollten nicht erlaubt sein.

11 Fill in: **shall, should** or **ought to**

1. ... I buy you a drink, Harry?
2. Harry ... be more careful with alcohol.
3. He ... not to drink so much.
4. He ... take more care of his health.
5. ... I order a taxi for you?
6. You ... do that.
7. You ... book the flight in advance.
8. When ... I be at the airport? At 7.30 p.m.
9. You ... be there a bit earlier.
10. ... I phone you when I have arrived? Please do so.

10 Translate into English:

1. Robin soll um 9 Uhr auf dem Flugplatz sein.
2. Er soll Dolly abholen.
3. Er soll mit dem Wagen seines Vaters fahren.
4. Er sollte ihr die Sehenswürdigkeiten von San Francisco zeigen.
5. Miriam sollte sich nach Preisen und Flügen nach Seattle erkundigen.
6. Sie sollte ein Telegramm an Mr Hopkins aufgeben.
7. Fox & Drake sollten Hunter & Co ein Angebot unterbreiten.
8. Sie sollten akzeptable Vorschläge machen.
9. Der Exporteur sollte sich sofort entscheiden.
10. Hunter & Co sollen die Rechnung sofort begleichen.

„Sollte" im Sinn eines **Ratschlags, einer Empfehlung oder einer Verpflichtung** wird durch

„**SHOULD**"

wiedergegeben. (nur im „past tense")

Man sollte eigentlich etw. tun.

Der Engländer gibt „sollte" durch „ought to" statt durch „should" wieder, wenn „**du solltest eigentlich etw. tun**" mehr Nachdruck verliehen werden soll.

„Ought to" wird nur im „past tense" gebraucht!

12 Translate into English:

1. Mr Robinson sollte das Risiko nicht eingehen; es ist zu groß.
2. Er sollte vorsichtiger sein.
3. Sie sollten es sich noch einmal überlegen.
4. Er sollte sich sofort entschließen.
5. Trevor sollte zum Arzt gehen.
6. Er hätte es früher tun sollen.
7. Er sollte nicht so viel rauchen.
8. Er sollte die Sache ernster nehmen.
9. Er sollte den Rat des Arztes befolgen.
10. Sie sollten sich mehr um Ihre Gesundheit kümmern.

Specific texts dealing with commerce and trade

1 Working in an export firm

Hans Kuhn is employed in an export firm in Hamburg. When he was a trainee, he had to sort and to file the correspondence, to learn how to write business letters and to calculate prices. When he had finished his vocational training, he had to deal with exports to Nigeria.

On his first day Hans received an enquiry for refrigerators from Hicks & Co Lagos. He immediately contacted German firms which produce refrigerators. When he had received offers from several firms, he worked out an offer for Hicks & Co. In the offer he quoted prices, the terms of payment and delivery, discounts and the delivery date. He also enclosed leaflets and brochures from different German firms in order to give Hicks & Co an idea of their refrigerators.

After two weeks Hans received an order for 40 refrigerators "Freezy" from the firm in Lagos. He placed the order with Hauser AG at once. He also phoned shipping agents requesting them to inform him when ships were leaving Hamburg for Lagos. Then he sent an advice of despatch to Hicks & Co informing them about the date of arrival of the refrigerators.

When the refrigerators had arrived in Lagos, Hicks & Co settled the invoice.

COMPREHENSION TESTS

1 Translate the text into German.

2 Answer the following questions:

1. Where is Hans Kuhn employed?
2. What did he have to do as a trainee?
3. What was his job when he had finished his vocational training?
4. What did he receive on his first day?
5. What did he quote in the offer?
6. Why did he enclose leaflets from different German firms?
7. How many refrigerators did Hicks & Co order?
8. Why did Hans phone shipping agents?

3 Complete the following sentences:

1. When he was a trainee, he had to ... and to file the ... .
2. He had to learn how to write ... and to ... prices.
3. When he had finished his vocational ..., he had to ... with exports to Nigeria.
4. When he had ... offers from several firms, he ... an offer for Hicks & Co.
5. He ... leaflets from different firms.

4 Make a summary of the text: "Working in an export firm."

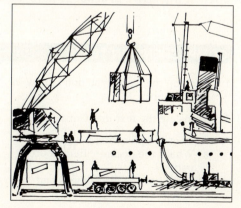

2 At the port of London (Shipping goods)

Life in the port of London is very busy. Ships are coming and going. Dockworkers are loading and unloading cargo or taking it to the warehouses. Here lorries are waiting to transport it to customers (wholesalers, importers, etc.).

There is the MS Queensland at the quay. It has brought coffee from Brazil and is being unloaded. The goods, which it has to transport to Bombay, first have to pass through customs. Then the dockworkers take the goods, which are packed in seaworthy cases and sacks or stowed in containers, to the ship. When the captain has examined the shipping documents such as the Bill of Lading, and has made sure that the cargo has been properly stowed, the MS Queensland leaves for Bombay where it will arrive in about 25 days' time.

COMPREHENSION TESTS

1. Look up the words you don't know in a dictionary.
2. Translate the text into German.
3. Answer the following questions:
   a) What's the dockers' field of occupation?
   b) What has the MS Queensland brought from Brazil?
   c) What are the goods packed in?
   d) What does the captain do before the ship leaves for the port of destination?
   e) How long does it take to sail from Hamburg to Bombay?
4. Name the means of transport and the other things which are to be seen in the picture.

3 A business talk

Mr Fowler, who is a manager at a London department store, has received a circular from Barner & Co. As this letter has attracted his interest, he is phoning Barner & Co.

Voice	Barner & Co.
Mr Fowler	This is Mr Fowler of Harrods, London. Can I speak to your sales manager Mr Sherman, please?
Voice	Yes, Mr Fowler. Just a moment, please.
Mr Sherman	Sherman speaking.
Mr Fowler	Good morning, Mr Sherman. This is John Fowler of Harrods, London. We have received your circular in which you offer a new collection of tropical wear and are very interested in finding out more about it.
Mr Sherman	How can I help you?
Mr Fowler	Well, Mr Sherman. We are going to extend our range of tropical wear and would find it most helpful if a representative of yours would call on us and make us familiar with your new tropical wear.
Mr Sherman	With pleasure, Mr Fowler. Can you suggest a date and time when our Mr Fox may call on you?
Mr Fowler	Monday next at half past two would be convenient. Would it also be convenient for you?
Mr Sherman	Yes, it would, Mr Fowler. Our Mr Fox will call on you in your office on Monday the 12th at half past two.
Mr Fowler	Fine, Mr Sherman. Goodbye.
Mr Sherman	Goodbye, Mr Fowler. And many thanks for your call.

1. Read the text in roles.
2. Translate it into German.
3. Ask questions on it and answer them.
4. Make a summary of the text.

4 A business letter
(MAKING A COUNTERPROPOSAL)

VÖLKERS & CO

Langenhorner Chaussee 134 – 22415 Hamburg
Telefon: 040 3781256 – Fax: 040 3781467
Internet: www.voelkers-wvd.de – E-Mail: voelkers-wvd@t-online.de

R.D. Marshall Company
10 Walker Street
LOS ANGELES Ca 90019
USA

16 June 20..

Our ref: SM/VO

Dear Mrs Baxter

We thank you for your quotation for jeans of 8th of this month.

You will be pleased to hear that the quality and the colours of the jeans appeal to us very much. We must point out, however, that several foreign firms are also offering jeans of good quality, but at much lower prices. It is true that our customers like to buy jeans which are made in the United States, but only if prices are acceptable.

Therefore you will understand that, in these circumstances, it is only possible for us to place an order with you if you are able to grant us a reduction of 10% on the list prices.

We look forward to your reply.

Yours sincerely
VÖLKERS & CO

Susanne Meister
Leiterin der Importabteilung

---

1. Read the letter.
2. Translate it into German.
3. Ask questions on the letter and answer them.
4. Reproduce the letter in your own words.

5 A business letter
(MAKING A COMPLAINT)

WATSON LIMITED

10 Corner Street – Oxford O5 PL 5GE
Tel.: 018569512142
Fax: 018562936985
Internet: www.watson-wvd.uk
e-mail: watson-wvd@net.uk

BS/DO

Hillman Bros
5 Baker Street
LONDON RS5 LE 4   14 March 20..

Dear Mr Hurd

We thank you for the prompt execution of our order of 8 March.

On opening the parcel, which arrived this morning, we found that you delivered maps of Oxford instead of guidebooks to Oxford. As the guidebooks to Oxford are currently out of stock, we would ask you to deliver them at once.

The maps of Oxford are held at your disposal.

Yours sincerely
WATSON LIMITED

Betty Smith
Chief Secretary

---

1. Read the letter.
2. Translate it into German.
3. Ask questions on it and answer them.
4. Reproduce the letter in your own words.

6 Visitors at the Hanover Fair

The Hanover Fair is one of the most important in the world. Manufacturers, engineers, mechanics, tradesmen and businessmen such as exporters, importers, wholesalers and retailers visit a fair in order to display and sell their products there or to see what is on display.

One of them is Mr Harriman, a sales manager from London. He is the head of the sales department. He has to see that incoming letters are answered promptly and that the company is competitive on the market. He has also to see that orders are executed carefully and punctually, that customers get the best possible service and that complaints, if any, are settled to the customers' satisfaction.

Then there is Mr Shriver. He is a mechanical engineer. It is his job to design and construct tools and machinery. Mechanical engineers are engaged in manufacturing plants in which aircraft, locomotives, cranes, drilling machines, combustion engines, etc. are produced.

Mr Blake is an electrical engineer. At college he studied how to design and construct motors, generators, etc. He is a specialist in everything that has something to do with electricity. An electrical engineer is engaged in manufacturing plants, radio and TV companies and others.

COMPREHENSION TESTS

1 Translate the text into German.

2 Answer the following questions:

1. Who visits fairs?
2. Why do people visit fairs?
3. Who is Mr Harriman?
4. What kind of work has he to do?
5. Who are Mr Shriver and Mr Blake?
6. What kind of work do they do?
7. Where do mechanical engineers work?
8. Where do electrical engineers work?

3 Complete the following sentences:

1. The Hanover ... is one of the most important in the ... .
2. Businessmen ... fairs in order to ... and sell their goods there.
3. Mr Harriman is the head of the ... .
4. He has to ... that the company is ... on the market.
5. An electrical ... is a specialist in everything that has something to do with ... .
6. It is the ... engineer's job to ... and construct tools and ... .

4 Fill in the missing letter(s):

wholes.ler, ret.ler, to be comp.tit.ve, ma.inery, man.fact.ring pl.nt, air.raft, cr.ne, comb.stion eng.ne, gen.rat.r, to the c.st.mers' s.tisfaction, visit.r, me.anic, to displ. sth, p.nctu.lly, to des.gn sth

5 Make a summary of the text "Visitors at the Hanover Fair".

7 What do you know about modern communications systems?

Kevin has attended the Technical College in Manchester for four years. This morning he has to take the final examination.

Teacher: Well, Kevin. You will remember that we dealt with communications systems. Would you please name some?

Kevin: Yes, sir. There is fax, for instance. Then there is satellite communication, Internet and e-mail.

Teacher: What do you know about fax?

Kevin: By means of fax you can transmit copies of letters and other things to other fax users. If you want to communicate by fax, you need a fax machine which is connected to your telephone.

Teacher: Good, Kevin. And what can you tell me about satellite communication?

Kevin: By means of satellite communication telephone conversations, television pictures and the like are transmitted.

Teacher: We also dealt with computers. Can you tell me what a computer is composed of?

Kevin: It is mainly composed of the keyboard, the central processing unit, the monitor and the printer.

Teacher: What's the function of the software?

Kevin: The software instructs the computer how to carry out the orders given to it.

Teacher: Good, Kevin. Can you name in one or two sentences the advantages of computers?

Kevin: Computers work very fast and economically. Only a little space is required to store a large volume of data. They are a great help to managers because it is often necessary to take quick decisions.

Teacher: Well, Kevin. Which are the latest communications systems?

Kevin: They are Internet and e-mail.

Teacher: What can you tell us about them?

Kevin: The Internet has revolutionized telecommunications. On the homepages of the Internet you can find any kind of information of general interest. You can book journeys, transfer money, have your own homepage or surf round the world.
There is also e-mail, which allows you to communicate with other e-mail users by sending letters and the like.

Teacher: Good, Kevin. That will do. You have done very well. I wish you all the best for your future.

COMPREHENSION TESTS

1 Translate the dialogue text into German.

2 Answer the following questions:

1. What kind of school did Kevin attend?
2. How did he explain fax?
3. What is a computer composed of?
4. What's the function of the software?
5. Name some advantages of computers.
6. What's the Internet good for?

3 Complete the following sentences:

1. This morning Kevin has to ... the ... examination.
2. You will remember that we ... with modern communications systems.
3. If you want to ... by fax, you need a ... which is connected to your telephone.
4. Computers work very ... and very ... .
5. Computers are also a great ... to managers because it is often ... to take quick ... .
6. Internet makes it possible to ... round the world.

4 Fill in the missing letter(s):

fin.l ex.min.tion, Technic.l Coll.ge in Man.ester, sate.ite, to be transmi.ed, k.board, ad.ant.ge, sp.ce, vol.me of d.ta, to revol.tioni.e, centr.l proce.ing un.t, ne.ess.ry

8 How a house is built

Mr Hunt is a bricklayer and has decided to build a house of his own. He has already bought a building site on the outskirts of Newcastle where sites are not so expensive. Mr Shilvers is an architect. He has made the construction plans for Mr Hunt's new house. Before work on the house begins, Mr Shilvers and Mr Hunt discuss everything in detail.

Mr Hunt is the one who begins the work on the house. When he has finished laying the bricks, he calls Mr Gibbs, the carpenter, and Mr Calder, the tiler, who make the roof. After that the plumber fits the gas and water pipes. Then the electrician, Mr Brown, continues the work on the house. He does the electrical wiring in the rooms and installs the electrical equipment. After that Mr Hunt plasters the walls. Then the central heating system with the radiators and gas boilers is installed by the fitter. The joiner fits in the window frames and doors. The glazier glazes the windows. The painter, who is the last tradesman, whitewashes the ceilings and papers the walls. Now the work on Mr Hunt's house is finished.

(Exercises page 166)

TRADESMEN

1. What are these people's jobs?
2. What do these people do in their jobs?

COMPREHENSION TESTS

1 Translate the text "How a house is built" into German.

2 Answer the following questions:

1. Who is Mr Hunt?
2. What has he decided to do?
3. Where has he bought a site?
4. Why did he buy a site there?
5. What kind of work do joiners and glaziers do?
6. What is done when the walls have been plastered?
7. Who is the last tradesman?

TOOLS
Who uses it/them?

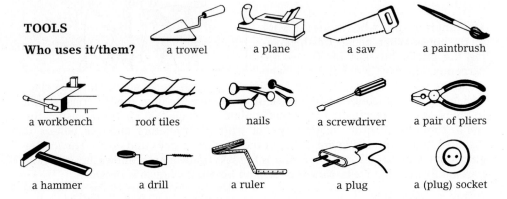

a trowel — a plane — a saw — a paintbrush

a workbench — roof tiles — nails — a screwdriver — a pair of pliers

a hammer — a drill — a ruler — a plug — a (plug) socket

9 A farmer's activities

What are the farmer and his wife doing?

166

VOCABULARY AIDS

to rake
to plough the land
to sow wheat/barley/oats
to fertilize the soil
to harvest potatoes/the crop

to thresh grain
to feed cattle
to milk cows
(siehe auch Vokabelverzeichnis)

10 Sarah learns how to cook

Sarah is a trainee at the Jolly Hotel where she is learning how to cook. At the beginning she has a lot of trouble with the cooking because almost everything goes wrong. But very soon Michael, the head cook, is very satisfied with her. "Cooking is very easy", he usually says. "If you use cream, sherry, the right spices and other wonderful ingredients, you will be all right, no matter whether you practise the French, Italian, Chinese or English style of cooking."

Today yogurt soup, duck with pears and chocolate mousse are, among other things, on the menu. "Well", Michael says to Sarah, "for the yogurt soup let me have five tablespoons of rice, 1.8 litres of chicken stock, salt and pepper, 600 ml yogurt, two egg yolks, two tablespoons of dried mint, 50 g of butter and two teaspoons of paprika. For duck with pears I need a duck (about 2.25 kg), olive oil, six unripe pears peeled and cut in half, one cinnamon stick, two sliced onions, one sliced carrot, two ripe tomatoes peeled and cut in pieces, a pinch of dried thyme, salt and 125 g of Spanish brandy. For the chocolate mousse let me have 180 g of semi-sweet chocolate, three eggs, three tablespoons of liqueur and two cups of whipped cream."

When Sarah had brought the necessary ingredients, Michael said, "Now look how these things are prepared!"

(First deal with exercises 1 – 3, page 169)

YOGURT SOUP

Boil the rice in the stock until soft. Add salt and pepper. Beat the yogurt with the egg yolks, add a little stock and beat well. Then pour the mixture into the soup, stirring. Add 1 tablespoon mint and cook, stirring all time, until the soup thickens. Before serving, melt the butter, stir in the paprika and the rest of the mint.

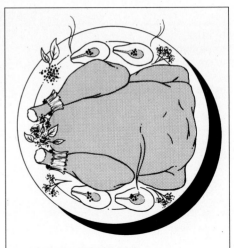

DUCK WITH PEARS

Brown the duck pieces in two tablespoons of oil in a frying pan. Cover the pears in water and boil them with the cinnamon for about 20 minutes. To make the sauce, cook the onions, carrots and tomatoes in three tablespoons of oil until they soften. Add the thyme, salt, brandy and the stock and simmer for about 30 minutes. Add the duck and cook gently for about 45 minutes.

Serve the duck pieces with the sauce poured over them and decorate with the warmed pear halves.

CHOCOLATE MOUSSE

Chop and melt chocolate. Then beat eggs over hot water until frothy and beat in liqueur.

Then stir in melted chocolate until thoroughly combined. After that beat cream in a separate bowl. Then stir one third whipped cream into mixture, fold in remaining cream.

COMPREHENSION TESTS

1 **Answer the following questions:**

1. What is Sarah learning?
2. Where does she learn it?
3. Why does she have a lot of trouble at the beginning?
4. What does Michael, the head cook, usually say?
5. What did Michael cook?
6. What do you need to cook duck with pears.

2 **Complete the following sentences:**

1. Sarah is a ... at the Jolly Hotel.
2. Very soon Michael, the head cook, is very ... with Sarah.
3. If you ... cream, sherry and the right ..., you will be ... .
4. Today chocolate ..., duck with ... and ... soup are on the ... .
5. Sarah brought the necessary ... .
6. What did Michael say when Sarah had ... them?

3 **Fill in the missing letter(s):**

train., ingred.ents, wh.ther, w.ther, spi.e, to practi.e, egg .olks. dr.d mint, to p.l sth, ne.essary, oni.n, pa.rika, ca.ot, to have a lot of tr.ble, Itali.n, Chin.se st.le of c.king, unr.pe p.rs

4 **Translate the texts into German.**

For further study

THE PREPOSITIONS – Die Präpositionen

Prepositions in the sense of place
(Präpositionen mit örtlicher Bedeutung)

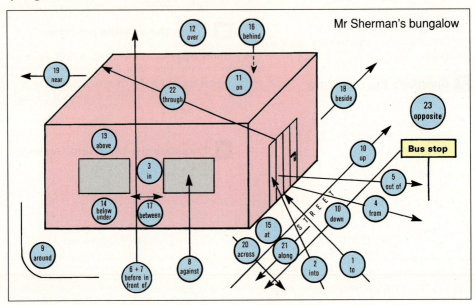

Mr Sherman's bungalow

1. Roy is going **to** the bungalow. (**zum** Bungalow **hin**, nicht hinein)
2. Roy is going **into** the bungalow. (er geht **hinein**)
3. Roy is **in** the bungalow. (er ist **drin**) R. is **at** the bungalow. (**am/beim** Bungalow). He was born **in** Hull. (**in**)
4./5. Roy is coming **from (out of)** the bungalow. (er kommt **vom** Bungalow /**aus** dem Bungalow **heraus**)
6. Roy is standing **before** the bungalow. (er steht **davor**)
7. There are some trees **in front of** the bungalow. (sie stehen **vor** dem Bungalow)
8. The rain is beating **against** the windows. (**gegen** die Fenster schlagen)
9. Roy is going **around** the bungalow. (um den Bungalow **herum**gehen)
10. Roy is running **up and down** the street. (**auf-** und **ab**laufen – **hinauf** und **herunter**)
11. Roy's ball is **on** the roof. (**auf** dem Dach sein)
12. The plane is just flying **over** the bungalow. (**über** dem Bungalow)
13. The burglar alarm is **above (over)** the left window. (**oberhalb [über]** des [dem] linken Fenster[s])
14. The flower bed is **below (under)** the left window. (**unterhalb [unter]** des [dem] linken Fenster[s])
15. Roy is **at** the bungalow. (**beim** Bungalow)
16. Roy is **behind** the bungalow. (**hinter** dem Bungalow)
17. There is a lamp **between** the two windows. (**zwischen 2** Dingen oder

Personen)
aber: There is only one bungalow **among** these houses. (**unter mehreren** Häusern)
18. There is a garage **beside** the bungalow. (**neben** dem Bungalow)
19. There is a shop **near** the bungalow. (**nahe** beim Bungalow)
20. There is a shop **across** the street. (**quer über** der Straße)
21. Roy is going **along** the street. (die Straße **entlang**)
22. Roy is going **through** the house. (**durch** das Haus gehen, **hindurch**)
23. There is a bus stop **opposite** our house. (**gegenüber** dem Haus)

1 Fill in an appropriate preposition:

1. Oliver comes ... Australia.
2. He was born ... Sydney.
3. Anne wanted to go on a tour ... Scotland.
4. A second-class return ticket ... Edinburgh, please.
5. The train leaves ... platform 2.
6. It arrived ... Edinburgh on time.
7. The taxi stand is ... the station.
8. He bought a magazine ... the kiosk.
9. They went shopping ... Harrods.
10. Is there a bus stop ... the store.
11. He met Jimmy when he went ... the store.
12. He was coming ... it when the ambulance arrived.
13. Oxford Street is ... Hyde Park.
14. Haymarket lies ... Piccadilly Circus and Trafalgar Square.
15. The river Thames flows ... London.
16. We had lunch ... a fast-food restaurant.
17. The restaurant is ... the cinema.
18. There were a lot of newspapers ... the table.
19. They went on a sightseeing tour ... London.
20. There are only three Englishmen ... the tourists.
21. Is there an underground station ... your house? (on the other side)
22. Is there a bridge ... the river?
23. There are trees ... the river bank.
24. The bedroom is ... the first floor, the dining room ... the ground floor. The bedroom is ... the dining room, the dining room ... the bedroom.
25. The burglar came in ... the window.

Prepositions in the sense of time
(Präpositionen mit zeitlicher Bedeutung)

1. It is **about** six o'clock. (**ungefähr**)
2. I met him two hours **ago**. (**vor**)
3. I will leave **after** lunch. (**nach**)
4. I will come **before** two o'clock. (**vor**)
5. I will be ready **in** a minute or two. (**in**)
6. It is a quarter **past** nine. (**nach**)
7. It is a quarter **to** nine. (**vor**)
8. The goods will arrive **by** the end of this month. (**bis ... spätestens**)
9. He was born **on** March 3, 1970. (**am**)
10. The film begins **at** eight o'clock. (**um**)
11. I waited for you **until** (**till**) eight o'clock. (**bis**)
12. I attended a holiday course **during** the summer holidays. (**während**) aber: While I was staying in Bournemouth, I attended a holiday course. (while – Konjunktion)
13. I have been waiting for you **since** two o'clock. (**seit** – Zeitpunkt)
14. I have been waiting for you **for** half an hour. (**seit** – Zeitspanne)

2 Fill in an appropriate preposition:

1. When does the party begin? ... 9 o'clock.
2. When are you leaving for Spain? ... Wednesday.
3. When will you be back? I'll be back ... the end of July.
4. When will Mr Hurt come to Hamburg? He will come ... March 3.
5. When are you going to the beach? ... breakfast.
6. How long have you been waiting for me? I have been waiting ... half ... eight.
7. When did you last see him? Three days ... .
8. How long will it take to repair the car? ... four hours.
9. Were you at Harrods ... or ... eleven o'clock?
10. When did you attend the holiday course in Brighton? I attended it ... the summer holidays.

THE CONJUNCTIONS – Die Konjunktionen

Eine **Konjunktion** verbindet Satzteile und Sätze; sie leitet Haupt- und Nebensätze ein.

Eine **Präposition** steht vor einem Substantiv oder Pronomen.

Preposition	Conjunction
After breakfast I played golf. I usually go jogging **before** breakfast.	**After** I had had breakfast, I played golf. I usually go jogging **before** I have breakfast.

Daniel **and** Carol have gone to the horse race. I'll watch television **or** read a book.	Konjunktionen, die Wörter miteinander verbinden, sind: **and** **or**

Mary went shopping **after** she had done her housework.	Konjunktionen, die Sätze miteinander verbinden:	
You will be successful **if** you work hard.	after	– nachdem
	when	– wenn, als
	for	– denn
Arthur failed the exam **although** he is a clever boy.	before	– bevor
	while (whilst)	– während
I know **that** he is in a very bad way.	though	– obwohl
	although	– obgleich
I was having a chat with Ann **while** Bob was playing tennis.	in order to	– um zu
	as	
	because	– da, weil
He went to the disco **in order to** meet friends there.	if	– wenn, falls
	unless	– wenn nicht
We will stay at home **because** it is raining. („Because" steht in der Mitte des Satzes!)	that	– dass, damit
	but	– aber
	since	– da (seit)
	whether	– ob
I'll do my homework **before** I go to the cinema.	as soon as u. a.	– sobald (wie)

Fill in an appropriate conjunction:

1. What would you like to have? Tea ... coffee? Tea.
2. After the news I drove to the airport ... pick up Sandra.
3. ... I am about to leave for Bristol, I will ring you up.
4. Everybody knows ... he is a bit clumsy.
5. You will hear from me ... I have arrived in New York.
6. ... she had caught a cold, she went out.
7. You will be fined ... you observe the traffic rules.
8. Alice will drop you ... you flirt with other girls.
9. Gerald was fired ... he was often drunk.
10. Anthony ... James were arrested ... they broke into a house and pinched money and cheques.
11. He asked me ... I could tell him the nearest way to the station.
12. ... Mr Perkins had been questioned by the constable, he had a drink.
13. ... Anne was watching a video, I was dropping a line to Mark.
14. He said ... he had heard a pack of lies today.
15. I wonder ... the penny will drop.
16. You will be successful ... you seize the bull by the horns.
17. You should think it over ... you are going to cause a storm in a teacup.
18. You should do it ... it is too late.
19. ... she had won in the lottery, she had a party with lots of alcohol.
20. Jack attended evening classes ... polish up his English.
21. ... he is a good tennis player, he lost the match.
22. He would have helped me ... he had not been short of money.
23. ... he does not play football, he does crossword puzzles.
24. Everybody dislikes him ... he often tricks other people.
25. We know ... she is a very modest person.

THE "IF-CLAUSES" – Die Bedingungssätze

1. Im Englischen unterscheidet man drei Arten von Bedingungssätzen:
   a) **den realen Bedingungssatz:** Er beinhaltet, dass das, was man voraussetzt, **durchaus** realisierbar ist.
   b) **den potenzialen Bedingungssatz:** Er beinhaltet, dass das, was man voraussetzt, **reell oder möglicherweise** realisierbar ist.
   c) **den irrealen Bedingungssatz:** Er beinhaltet, dass das, was gedacht oder vorausgesetzt wird (wurde), **nicht** oder **nur theoretisch** realisierbar ist.

2. Die **Bedingungssätze** werden in der Regel mit der Konjunktion **„if"** eingeleitet.

The use of the "if-clauses" – die Anwendung der „if-clauses"

	if-Satz (Nebensatz/if-clause)	**Hauptsatz** (main clause)
Etwas ist realisierbar	If you **pass** the exam, *Wenn du das Examen bestehst,*	I **will arrange** a party. *werde ich eine Party arrangieren.*
Zeitenfolge:	*present tense*	*will-future*

	if-Satz (Nebensatz/if-clause)	Hauptsatz (main clause)
Etwas ist reell oder möglicherweise realisierbar	If you **should** pass the exam, Wenn du das Examen bestehen solltest,	I **will (would) arrange** a party. werde (würde) ich eine Party arrangieren.
Zeitenfolge:	should	will-future or conditional
Etwas ist **nicht** oder nur theoretisch realisierbar	If you **passed** the exam, Wenn du das Examen beständest,	I **would arrange** a party. würde ich eine Party arrangieren.
Zeitenfolge:	past tense	conditional
	If you **had passed** the exam, Wenn du das Examen bestanden hättest,	I **would have arranged*** a party. hätte ich eine Party arrangiert.
Zeitenfolge:	past perfect	conditional perfect

* Die Zeiten des „conditional perfect" siehe Seite 190

MAN MERKE SICH

Man kann auch mit dem Hauptsatz beginnen, wobei allerdings das Komma entfällt.

I will arrange a party if you pass the exam.

The sequence of tenses – die Zeitenfolge

	if-clause	main clause
1.	present	will-future
2.	should	will-future or conditional
3.	past	conditional
4.	past perfect	conditional perfect

1 Fill in the correct tenses in line with the pattern:

PATTERN

If you **(to borrow)** too much money, you will **(to get)** into trouble.

If **you borrow** too much money, **you will get** into trouble.

1. If you (to need) any/some money, I (to lend) you some.
2. If you (to have) any trouble, I (to help) you.
3. If you (to work) hard, you (to be) successful.
4. If I (to receive) an invitation, I (to go) to the party.
5. If you (to hire) a taxi, you (to arrive) in time.
6. If you (to visit) me, I (to show) you the sights of the city.
7. You (to get) tickets for the show if you (to book) in advance.
8. You (to reach) your goal if you (to do) your best.
9. If I (to win) a lot of money in the lottery, I (to go) on a trip around the world.
10. You perhaps (to win) a lot of money if you (to do) the football pools.

2 Fill in the correct tenses in line with the pattern:

PATTERN

If you **(to borrow)** too much money, you **(to get)** into trouble.

If you **should borrow** too much money, **you will (would)** get into trouble.

Use the sentences of exercise 1.

3 Fill in the correct tenses in line with the pattern:

PATTERN

If you **(to borrow)** too much money, you **(to get)** into trouble.

If you **borrowed** too much money, **you would get** into trouble.

Use the sentences of exercise 1.

4 Fill in the correct tenses in line with the pattern:

PATTERN

If you **(to borrow)** too much money, you **(to get)** into trouble.

If **you had borrowed** too much money, **you would have got** into trouble.

Use the sentences of exercise 1.

5 Put the verbs in brackets into the correct tense:

PATTERN

I'll take part in the stag party if I (to get) an invitation.

I'll take part in the stag party if **I get** an invitation.

1. If you try your luck, you (to win) certainly the prize.
2. I would be angry with you if you (to waste) all your money.
3. I (to give) you some more wine if there was any left in the bottle.
4. If you (to drink) too much, you will have a hangover the next day.
5. If you had told the truth, nothing (to happen).
6. If you should disagree to the conditions, we (to look) for another partner.
7. If you had come across difficulties, I (to assist) you.
8. You must wait a few minutes if you (to want) to speak with him.
9. If it (to rain) cats and dogs, I would stay at home.
10. If you (to take) this opportunity, you will be successful.
11. If you had blackmailed me, I (to report) you to the police.
12. If you should try to bribe him, he (to tell) me.
13. You would not have got yourself into a fix if you (to be) more careful.
14. If the engine had stood the test, it (to be launched) on the market.
15. You (to get) a guarantee on the car if it had been new.

6 Translate into English:

1. Ich hätte dir geholfen, wenn du mich darum gebeten hättest.
2. Sarah würde es tun, wenn du damit einverstanden bist.
3. Ich werde an der „Moonlight party" teilnehmen, wenn das Wetter gut ist.
4. Ich wäre ärgerlich auf dich, wenn du dich in die Sache einmischen würdest.
5. Du wirst die Maschine bekommen, wenn du ein Taxi nimmst.
6. Wenn du im Fußballtoto spielst, kannst du viel Geld gewinnen.
7. Ich würde eine Weltreise machen, wenn ich viel gewänne.
8. Wir werden die Bedingungen annehmen, wenn sie gut sind.
9. Wenn das Angebot günstig gewesen wäre, hätten wir es angenommen.
10. Die Bank hätte den Kredit nicht gewährt, wenn die Auskunft ungünstig gewesen wäre.

THE INDIRECT SPEECH (QUESTION) – Die indirekte Rede (Frage)

The sequence of tenses 1 – die Zeitenfolge 1

Direkte Rede: Indirekte Rede:	He says, "Liz **is/was** a sport." He **says** that Liz **is/was** a sport. **(Bezugsverb)**	**PRESENT / PAST** into into **PRESENT / PAST**
Direkte Frage: Indirekte Frage:	He asks, "**Is/was** Liz a sport?" He **asks** if Liz **is/was** a sport. **(Bezugsverb)**	**PRESENT / PAST** into into **PRESENT / PAST**

MAN MERKE SICH

Steht das **Bezugsverb** des Hauptsatzes im „**present**" / „**present perfect**", so werden im Nebensatz der indirekten Rede (Frage) die **gleichen Zeiten** gebraucht wie in der **direkten Rede/Frage**.

→ **Es sind also im Nebensatz sämtliche Zeiten möglich!**

The sequence of tenses 2 – Die Zeitenfolge 2

He said, "I **am** tipsy." (beschwipst) He said that he **was** tipsy.	**PRESENT** into **PAST**
He said, "I **was** tipsy." He said that he **had been** tipsy.	**PAST** into **PAST PERFECT**
He said, "I **will** phone you on Sunday." He said that he **would** phone me on Sunday.	**WILL-FUTURE** into **CONDITIONAL**
He said, "I **have phoned** Sarah." He said that he **had phoned** Sarah.	**PRESENT PERFECT** into **PAST PERFECT**
He asked me, "**Are** you tipsy?" He asked me if I **was** tipsy.	**PRESENT** into **PAST**
He asked me, "**Were** you tipsy?" He asked me if I **had been** tipsy.	**PAST** into **PAST PERFECT**
He asked me, "**Will you phone** him?" He asked me if I **would phone** him.	**WILL-FUTURE** into **CONDITIONAL**
He asked me, "**Have you phoned** him?" He asked me if I **had phoned** him.	**PRESENT PERFECT** into **PAST PERFECT**

MAN MERKE SICH

1. Steht das **Bezugsverb** des Hauptsatzes im **PAST** oder **PAST PERFECT**, so steht das Verb des Nebensatzes in folgenden Zeiten:
   PAST oder **PAST PERFECT** oder **CONDITIONAL**
   Welche dieser drei Zeiten im Nebensatz der indirekten Rede (Frage) steht, **richtet sich nach der Zeit, in der das Verb in der direkten Rede steht.**

2. Bei der Umwandlung der direkten Rede in die indirekte wird:
this zu **that**, **these** zu **those**	**yesterday** zu **the day before**
today zu **that day**	**last week** zu **the week before**
now zu **then**	**next week** zu **the following week**
tomorrow zu **the next (following) day**	**three weeks ago** zu **three weeks before**

1 Make sentences in line with the pattern and use the correct tense(s):

PATTERN

He **says (said)**, "I work for Calder & Co."
He **says** that **he works** for Calder & Co.
He **said** that **he worked** for Calder & Co.

a) **He says:**
b) **He said:**

1. "I am a bank clerk."
2. "I get up at half past six in the morning."
3. "We have breakfast at seven o'clock."
4. "I leave for the office at a quarter past seven."
5. "I go to the office by bus."
6. "I was at a disco last night."
7. "I met a lot of friends there."
8. "We had a lot of fun."
9. "I was merry."
10. "A taxi took him home."
11. "I will buy a new camera."
12. "I will take photos of the sights of Boston."
13. "Harry will spend his next holidays in California."
14. "He will go there by caravan."
15. "He and his friends will have a good time there."
16. "Maureen has applied for that job."
17. "She has had good luck."
18. "She has arranged a party."
19. "She has invited a lot of friends."
20. "Most of them have accepted the invitation."

2 Make sentences with "he asks if" and "he asked if" in line with the pattern:

PATTERN

He **asks (asked)**, "Do you work for Calder & Co?"
He **asks** if **I work** for Calder & Co.
He **asked** if **I worked** for Calder & Co.

a) **He asks:**
b) **He asked:**

1. "Are you a bank clerk?"
2. "Do you like your job?"
3. "Do you go to your office by bus or by tube?"
4. "Were you in the disco last night?"
5. "Did you meet a lot of friends?"
6. "Did you have a lot of fun?"
7. "Will Helen buy a new camera?"
8. "Will you take photos of Boston?"
9. "Will you go to Miami by caravan?"
10. "Has Sarah applied for that job?"
11. "Has she had good luck?"
12. "Has she celebrated it?"

3 Make sentences in line with the pattern:

PATTERN

He **says / said** –
I will go on holiday in July.

He **says** that **he will go** on holiday in July.
He **said** that **he would go** on holiday in July.

1. **Tom says / said** –
   I booked a package holiday to Florida yesterday.
2. **He told us** –
   Susan has already made the necessary arrangements.
3. **The clerk says / said** –
   The ship leaves Miami for the Caribbean Islands on Monday.
4. **He says / said** –
   We will buy cigarettes and spirits in the duty-free shop.
5. **They say / said** –
   The voyage was marvellous.
6. **He says / said** –
   The next plane to New York leaves at 8.15 a.m.
7. **Ronald says / said** –
   I have changed 200 pounds into dollars.
8. **Anne says / said** –
   I will cash my traveller's cheque at the airport.
9. **The clerk says / said** –
   The exchange rate of the euro is very favourable.
10. **Kevin told us** –
    I rented a Ford at this car-rental office last week.

11. **Helen says / said** –
    San Francisco is really worth a visit.
12. **Maureen says / said** –
    The tour of the United States will be a great experience.
13. **Arthur told us** –
    I enjoyed my stay in California.
14. **Mark says / said** –
    We went out last night and had a lot of fun.

4 **Translate into English:**

1. Henry sagt(e), dass er morgen nach Los Angeles fliegen werde.
2. Susan sagt(e), dass sie mich nächste Woche besuchen werde.
3. Mr Fox sagt(e), dass er mich angerufen habe.
4. Robert erzählte mir, dass er in Miami eine nette Amerikanerin kennen gelernt habe.
5. Mark sagt(e), dass er in New York sehr viele Aufnahmen machen werde.
6. Irene erzählte mir, dass ihr Freund einen Unfall gehabt habe.
7. Tim fragte mich, ob ich Mr Pitt kenne.
8. Sarah fragte mich, ob Jack krank sei.
9. Anne fragte mich, ob ich zu der Party gehen werde.

THE INFINITIVE – Der Infinitiv, die Grundform

The forms of the infinitive – Die Formen des Infinitivs

AKTIV (active)	PASSIV (passive)
to ask	to be asked
to have asked	to have been asked

The infinitive as subject, object and an adverbial clause
(Der Infinitiv als Subjekt, Objekt und als adverbialer Satz)

To read is instructive.
(Reading is instructive.)
Lesen ist lehrreich.

It was impossible for me **to help** him out of his difficulties.
Es war mir nicht möglich, ihm aus seinen Schwierigkeiten herauszuhelfen.

It was interesting **to listen** to him.
Es war interessant, ihm zuzuhören.

They intended **to travel to** Wales.
Sie beabsichtigten eine Reise nach Wales zu machen.

Susan continued **to crack** jokes.
Susan machte weiter Witze.
(Susan fuhr fort Witze zu machen.)

Der Infinitiv als Subjekt

Ein **substantiviertes Verb** (Subjekt) wird im Englischen u. a. durch **den Infinitiv** wiedergegeben. (Siehe auch Gerundium – Seite 183)

Der Hauptsatz wird häufig durch „it" eingeleitet; der Infinitiv folgt häufig auf ein Adjektiv, wie bei:

it is difficult (for me), **it is important** (for me), **it is (im-)possible** (for me) usw.

Der Infinitiv als Objekt

Er steht meistens nach Verben wie:

to intend	to prefer
to love	to begin
to start	to continue
to hate	to forget
to learn	to regret

u. a.

I will do everything in my power **to help** him.
Ich werde alles in meiner Macht Stehende tun, um ihm zu helfen.

Steve did his (very) best **(in order) to reach** his goal.
Steve tat sein (Aller-)Bestes, um sein Ziel zu erreichen.

Would you be **so** kind **as to pass** me the ashtray?
Würden Sie bitte so freundlich sein und mir den Aschenbecher reichen?

Der Infinitiv wird in Nebensätzen verwendet, die einen **Zweck** beinhalten. Diese Nebensätze werden eingeleitet durch:

to	– zu, um zu
in order to	– um zu
so ... as to	– (so ...) das, und, um

Steht im Hauptsatz „**so**", muss man den Infinitiv mit „**as to**" anschließen.

1 Translate the following sentences into English:

1. Es ist nicht immer leicht, sich zu beherrschen.
2. Es wäre ratsam, es nicht zu tun.
3. Es wäre riskant, ihm Geld zu leihen.
4. Es wäre leichtsinnig, ihm zu trauen.
5. Es ist oft schwierig, das Richtige zu tun.
6. Es wäre unklug, ihn zu provozieren.
7. Er beabsichtigte sich mit ihm zu einigen.
8. Sie waren bereit einen Kompromiss zu schließen.
9. Er will das Angebot nicht annehmen.
10. Mr Newman bat die Firma, den Auftrag zu stornieren.
11. Die Firma lehnte es ab, dies zu tun.

The infinitive as part of the object – Der Infinitiv als Teil des Objekts

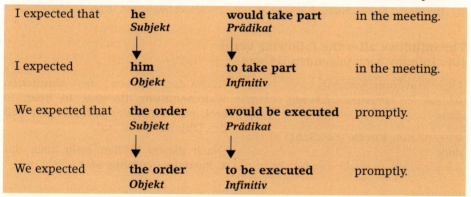

MAN MERKE SICH

Diese Infinitivstruktur **(Subjekt wird zum Objekt; Prädikat wird zum Infinitiv)** wird angewendet, wenn im Hauptsatz folgende Verben stehen:
to expect, to order, to want, to wish, to prefer, to cause (verursachen), **to require, to allow, to think** (jmdn. halten für), **to advise** (jmdm. raten) u. a.

2 Make sentences in line with the pattern:

PATTERN
I asked –
Bobby should buy me a Guinness.
I asked Bobby to buy me a Guinness.

1. Oliver expected –
   I would invite him to the party.
2. Susan asked –
   I should buy her a drink.
3. Mr Hopkins advised –
   He should think it over again.
4. We expect –
   She will change her mind.
5. She wants –
   He picks Mike up from the airport.
6. Father allowed –
   I go to the disco.
7. Thomas asked –
   Susan should keep it to herself.
8. The doctor ordered –
   The injured woman should be taken to hospital.
9. Mark requested –
   Bob should lend him some money.
10. He advised –
    He should raise a loan.
11. We expect –
    The prices will rise next month.
12. I requested –
    He should settle the bill at once.

3 Translate the following sentences into English:

1. Harold erwartete, dass ich Jane zum Bahnhof bringe.
2. Joan wollte, dass ich mir ein Taxi nehme.
3. Sheila wollte, dass wir einen Wagen mieten.
4. Er erwartete, dass ich ihm Geld leihe.
5. Ich wünsche, dass Sie ihm die Wahrheit sagen.
6. Mutter erlaubte, dass ihre Tochter zu der Party geht.
7. Der Arzt ordnete an, dass der verletzte Mann ins Krankenhaus gebracht wird.
8. Wir erwarten, dass die Preise demnächst steigen.
9. Wir wünschen, dass die Fa. Huxley Co. den Auftrag sofort ausführt.
10. Er ordnete an, dass die Rechnung sofort beglichen wird.

The infinitive after the following verbs
(Der Infinitiv nach folgenden Verben)

I saw **him come** (coming).
Ich sah ihn kommen. / Ich sah, wie er kam.

I heard **him knock** (knocking) at the door.
Ich hörte, wie er an die Tür klopfte.

Nach den Verben der **sinnlichen Wahrnehmung** (**to see, to hear, to feel,** etc.) steht **der Infinitiv als Teil des Objekts ohne „to".**

(Nach diesen Verben steht auch das **1. Partizip – coming**, etc.)

4 Make sentences in line with the pattern:

PATTERN
I saw – he pinched the lighter.
I saw him **pinch (pinching)** the lighter.

1. **I heard**
   – Mark quarrelled with his friend.
   – She cried.
   – She ran away.

2. **I saw**
   – Some men broke into the bank.
   – The police seized the gangsters.
   – One man escaped in a car.

The infinitive with interrogative – Der Infinitiv mit Fragewort

I did not **know what to answer**.
Ich wusste nicht, was ich antworten sollte.

He could not **decide whether to go** by bus or by taxi.
Er konnte sich nicht entscheiden, ob er mit dem Bus oder einem Taxi fahren sollte.

The policeman **told** me **how to get** to the nearest bus stop.
Der Polizist sagte mir, wie ich zur nächsten Bushaltestelle komme.

Der Infinitivsatz mit Fragewort steht hauptsächlich nach den Verben:

to ask, to forget, to decide, to wonder, to explain, to find out, to know, to learn, to remember, to see, to show, to tell u. a.

(Im Deutschen steht oft „sollen" oder „können" im Nebensatz.)

Gebräuchliche Fragewörter sind:
when, what, where, how, whether u. a.

5 Translate into English:

1. Andrew fragte mich, wann er Sally anrufen soll.
2. Ich sagte ihm, wann er sie anrufen soll.
3. Jane fragte mich, wie man zum Trafalgar Square kommt.
4. Er zeigte ihr, wie man dorthin kommt.
5. Ich wusste nicht, wie man es macht.
6. Miriam erklärte ihm, wie man es macht.
7. Jack hatte vergessen, wo er Maureen abholen sollte.
8. Er erinnerte sich nicht daran, wo er Catherine treffen wollte.
9. Humphrey erklärte mir, wie man Baseball spielt.
10. Gregory zeigte mir, wie man einen Computer programmiert.

THE PARTICIPLE / THE GERUND – Das Partizip / das Gerundium

THE PARTICIPLE

The forms of the participle – Die Formen des Partizips

	Aktiv (active)	Passiv (passive)
1. **PRESENT PARTICIPLE** (1. Partizip)	asking	being asked, asked
2. **PAST PARTICIPLE** (2. Partizip)	having asked	having been asked

work**ing**	(to work)
ask**ing**	(to ask)
go**ing**	(to go)
catch**ing**	(to catch)

work**ed**	(to work)
ask**ed**	(to ask)
gone	(to go)
caught	(to catch)

Das „**present participle**" wird durch Anhängen der **Endung „ing"** an den **Infinitiv** des Verbs (ohne to) gebildet.

Das „**past participle**" wird bei den **regelmäßigen Verben** durch Anhängen von „**ed**" gebildet.

Bei den **unregelmäßigen Verben** ist die **3. Form** der Stammformen das **2. Partizip** (past participle).

Points to note with the spelling – Besonderheiten in der Rechtschreibung

si**tt**ing	(to sit)	Auslautender einfacher **Mitlaut** wird nach **kurzem, betontem Selbstlaut verdoppelt.**
pu**tt**ing	(to put)	
ru**nn**ing	(to run)	
swi**mm**ing	(to swim)	
refe**rr**ing	(to refer)	
submi**tt**ing	(to submit)	
sto**pp**ing	(to stop)	

hav**ing**	(to have)	Auslautendes „**e**" fällt vor der Endung „**ing**" fort.
writ**ing**	(to write)	

l**y**ing	(to lie)	Verben auf „**ie**" verwandeln vor „**ing**" das „**ie**" in „**y**".

try**ing**	(to try)	Verben auf „**y**" verwandeln das „**y**" bei **vorangehendem Mitlaut** in „**ie**".
tried		

The predicative use of the participle
(Der prädikative Gebrauch des Partizips)

I have **forgotten** his telephone number. This cheque was **cashed** yesterday. Margaret had **lost** the tickets.	Das „**past participle**" wird in den **zusammengesetzten Zeiten** (wie z. B. *present perfect, past perfect*) gebraucht.
Henry **is doing** the crossword puzzle. The bill **is being typed**. Wait a moment, please.	Das „**present participle**" wird in der **Verlaufsform** gebraucht.

The attributive use of the participle
(Der attributive Gebrauch des Partizips)

Sarah is a **charming** woman. attributiv The **advised** (avisierte) fax arrived. attributiv	Das „**present participle**" und „**past participle**" werden auch **attributivisch** gebraucht.

MAN MERKE SICH

Das „**present participle**" steht auch nach den Verben der **sinnlichen Wahrnehmung** (to see, to hear, to feel, etc.) sowie nach den Verben der **Ruhe und Bewegung** (to sit, to stand, to come, to leave, to go, to stay, etc.).

I <u>saw</u> the men **playing** cards. Father was <u>sitting</u> in his armchair **smoking** a pipe.

1 Fill in the correct participle of the verb in brackets:

PATTERN:
What is Joyce ... ? She is ... a cheque. **(to do, to make out)**
What is Joyce **doing**? She is **making out** a cheque.

1. Has Oliver ... this hotel? Yes. **(to recommend)**
2. Was the hotel ... ? No. **(to air-condition)**
3. What is Irene ... ? She is ... the registration form. **(to do, to fill in)**
4. I saw her ... money at the cashier's. **(to change)**
5. Has the telephonist ... a taxi for Mrs Pitt? Yes, he has. **(to call)**
6. Has she ... Mr Hopkins a wake-up call? Yes. **(to give)**
7. Have you ... a car? Yes, I have. **(to rent)**
8. Have you ... a road map of Cornwall? Yes. **(to buy)**
9. What has ... to your car? I had an accident. **(to happen)**
10. Was anyone ... in the accident? Yes, I was. **(to injure)**
11. Was an ambulance ... ? Yes. **(to call)**
12. What hospital were you ... to? To St Mary's. **(to take)**
13. Henry told me an ... story about yesterday's football match. **(to interest)**
14. Is it really true that the match was ... by the Rangers? **(to win)**
15. Was it an ... match? Yes. **(to excite)**
16. The victory was ... by young and old. **(to celebrate)**
17. Have you ... Matthew? **(to see)**
18. Yes. I saw him ... away. **(to run)**
19. Jack has ... the exam. **(to pass)**
20. His friends came ... to congratulate him on his success. **(to run)**

THE GERUND

The forms of the gerund – Die Formen des Gerundiums

AKTIV (active)	PASSIV (passive)
catching	being caught
having caught	having been caught

Die Formen des Gerundiums und des Partizips sind **gleich**.

The gerund as "subject" – Das Gerundium als Subjekt

Swimming is healthy.
Schwimmen ist gesund.

Dancing is enjoyable.
Tanzen macht viel Spaß.

Learning English idioms is important.
Das Lernen von englischen Redewendungen ist wichtig.

Das deutsche substantivierte Verb wird im Englischen durch die „ing"-Form (Gerundium) wiedergegeben.

Der Artikel entfällt im Englischen.

(Das substantivierte Verb kann im Englischen auch durch den Infinitiv wiedergegeben werden. Siehe auch Seite 178.)

The gerund as "object" – Das Gerundium als Objekt

Arthur avoided **answering** my questions.
Arthur vermied es, meine Fragen zu beantworten.

They enjoyed **dancing**.
Sie hatten Freude am Tanzen.

Tom gave up **smoking**.
Tom gab das Rauchen auf.

I can't help **taking** drugs.
Ich kann nicht umhin Drogen zu nehmen. (Es ist nun einmal so.)

I haven't finished **reading** that book yet.
Ich habe das Buch noch nicht zu Ende gelesen.

Nach bestimmten Verben steht im Englischen das Gerundium als **Objekt** (im Deutschen häufig Infinitiv), z. B.:

to enjoy	– Spaß/Freude haben, etw. genießen
to avoid	– vermeiden
I can't help	– ich kann nicht umhin
to admit	– zugeben
to give up	– aufgeben
I don't mind	– ich habe nichts dagegen
to finish	– beenden
to imagine	– sich einbilden, sich vorstellen
to suggest	– vorschlagen

u. a.

2 Make sentences in line with the pattern:

PATTERN
It is unfair to trick other people.
Tricking other people is unfair.

1. It is enjoyable to dance.
2. It is interesting to visit foreign countries.
3. It is advisable to book tickets for "Cats" in advance.
4. It is frivolous to borrow so much money.
5. It is fascinating to listen to her.
6. It is foolish to quarrel with him about it.
7. It is dangerous to skate on the lake.
8. It is stupid to stick one's nose into other people's business.
9. It is risky to speculate on the Stock Exchange.
10. It is unfair to lead other people by the nose.

The gerund after prepositions – Das Gerundium nach Präpositionen

I succeeded **in winning** the race.
I am thinking **of emigrating** to Canada.
I am proud **of being** a member of this club.
There is no chance **of surviving** (überleben) the catastrophe.
I apologize **for having been** so rude (gemein) to you.

Folgt auf eine **Präposition** oder einen präpositionalen Ausdruck ein **Verb**, so tritt **es** in die „**ing-Form**" (Gerundium).

Solche präpositionalen Ausdrücke sind:

to succeed in	– gelingen	to be good at	– gut sein in
to be interested in	– interessiert sein an	to be fond of	– etwas gern tun, mögen
to think of	– denken an	to be tired of	– etwas satt haben
to dream of	– träumen von	to be used to	– pflegen, gewohnt sein etwas zu tun
to apologize for	– sich entschuldigen wegen		
to be angry at (about)	– ärgerlich sein über	to have the chance (opportunity) of	– die Chance (Gelegenheit) haben
to be afraid of	– fürchten, sich fürchten vor	to have an interest in	– Interesse daran haben
to be proud of	– stolz sein auf	u. a.	

3 Find the correct combination:

1. I am interested in
2. I look forward to
3. He succeeded in
4. I apologize for
5. I am proud of
6. Arthur is fond of
7. Miriam is good at
8. I am afraid of
9. Ralph thought of
10. I am tired of
11. Charles is good at
12. Mark is proud of
13. I apologize for
14. They succeeded in
15. Henry is used to

to learn foreign languages
to learn the whole truth
to play with the computer
to emigrate to Canada
to pass the exam
to have been so rude to him
to work hard
to see you again
to be a Yorkshireman
to hurt his feelings
to hear such nonsense again and again
to come late
to be a member of this club
to play the piano
to talk me into the matter

SHORTENING SUBORDINATE CLAUSES BY USING THE PARTICIPLE PRESENT/GERUND (1)
Die Verkürzung von Nebensätzen durch das Partizip Präsens/Gerundium (1)

Arriving at the airport, I was interviewed by a reporter. **(Gleichzeitigkeit)**
Als ich am Flugplatz ankam, wurde ich von einem Reporter interviewt.

Crossing the road, Harry met Liz. **(Gleichzeitigkeit)**
Als Harry die Straße überquerte, traf er Liz.

(While) watching television, Tom had some whiskies. **(Gleichzeitigkeit)**
Während Tom fernsah, trank er einige Whiskys.

MAN MERKE SICH

1. Adverbiale Nebensätze können durch das **Partizip** verkürzt werden, wenn **Haupt-** und **Nebensatz** das **gleiche** Subjekt haben.
2. Der adverbiale Nebensatz wird durch das „**1. Partizip**" (present participle) verkürzt, wenn die Handlungen in **Haupt-** und **Nebensatz gleichzeitig** ablaufen.
3. Das **Subjekt** des verkürzten Nebensatzes steckt in der „**ing-Form**".

Verkürzte temporale Nebensätze kann man durch „**while**" und „**when**" kenntlich machen. Diese Konjunktionen stehen aber nur vor dem 1. Partizip.

4 Translate the following sentences into German:

1. Leaving the pub, I was tipsy.
2. (While) having breakfast, I read the sports news.
3. (While) doing the crossword puzzle, I consulted a dictionary.
4. While making a speech, Mrs Sherman fainted.
5. While giving the talk, she had a heart attack.

5 Make sentences according to the pattern:

PATTERN

to have a drink in a pub – to insult many people
(While) having a drink in a pub, he insulted many people.

1. to walk down Oxford Street – to meet Sarah
2. to leave the hotel – to see Bud Spencer
3. to drive along the coast – to see many beautiful places of interest
4. to have a swim in the open sea – to be skimmed by a surfer
5. to cross the road – to be stopped by a policeman

6 Translate into English:

1. Als Vivian bei Selfridges einkaufte, traf sie Thorsten.
2. Als Michael das Warenhaus verließ, bekam er einen Herzanfall.
3. Als der „Popstar" in die Musikhalle kam, wurde er von seinen Fans stürmisch begrüßt.
4. Als wir durch Eton fuhren, sahen wir das Eton College.
5. Als Edgar im Meer badete, wurde er von einem Surfer gestreift.
6. Während Maggie Videos sah, strickte sie.
7. Als er den Ford überholte, stieß er mit einem Rolls-Royce zusammen.
8. Als ich den Verletzten sah, rief ich einen Krankenwagen herbei.

SHORTENING SUBORDINATE CLAUSES BY USING THE PARTICIPLE PERFECT/GERUND (2)
Verkürzung von Nebensätzen durch das Partizip Perfekt/Gerundium (2)

After arriving at the airport, I phoned Irene. **(Gerundium)**

Als ich auf dem Flugplatz angekommen war, rief ich Irene an. (zeitliche Divergenz)

After crossing the road, we saw an accident. **(Gerundium)**

Als wir die Straße überquert hatten, sahen wir einen Unfall. (zeitliche Divergenz)

Ebenfalls möglich:

Having arrived at the airport, I phoned Irene. **(Partizip Perfekt)**

Having crossed the road, we saw an accident. **(Partizip Perfekt)**

Fallen die Handlungen in Haupt- und Nebensatz **zeitlich auseinander** (zeitliche Divergenz), wird der **adverbiale Nebensatz** (hier der Zeit) **bevorzugt** durch das <u>Gerundium</u> **verkürzt**.

(After arriving at the airport, I ...)

Auch in diesem Fall müssen die **Subjekte** in Haupt- und Nebensatz **gleich sein.**

Die Verkürzung von Nebensätzen der Zeit durch das **Partizip Perfekt** ist in diesem Fall auch möglich.

MAN MERKE SICH

> Durch das Gerundium werden auch Nebensätze verkürzt, die mit den Präpositionen **before, on, by, without, instead of** u. a. beginnen.
>
> **Before going** to the sauna, I posted a letter. He moved to Bristol **without saying** goodbye.

7 Translate the following sentences into German:

1. After leaving (having left) the bank, I noticed that someone was following me.
2. After returning (having returned) from the excursion, I was tired.
3. After finishing (having finished) my work, I went out.
4. After doing (having done) the housework mother went to a birthday party.
5. After getting (having got) the fax, I answered it.

8 Make sentences according to the pattern:

PATTERN

to arrive at the airport – to check in
After arriving (having arrived) at the airport, I checked in.

1. to wash the car
   – to drive downtown
2. to leave the pub
   – to faint
3. to cash the cheque
   – to go shopping
4. to pass the driving test
   – to buy a car
5. to make a speech
   – to be interviewed by a reporter

9 Translate the following sentences into English:

1. Als Mr Harris bei Harrods eingekauft hatte, ging er ins Fitnesscenter.
2. Als er das Warenhaus verlassen hatte, erblickte er Julia Roberts.
3. Als Susan das Kreuzworträtsel gelöst hatte, ging sie zum Friseur.
4. Als Harry sich rasiert hatte, frühstückte er.
5. Als er Mr Miller gefaxt hatte, sah er sich das Fußballspiel Liverpool gegen Manchester an.
6. Als sich Robert das Video angesehen hatte, rief er Miriam an.
7. Als Nicole den Wetterbericht gehört hatte, trank sie einen Cognac.
8. Als Jack einige Drinks zu sich genommen hatte, war er beschwipst.
9. Als Mary den Haushalt erledigt hatte, ging sie in die Sauna.
10. Als Jimmy Mr Sherman eine E-Mail geschickt hatte, spielte er mit Susan Schach.

SHORT FORMS OF THE AUXILIARY VERBS
(Kurzformen der Hilfsverben)

TO BE

the present tense

I	am	I'm		I'm not		–*	
you	are	you're		you	aren't	aren't	you?
he	} is	he's[1]		he	} isn't	isn't {	he?
she		she's[1]		she			she?
it		it's[1]		it			it?
we	are	we're		we	aren't	aren't	we?
you	are	you're		you	aren't	aren't	you?
they	are	they're		they	aren't	aren't	they?

the past tense

I	was	–	I	wasn't	wasn't I?	
you	were		you	weren't	weren't you?	
etc.			etc.		etc.	

* In der Umgangssprache: aren't I? (Slang: ain't I?)

TO HAVE

the present tense

I	have	I've		I	haven't	haven't	I?
you	have	you've		you	haven't	haven't	you?
he	} has	he's[1]		he	} hasn't	hasn't {	he?
she		she's		she			she?
it		it's		it			it?
we	have	we've		we	haven't	haven't	we?
you	have	you've		you	haven't	haven't	you?
they	have	they've		they	haven't	haven't	they?

the past tense

I	had	I'd[1]	I	hadn't	hadn't	I?
you	had	you'd[1]	you	hadn't	hadn't	you?
etc.		etc.	etc.		etc.	

TO DO

the present tense

I	do	I	don't	don't	I?		
you	do	you	don't	don't	you?		
he	} does	he	} doesn't	doesn't {	he?		
she		she			she?		
it		it			it?		
we	do	we	don't	don't	we?		
etc.		etc.		etc.			

the past tense

I	did	I	didn't	didn't	I?
etc.		etc.		etc.	

FURTHER SHORT FORMS (Weitere Kurzformen)

I shan't	– I shall not	I mustn't	– I must not
I won't	– I will not	I shouldn't	– I should not
I can't	– I cannot	I'll	– I will / I shall
I couldn't	– I could not	I'd	– I would / I should

---

1 Die Kurzformen werden nur angewandt, wenn der Textzusammenhang keine Verwechslung mit anderen Hilfsverben zulässt (z. B. he's – he is, I'd – I should, you'd – you would).

CONJUGATION TABLE – Konjugationstabelle

	Active			Passive
	to be	to have	to ask	to ask
Present	I am ich bin you are he she } is it we are you are they are	I have ich habe you have he she } has it we have you have they have	I ask ich frage you ask he she } asks it we ask you ask they ask	I am asked ich werde gefragt you are asked he she } is asked it we are asked you are asked they are asked
Past	I was ich war you were he she } was it we were you were they were	I had ich hatte you had he she } had it we had you had they had	I asked ich fragte you asked he she } asked it we asked you asked they asked	I was asked ich wurde gefragt you were asked he she } was asked it we were asked you were asked they were asked
Future	I will* be ich werde sein you will be he she } will be it we will* be you will be they will be	I will* have ich werde haben you will have he she } will have it we will* have you will have they will have	I will* ask ich werde fragen you will ask he she } will ask it we will* ask you will ask they will ask	I will* be asked ich werde gefr. werden you will be asked he she } will be asked it we will* be asked you will be asked they will be asked
Conditional	I would* be ich würde sein you would be he she } would be it we would* be you would be they would be	I would* have ich würde haben you would have he she } would have it we would* have you would have they would have	I would* ask ich würde fragen you would ask he she } would ask it we would* ask you would ask they would ask	I would* be asked ich würde gefr. werden you would be asked he she } would be asked it we would* be asked you would be asked they would be asked
Present perfect	I have been ich bin gewesen you have been he she } has been it we have been you have been they have been	I have had ich habe gehabt you have had he she } has had it we have had you have had they have had	I have asked ich habe gefragt you have asked he she } has asked it we have asked you have asked they have asked	I have been asked ich bin gefragt worden you have been asked he she } has been asked it we have been asked you have been asked they have been asked

* In der Schriftsprache findet man auch I (we) shall bzw. I (we) should statt I (we) will bzw. I (we) would.

	Active			Passive
	to be	to have	to ask	to ask
Past perfect	I had been ich war gewesen you had been he ⎫ she ⎬ had been it ⎭ we had been you had been they had been	I had had ich hatte gehabt you had had he ⎫ she ⎬ had had it ⎭ we had had you had had they had had	I had asked ich hatte gefragt you had asked he ⎫ she ⎬ had asked it ⎭ we had asked you had asked they had asked	I had been asked ich war gefr. worden you had been asked he ⎫ she ⎬ had been asked it ⎭ we had been asked you had been asked they had been asked

Future perfect (active)

to be	to have	to ask
I will* have been ich werde gewesen sein you will have been he ⎫ she ⎬ will have been it ⎭ we will* have been you will have been they will have been	I will* have had ich werde gehabt haben you will have had he ⎫ she ⎬ will have had it ⎭ we will* have had you will have had they will have had	I will* have asked ich werde gefragt haben you will have asked he ⎫ she ⎬ will have asked it ⎭ we will* have asked you will have asked they will have asked

Conditional perfect (active)

to be	to have	to ask
I would* have been ich würde gewesen sein you would have been he ⎫ she ⎬ would have been it ⎭ we would* have been you would have been they would have been	I would* have had ich würde gehabt haben you would have had he ⎫ she ⎬ would have had it ⎭ we would* have had you would have had they would have had	I would* have asked ich würde gefragt haben you would have asked he ⎫ she ⎬ would have asked it ⎭ we would* have asked you would have asked they would have asked

Future and conditional perfect (passive)

Future perfect	Conditional perfect
I will* have been asked ich werde gefragt worden sein you will have been asked he ⎫ she ⎬ will have been asked it ⎭ we will* have been asked you will have been asked they will have been asked	I would* have been asked ich würde gefragt worden sein you would have been asked he ⎫ she ⎬ would have been asked it ⎭ we would* have been asked you would have been asked they would have been asked

* In der Schriftsprache findet man auch I (we) shall bzw. I (we) should statt I (we) will bzw. I (we) would.

LIST OF THE IRREGULAR VERBS
(Verzeichnis der unregelmäßigen Verben)

Infinitive	Past Tense	Past Participle	
to arise [aɪz]	arose [əʊ]	arisen [ɪ]	sich erheben
to awake [eɪ]	awoke [əʊ]*	awoken*	erwachen
to be	was	been	sein
to bear [eə]	bore [ɔː]	borne [ɔː]	(er)tragen; born: geboren
to beat [iː]	beat [iː]	beaten [iː]	schlagen
to become [ʌ]	became [eɪ]	become	werden (z. B. Ingenieur)
to begin [ɪ]	began [æ]	begun [ʌ]	beginnen, anfangen
to bend [e]	bent [e]	bent	beugen, biegen
to bet [e]	bet*	bet*	wetten
to bid [ɪ]	bade [æ]	bidden [ɪ]	heißen, gebieten
to bind [aɪ]	bound [aʊ]	bound	binden
to bite [aɪ]	bit [ɪ]	bit(ten) [ɪ]	beißen
to bleed [iː]	bled [e]	bled	bluten
to blow [əʊ]	blew [uː]	blown [əʊ]	blasen
to break [eɪ]	broke [əʊ]	broken [əʊ]	(zer)brechen
to breed [iː]	bred [e]	bred	brüten; züchten
to bring [ɪ]	brought [ɔː]	brought	bringen
to broadcast	broadcast	broadcast	(im Rundfunk) senden
to build [ɪ]	built [ɪ]	built	bauen
to burn [ɜː]	burnt [ɜː]*	burnt*	(ver)brennen
to buy [aɪ]	bought [ɔː]	bought	kaufen
to catch [æ]	caught [ɔː]	caught	fangen, erreichen (z. B. den Zug)
to choose [uːz]	chose [əʊz]	chosen [əʊ]	wählen, (sich) aussuchen
to come [ʌ]	came [eɪ]	come	kommen
to cost [ɒ]	cost [ɒ]	cost	kosten
to creep [iː]	crept [e]	crept	kriechen
to cut [ʌ]	cut	cut	schneiden
to deal [iː]	dealt [e]	dealt [e]	handeln, sich befassen (mit)
to dig [ɪ]	dug [ʌ]	dug	graben
to do [uː]	did [ɪ]	done [ʌ]	tun
to draw [ɔː]	drew [uː]	drawn [ɔː]	ziehen, zeichnen
to dream [iː]	dreamt*	dreamt*	träumen
to drink [ɪ]	drank [æ]	drunk [ʌ]	trinken
to drive [aɪ]	drove [əʊ]	driven [ɪ]	treiben, fahren
to eat [iː]	ate [eɪt]	eaten [iː]	essen
to fall [ɔː]	fell [e]	fallen [ɔː]	fallen
to feed [iː]	fed [e]	fed	füttern
to feel [iː]	felt [e]	felt	(sich) fühlen
to fight [aɪ]	fought [ɔː]	fought	kämpfen
to find [aɪ]	found [aʊ]	found	finden
to flee [iː]	fled [e]	fled	fliehen
to fling [ɪ]	flung [ʌ]	flung	schleudern, werfen
to fly [aɪ]	flew [uː]	flown [əʊ]	fliegen
to forbid [ɪ]	forbade [eɪ]	forbidden [ɪ]	verbieten
to forget [e]	forgot [ɒ]	forgotten	vergessen
to forgive [ɪ]	forgave [eɪ]	forgiven [ɪ]	vergeben
to freeze [iː]	froze [əʊ]	frozen [əʊ]	(ge)frieren
to get [e]	got [ɒ]	got	bekommen, werden
to give [ɪ]	gave [eɪ]	given [ɪ]	geben

* bedeutet, dass auch die regelmäßige Form auf „ed" vorkommt.

Infinitive	Past Tense	Past Participle	
to go [əʊ]	went [e]	gone [ɒ]	gehen
to grow [əʊ]	grew [uː]	grown [əʊ]	wachsen; anbauen
to hang [æ]	hung [ʌ]*	hung*	(auf)hängen
to have	had	had	haben
to hear [ɪə]	heard [ɜː]	heard	hören
to hide [aɪ]	hid [ɪ]	hidden [ɪ]	(sich) verstecken
to hit [ɪ]	hit	hit	schlagen; treffen
to hold [əʊ]	held [e]	held	halten
to hurt [ɜː]	hurt	hurt	verletzen; wehtun
to keep [iː]	kept [e]	kept	(be)halten, aufbewahren
to know [nəʊ]	knew [njuː]	known [nəʊn]	kennen, wissen
to lay [eɪ]	laid [eɪ]	laid	legen
to lead [iː]	led [e]	led	leiten, führen
to lean [iː]	leant [e]*	leant*	lehnen
to learn [ɜː]	learnt [ɜː]*	learnt*	lernen; erfahren
to leave [iː]	left [e]	left	(ver)lassen
to lend [e]	lent	lent	leihen
to let [e]	let	let	lassen
to lie [aɪ]	lay [eɪ]	lain [eɪ]	liegen
to light [aɪ]	lit [ɪ]*	lit*	anzünden, erleuchten
to lose [luːz]	lost [ɒ]	lost	verlieren
to make [eɪ]	made [eɪ]	made	machen
to mean [iː]	meant [e]	meant	meinen, bedeuten
to meet [iː]	met [e]	met	begegnen, treffen, kennen lernen
to pay [eɪ]	paid [eɪ]	paid	(be)zahlen
to put [ʊ]	put	put	setzen, legen, stellen
to read [iː]	read [e]	read	lesen
to rid [ɪ]	rid	rid	freimachen, befreien
to ride [aɪ]	rode [əʊ]	ridden [ɪ]	reiten, fahren
to ring [ɪ]	rang [æ]	rung [ʌ]	läuten, anrufen (Telefon)
to rise [aɪz]	rose [əʊ]	risen [ɪ]	aufstehen, steigen (z. B. Preise)
to run [ʌ]	ran [æ]	run [ʌ]	rennen, laufen
to say [eɪ]	said [e]	said	sagen
to see [iː]	saw [ɔː]	seen [iː]	sehen
to seek [iː]	sought [ɔː]	sought	suchen
to sell [e]	sold [əʊ]	sold	verkaufen
to send [e]	sent	sent	senden, (ver)schicken
to set [e]	set	set	setzen, stellen
to sew [əʊ]	sewed [əʊ]	sewn [əʊ]*	nähen
to shake [eɪ]	shook [ʊ]	shaken [eɪ]	schütteln
to shine [aɪ]	shone [ɒ]	shone	scheinen, glänzen
to shoot [uː]	shot [ɒ]	shot	schießen
to show [əʊ]	showed [əʊ]	shown [əʊ]*	zeigen
to shut [ʌ]	shut	shut	schließen
to sing [ɪ]	sang [æ]	sung [ʌ]	singen
to sink [ɪ]	sank [æ]	sunk [ʌ]	sinken, versenken
to sit [ɪ]	sat [æ]	sat	sitzen
to sleep [iː]	slept [e]	slept	schlafen
to slide [aɪ]	slid [ɪ]	slid	gleiten
to smell [e]	smelt [e]*	smelt*	riechen

* bedeutet, dass auch die regelmäßige Form auf „ed" vorkommt.

Infinitive	Past Tense	Past Participle		
to speak [iː]	spoke [əʊ]	spoken [əʊ]		sprechen
to speed [iː]	sped [e]*	sped*		sich beeilen
to spell [e]	spelt [e]*	spelt*		buchstabieren
to spend [e]	spent	spent		ausgeben (Geld); verbringen
to spill [ɪ]	spilt*	spilt*		verschütten
to spin [ɪ]	spun [ʌ]	spun		spinnen
to spit [ɪ]	spat [æ]	spat		spucken
to split [ɪ]	split	split		spalten
to spoil [ɔɪ]	spoilt [ɔɪ]*	spoilt [ɔɪ]*		verderben, verwöhnen
to spread [e]	spread	spread		(sich) aus-, verbreiten
to spring [ɪ]	sprang [æ]	sprung [ʌ]		springen
to stand [æ]	stood [ʊ]	stood		stehen
to steal [iː]	stole [əʊ]	stolen [əʊ]		stehlen
to stick [ɪ]	stuck [ʌ]	stuck		(an)stecken, (an)kleben
to stink [ɪ]	stank [æ]	stunk [ʌ]		stinken
to strike [aɪ]	struck [ʌ]	struck		stoßen, schlagen
to swear [eə]	swore [ɔː]	sworn		schwören; fluchen
to sweep [iː]	swept [e]	swept		fegen, kehren
to swim [ɪ]	swam [æ]	swum [ʌ]		schwimmen
to swing [ɪ]	swung [ʌ]	swung		schwingen, schwenken
to take [eɪ]	took [ʊ]	taken [eɪ]		nehmen; bringen
to teach [iː]	taught [ɔː]	taught [ɔː]		lehren, unterrichten
to tear [eə]	tore [ɔː]	torn [ɔː]		zerreißen
to tell [e]	told [əʊ]	told		erzählen; (es) sagen
to think [ɪ]	thought [ɔː]	thought		denken, glauben
to throw [əʊ]	threw [uː]	thrown [əʊ]		werfen
to thrust [ʌ]	thrust	thrust		stoßen
to tread [e]	trod [ɒ]	trodden [ɒ] (trod)		treten
to understand [æ]	understood [ʊ]	understood		verstehen
to wake up [eɪ]	woke [əʊ]*	woke(n) [əʊ]*		(auf)wecken, -wachen
to wear [eə]	wore [ɔː]	worn		tragen (Kleider)
to weave [iː]	wove [əʊ]	woven [əʊ]		weben
to weep [iː]	wept [e]	wept		weinen
to win [ɪ]	won [ʌ]	won		gewinnen
to write [aɪ]	wrote [əʊ]	written [ɪ]		schreiben

* bedeutet, dass auch die regelmäßige Form auf „ed" vorkommt.

VOCABULARY

1 WORKING FOR FOWLER & CO

a full-time job [fʊl], [taɪm]	Do you have a full-time job? No, a part-time (Teilzeit) job.	eine Vollzeitbeschäftigung
Fowler & Co		Firma Fowler & Co.
typist [ˈtaɪpɪ̯st]		Stenotypistin
to type sth [taɪp]		etwas mit der Maschine schreiben, tippen
business letter [ˈbɪznɪ̯s]		Geschäftsbrief
a flat [flæt]		eine (Etagen-)Wohnung
cooking [ˈkʊkɪŋ]	Do you like (the) English cooking? So-so.	Kochen, Küche, Kochkunst
to travel/travelling [ˈtrævəl]		reisen/Reisen
to be a sales manager [seɪlz]		Verkaufsleiter sein
to telephone/to phone [ˈtelɪ̯fəʊn]		telefonieren
to offer sth [ˈɒfə]	What products does this firm offer? Cameras.	etwas anbieten
product [ˈprɒdʌkt]		Erzeugnis, Produkt
to sell sth [sel]		etwas verkaufen
to be married [ˈmærɪd]	Are you single or married? I'm single.	verheiratet sein
hobby		Hobby
to read/reading		lesen/Lesen
to play squash [skwɒʃ]		Squash spielen
to drive a car [draɪv]		Auto fahren
a computer specialist [ˈspeʃəlɪ̯st]		ein Computerspezialist
programmer [ˈprəʊɡræmə]	What's your job? I am a computer programmer.	Programmierer
real [rɪəl]		hier: echt, wirklich
a freak		ein Freak
to live [lɪv]	Do you live in the country or in a town? In the country.	wohnen
suburb [ˈsʌbɜːb]		Vorort (einer Stadt)
to cycle/cycling [ˈsaɪkəl]		Rad fahren/Radfahren
to collect stamps [kəˈlekt]		Briefmarken sammeln
to be a junior clerk [ˈdʒuːnɪə], [klɑːk]		Anfänger in einer Firma sein (ähnlich einem kaufmännischen Lehrling)
a beginner		ein Anfänger
to sort the correspondence [sɔːt], [kɒrɪ̯ˈspɒndəns]		die Korrespondenz sortieren
to post a letter [pəʊst]		einen Brief aufgeben
to be engaged to sb [ɪnˈɡeɪdʒd]		mit jemandem verlobt sein
chap [tʃæp]	Old chap!	Kerl, Junge
to like doing sth	Do you like cycling? Yes, I really do.	etwas gern tun
to knit/knitting [nɪt]		stricken, Stricken

COMPREHENSION TESTS / GRAMMATICAL EXERCISES

1
What kind of work?   Was für eine Arbeit?

2
to complete sth [kəmˈpliːt]   etwas vervollständigen

3
to rewrite sth	You must rewrite it.	etwas nochmals schreiben
to add sth [æd]		etwas hinzufügen, einfügen
to be missing [ˈmɪsɪŋ]	Two pound notes are missing.	fehlen
letter		hier: Buchstabe

4
job	Do you like your job? Yes.	Job
activities [ækˈtɪvₜtiːz]		Aktivitäten
lovely	Anne has a lovely voice.	herrlich, wunderschön
voice [vɔɪs]		Stimme
a lot of fans	Does she have a lot of fans? Yes.	viele Fans
to repair sth [rɪˈpeə]		etwas reparieren
usual [ˈjuːsʊəl; -ʒəl]		üblich
inspection [ɪnˈspekʃən]		Inspektion
a store [stɔː]		ein Warenhaus
to work	Who do you work for? For Calder & Co.	arbeiten
department [dɪˈpɑːtmənt]		Abteilung
a TV set	Have you got a TV set? Yes.	ein Fernsehapparat
a video recorder [ˈvɪdɪəʊ] [rɪˈkɔːdə]		ein Videorekorder

5
to fill in sth	Jack is filling in a cheque.	etwas eintragen, ausfüllen
a bank clerk [klɑːk]		ein Bankangestellter
to be pretty	Is Judy a pretty woman? Yes.	hübsch sein
a disco		eine Disko(thek)
to be a student [ˈstjuːdənt]		Student (Schüler) sein
a technical college[1] [ˈteknɪkəl]	Eric attends the Technical College in Brighton.	eine berufsbildende Lehranstalt (technisch)

6
to be beautiful		schön sein
child/children		Kind/Kinder
girlfriend	Sally is my girlfriend.	Freundin
cat [kæt]		Katze
to be called	I am called Frank. (My name is ...)	heißen
dog [dɒg]		Hund
to be interesting	Is this book interesting? Yes, it is.	interessant sein

---

[1] Wenn Lehranstalten nicht näher bezeichnet sind, schreibt man sie klein.

7

to call on sb	When shall I call on you? At 10 a. m.	jemanden aufsuchen
to leave (for)		sich begeben nach, fahren
to take	Mary usually takes the bus.	nehmen
to dictate sth [dɪkˈteɪt]	He dictates business letters to his secretary.	etwas diktieren
to get up	When do you get up? At seven o'clock in the morning.	aufstehen
to watch TV		fernsehen
to prepare sth [prɪˈpeə]		etwas vorbereiten
breakfast		Frühstück
bacon [ˈbeɪkən]	What do the English have for breakfast? Bacon and eggs.	Schinkenspeck
egg		Ei
office		Büro
underground (train) [ˌʌndəˈgraʊnd]	Do you go to the office by bus? No, by underground.	U-Bahn (in London: „tube" genannt)
bus		Bus
while		während
customer [ˈkʌstəmə]		Kunde
lunch	When do you have lunch? At one o'clock.	Mittagessen
afternoon		Nachmittag
evening		Abend
to go for a walk		spazieren gehen
usually [ˈjuːʒʊəli]	We usually have dinner at six o'clock in the evening.	
dinner		Hauptmahlzeit (Mittag-, Abendessen)

2 WHAT TO DO AT THE WEEKEND?

at last		endlich
to be glad [glæd]	I'm glad to see you.	sich freuen, froh sein
to want [wɒnt]		wünschen
cinema [ˈsɪnɪmə]		Kino
sport		Sport
to practise sth [ˈpræktɪs]	Do you practise sport? Yes. I do.	etwas ausüben
to visit sb [ˈvɪzɪt]		jemanden besuchen
to relax [rɪˈlæks]	What are you doing? I'm relaxing a bit.	sich entspannen, erholen
for instance [ˈɪnstəns]		zum Beispiel
an apprentice [əˈprentɪs]	He is an apprentice at (in) this garage (Werkstatt).	ein gewerblicher Auszubildender
to have a date with sb [deɪt]		mit jemandem eine Verabredung haben
fun [fʌn]	They had a lot of fun.	Spaß

nurse [nɜːs]	She is a nurse at (in) this hospital.	Krankenschwester
rather [ˈrɑːðə]	That's rather expensive.	ziemlich
to be boring [ˈbɔːrɪŋ]	This film is rather boring.	langweilig sein
theatre [ˈθɪətə]		Theater
to visit a show		sich eine Show ansehen
to spend the weekend		das Wochenende verbringen
cottage [ˈkɒtɪdʒ]		kleines Wohnhaus, Landhaus
country [ˈkʌntri]	He lives in the country.	das Land
life		das Leben
to be hectic [ˈhektɪk]	Life is hectic in cities.	hektisch sein
to work around the house		am Haus arbeiten
to paint [peɪnt]		streichen, anstreichen, malen
to put up wallpaper [wɔːl]		tapezieren
to build sth [bɪld]		etwas bauen
cupboard [ˈkʌbəd]	He likes to build cupboards.	Schrank
and so on		und so weiter
to buy sth		etwas kaufen
material [məˈtɪəriəl]		Material
to need sth [niːd]	Do you need any help? No, thank you.	etwas benötigen
nearby [ˌnɪəˈbaɪ]		nahe, nahe gelegen
shop		Geschäft
to be a stewardess	What do you do? I'm a stewardess.	Stewardess sein
horse race [reɪs]		Pferderennen
to spend one's free time		seine Freizeit verbringen
golf course [kɔːs]		Golfplatz
tennis court [kɔːt]		Tennisplatz

COMPREHENSION TESTS / GRAMMATICAL EXERCISES

3

to explain sth to sb [ɪkˈspleɪn]	Would you please explain it to me? With pleasure.	jemandem etwas erkären

4

to be great		toll, fantastisch sein
to have a drink		einen Drink nehmen
My goodness! [ˈɡʊdnəs]		Meine Güte!
to be funny [ˈfʌni]	Robert is a funny man.	lustig, komisch sein
That's no business of yours.		Das geht dich nichts an.
to be true [truː]	Is it true that she looks like her mother? Yes.	wahr sein, stimmen
Damn! [dæm]		Verdammt!

5

to reproduce sth [riːprəˈdjuːs]		etwas wiedergeben
contents [ˈkɒntents]	Can you describe (beschreiben) the contents of this bag? I'll try.	Inhalt

6

concert [ˈkɒnsət]		Konzert
to be outstanding [aʊtˈstændɪŋ]		überragend, hervorragend sein
to be magnificent [mægˈnɪfɪsənt]		großartig sein
ballet [ˈbæleɪ]	Have you seen the ballet "Romeo & Juliet?" Yes.	Ballett
booking fees [fiːz]		Reservierungskosten (-gebühren)
group [gruːp]		Gruppe
to cancel sth [ˈkænsəl]	They have cancelled the contract.	etwas absagen, stornieren
engagement [ɪnˈgeɪdʒmənt]		hier: Verabredung
to cry [kraɪ]		weinen, heulen, schreien
simple [ˈsɪmpəl]		einfach
plan [plæn]		Plan
starring [ˈstɑːrɪŋ]	Starring Harrison Ford.	es spielt/spielen
thriller [ˈθrɪlə]		Krimi, Thriller
action packed [ˈækʃən], [pækt]		voller Aktion
explosive [ɪkˈspləʊsɪv]		explosiv
to be brilliant [ˈbrɪljənt]	She is a brilliant woman.	brillant, glänzend, großartig sein
directed by ... [dɪˈrektɪd, daɪ-]		Regie ...
artistry [ˈɑːtɪstri]		Kunst
atmospheric [ˌætməsˈferɪk]		atmosphärisch
power [ˈpaʊə]		Kraft, Gewalt, Wucht
advertisement [ədˈvɜːtɪsmənt]	Have you read this advertisement? Yes.	Anzeige, Inserat
performance [pəˈfɔːməns]		Vorstellung
to take place [pleɪs]		stattfinden
leading actor (actress) [ˈliːdɪŋ], [ˈæktə], [ˈæktrəs]		Hauptdarsteller(in)

7

penfriend	Schreibfreund
aunt [ɑːnt]	Tante

8

to flirt with sb [flɜːt]	Jennifer likes flirting.	mit jemandem flirten
to play squash (badminton)		Squash (Badminton) spielen
to go for a walk		spazieren gehen
to go jogging		joggen
to watch the sports news [njuːz]		die Sportnachrichten hören

a talk show	Which talk show is the best?	eine Talkshow
to listen to the weather forecast ['fɔːkɑːst]		den Wetterbericht hören
a love story (thriller) ['θrɪlə]	What a thriller!	eine Liebesgeschichte (ein Krimi)
a love letter		ein Liebesbrief
to send a fax (an e-mail) [fæx]		ein Fax (E-Mail) schicken

9

to play chess [tʃes]		Schach spielen
to disturb sb [dɪˈstɜːb]	Don't disturb me.	jemanden stören
to do a crossword puzzle		ein Kreuzworträtsel raten
to be noisy ['nɔɪzi]		laut sein
to leave for [liːv]	Is he leaving for Ireland tomorrow? Yes.	hier: sich begeben nach (zu)
a fitness centre		ein Fitnesscenter
to work out		hier: sich körperlich fit halten
to ride one's bike [raɪd]		Rad fahren
to wait [weɪt]	Who are you waiting for? For Henry.	warten
to wash a car		einen Wagen waschen

10

Discman		Discman
scooter ['skuːtə]		Motorroller
wristwatch [rɪst]	My (wrist)watch is fast (slow).	Armbanduhr
flat [flæt]		Wohnung
wallet [wɒlɪ̥t]		Brieftasche
credit card	Do you pay by credit card? Yes.	Kreditkarte
mobile phone ['məʊbaɪl]		Handy, schnurloses Telefon
computer	Does Liz program (Amer.) computers? Yes.	Computer

3 BY CARAVAN TO THE SEASIDE

to be an electrician [ɪˌlekˈtrɪʃən]		Elektriker sein
outskirts ['aʊtskɜːts]	Where do you live? I live on the outskirts of this town/city.	Stadtrand
a caravan ['kærəvæn]		Wohnwagen
abroad [əˈbrɔːd]	I haven't seen Jack for a long time. I think he has gone abroad.	Ausland, ins Ausland
bank holiday		englischer Feiertag
to decide to do sth [dɪˈsaɪd]	He decided to do it.	sich entschließen etwas zu tun
caravan site [saɪt]		Campingplatz f. Wohnmobile
seaside resort [rɪˈzɔːt]		Seebad
motorway ['məʊtəweɪ]	Let's take the motorway.	Autobahn
to arrive [əˈraɪv]		ankommen
about [əˈbaʊt]		ungefähr (bei Zahlen)

foreigner ['fɒrᵻnə]	There are about 20 foreigners in the bus.	Ausländer
France, Belgium, the Netherlands/ Denmark [frɑːns], ['beldʒəm], ['denmɑːk]		Frankreich, Belgien, die Niederlande, Dänemark
people ['piːpəl]		die Leute, Menschen, das Volk
tent [tent]		Zelt
beside sth [bɪ'saɪd]	Where is there a butcher('s)? A butcher('s) is beside the grocer('s).	neben etwas (örtlich)
to make friends		mit jemandem Freundschaft schließen
beach [biːtʃ]	Let's go to the beach.	Strand
to have a swim	Let's go for a swim.	baden gehen
magazine [mægə'ziːn]		Zeitschrift
either ... or ['aɪðə]	I'll go either to Brighton or to Eastbourne.	entweder ... oder
nearby	Where can I get a ballpoint? You'll get one in the nearby shop.	in der Nähe, nahe, nahe gelegen
to drive along sth		etwas entlangfahren
lovely	You should drive along the coast. It's lovely.	wunderschön
places of interest/sights		Sehenswürdigkeiten
to cook [kʊk]		eine Speise kochen, braten, etwas zubereiten
to stroll along sth [strəʊl]	They are strolling along the promenade.	etwas entlangschlendern, bummeln
sunset ['sʌnset]		der Sonnenuntergang
to miss sth [mɪs]	Hurry up. You'll miss the train.	etwas versäumen, verpassen
traffic ['træfɪk]	Mind the traffic, (achte auf ...)	der Verkehr
especially, specially [ɪ'speʃəli]		besonders
to leave sth	I'll leave the party after midnight.	etwas verlassen
early	Come as early as possible.	früh
afternoon		Nachmittag

COMPREHENSION TESTS / GRAMMATICAL EXERCISES

THE MAIN RADIO STATIONS

radio station ['reɪdiəʊ]		Rundfunksender
main [meɪn]	Is this the main street of the town? Yes, it is.	hauptsächlich, Haupt-
entertainment [ˌentə'teɪnmənt]		Unterhaltung
light music/classical music ['mjuːzɪk], ['klæsɪkəl]		leichte Musik/ klassische Musik
the news [njuːz]	Here's the news on BBC 1.	die Nachrichten
comedy ['kɒmᵻdi]		Komödie
play		Spiel, (Theater-)Stück, (Schau-)Spiel

5

nationality [ˌnæʃəˈnælɪti]	What's your nationality? I'm English.	Nationalität
Italy/Italian [ɪˈtæliən]		Italien/italienisch
Scotland/Scottish	Where do you come from? From Scotland.	Schottland/schottisch
Austria/Austrian [ˈɒstriə]		Österreich/österreichisch
Spain/Spanish [speɪn]		Spanien/spanisch
language		Sprache

6

cassette [kəˈset]		Kassette
This is Mr ... speaking.		Mr ... am Apparat.
to speak to sb		mit jemandem sprechen

7

to spell sth	Spell the word, please.	etwas buchstabieren
to try sth	I tried to phone you last night.	etwas versuchen
to be quiet [ˈkwaɪət]		ruhig sein
to go to the party		zu der Party gehen
to have a dance	May I have this dance?	tanzen
to have a swim		schwimmen
to have a smoke		rauchen
to leave [liːv]	I'm leaving in a minute or two.	hier: aufbrechen, losgehen

8

an e-mail address [əˈdres]	I'll send Lucy an e-mail.	eine E-Mail-Adresse
credit card [ˈkredɪt]		Kreditkarte
a mobile phone [ˈməʊbaɪl]	Do you have a mobile phone? No.	ein Handy
identity card [aɪˈdentɪti]		Ausweis
travel bag [ˈtrævəl], [bæg]		Reisetasche

9

bracket [ˈbrækɪt]		Klammer
in bold type [bəʊld], [taɪp]		in Fettschrift
to catch sb/sth [kætʃ]	They will catch the thief (Dieb).	jemanden/etwas fangen
to look for sb/sth	What are you looking for? I'm looking for Grace.	jemanden/etwas suchen
grocer('s) [ˈgrəʊsə]	Has Alice gone to the grocer's? I don't know.	der Lebensmittelhändler
tomato [təˈmɑːtəʊ]		Tomate
Mum [mʌm]		Mutter
to peel sth [piːl]	Have you peeled the potatoes, Sarah? No.	etwas schälen
to sharpen sth [ˈʃɑːpən]		etwas schärfen
to pull out sth [pʊl]		etwas herausziehen (Zahn)
dentist [ˈdentɪst]	I don't like going to dentists.	Zahnarzt
to sweep up [swiːp]		auffegen
leaf/leaves [liːf, liːvz]		Blatt/Blätter

4 GREAT BRITAIN AND ITS GEOGRAPHY

certain ['sɜːtn]	I'm certain that he will come.	sicher, gewiss
quite a lot [kwaɪt]	Sorry, I don't know any more. Oh, that's quite a lot.	sehr viel, eine ganze Menge
geography [dʒɪˈɒgrəfi]		Geografie
whether [ˈweðə]	I don't know whether I'll go to the party.	ob
difficulty/to be difficult [ˈdɪfɪkəlti]	Do you have any difficulties with Sarah? Oh, quite a lot.	Schwierigkeit/ schwierig sein
map [mæp]		Landkarte
to consult sb/sth [kənˈsʌlt]	You should consult a doctor/a dictionary.	jemanden/etwas befragen, konsultieren
capital [ˈkæpɪtl]		Hauptstadt
to be surrounded by [səˈraʊndɪd]	Britain is surrounded by water.	umgeben sein von
north, east, west, south		Norden, Osten, Westen, Süden
important [ɪmˈpɔːtənt]		wichtig, bedeutend
river [ˈrɪvə]	Name important rivers in Britain.	Fluss
mountain [ˈmaʊntɪn]		Berg
port [pɔːt]		Hafen
to be known for	Oxford is known for its university. (colleges)	bekannt sein durch
to connect [kəˈnekt]		verbinden

COMPREHENSION TESTS / GRAMMATICAL EXERCISES

1

inhabitant(s) [ɪnˈhæbɪtənt]		Einwohner
to consist of [kənˈsɪst]	Great Britain consists of England, Scotland and Wales.	bestehen aus
to be situated on (in) [ˈsɪtʃʊeɪtɪd]	Glasgow is situated on the Clyde (in Scotland).	gelegen sein am (in)

4

Channel Tunnel [ˈtʃænl], [ˈtʌnl]		Kanaltunnel

5

the world language [ˈlæŋgwɪdʒ]		die Weltsprache
it is spoken	English is spoken in many countries.	es wird gesprochen
to belong to sth [bɪˈlɒŋ]	Which club do you belong to?	zu etwas gehören
the Commonwealth of Nations [ˈkɒmənwelθ]		das Commonwealth (engl. Gemeinwesen, Völkergemeinschaft) (früher „British Empire")
Canada		Kanada

India ['ɪndɪə]		Indien
Australia		Australien
to play an important role [rəʊl]		eine wichtige Rolle spielen
business life		Geschäftsleben
businessman		Geschäftsmann
Norwegian [nɔːˈwiːdʒən]		Norweger
Dutch [dʌtʃ] (Dutchman)		Holländer (der Holländer)
Japanese [dʒæpəˈniːz]		Japaner
business letter		Geschäftsbrief
as well		ebenfalls
foreign [ˈfɒrən]	French is a foreign language.	ausländisch
to enjoy sth [ɪnˈdʒɔɪ]		hier: etwas gern tun, etwas genießen
gap [gæp]		Lücke

6

arithmetic [əˈrɪθmətɪk]	Arithmetik, Rechnen
to add/addition [æd], [əˈdɪʃən]	addieren/Addition
plus/minus [plʌs/ˈmaɪnəs]	plus, minus
five times	fünfmal
to subtract/subtraction [səbˈtrækt], [səbˈtrækʃən]	subtrahieren (Subtraktion)
to multiply/multiplication [ˈmʌltəplaɪ], [ˌmʌltəplɪˈkeɪʃən]	multiplizieren (Multiplikation)
to divide/division [dəˈvaɪd], [dəˈvɪʒən]	dividieren (Division)

8

What time is it?	Wie viel Uhr ist es?

9

departure(s) [dɪˈpɑːtʃə]		Abfahrt(-szeiten)
arrival(s) [əˈraɪvəl]	What are the times of departure and arrival?	Ankunft(-szeiten)

5 MAKING TRAVEL ENQUIRIES TO LONDON

to enquire about [ɪnˈkwaɪə]	I'll enquire about trains to Sheffield.	sich erkundigen nach
trip	I'll go on a trip to Scotland next week.	Reise, Fahrt
travel agency [ˈtrævəl], [ˈeɪdʒənsi]		Reisebüro
to depend [dɪˈpend]		abhängen, hier: darauf ankommen
to go by ship/by train		mit dem Schiff/Zug fahren
to catch the ferry [kætʃ]		die Fähre erreichen
of course [kɔːs]	Will you help him? Of course.	natürlich, selbstverständlich
to fly [flaɪ]		fliegen
a second-class return ticket [ˈsekənd]	Do you want a single or a return ticket? A return (ticket).	eine Rückfahrkarte 2. Klasse
via (lateinisch) [vaɪə]		über (Ostende)

to take	How long does it take to get to the station?	hier: dauern
company ['kʌmpəni]		Gesellschaft
to offer sth/offer ['ɒfə]	That's a good offer.	etwas anbieten/ das Angebot
to be cheap [tʃi:p]	Is that the cheapest ticket to Bristol? Yes, it is.	billig sein
charter flight ['tʃɑ:tə], [flaɪt]		Charterflug
including/to include [ɪn'klu:dɪŋ]	What does the price include? – Service and taxes (Steuern).	einschließlich/ etwas einschließen
bed and breakfast [bed]		Zimmer mit Frühstück
brochure ['brəʊʃə]		Broschüre, Katalog
rate [reɪt]		Preis, Tarif
to book sth	I'd like to book a flight to New York.	etwas buchen (im Sinne von bestellen)
single room ['sɪŋɡəl]	Would you like a single or a double room? – A double.	Einzelzimmer
total ['təʊtl]	What's the total price? £25.50.	Gesamt ...
to phone sb	I'll phone you tomorrow.	jemanden anrufen
airline company ['eəlaɪn]		Fluggesellschaft
to be lucky/lucky ['lʌki]	It's my lucky day./ You're lucky.	Glück haben/Glücks...
to be vacant (free) ['veɪkənt]	Are there any seats vacant? I'm sorry, there aren't.	frei sein
plane (aircraft) [pleɪn], ['eəkrɑ:ft]		Flugzeug
airport		Flugplatz
takeoff ['teɪk-ɒf]		Start (eines Flugzeugs)
at the latest ['leɪtʃst]		spätestens
to check in [tʃek]	Where do I have to check in? At the BA counter (desk) just over there.	einchecken
voucher ['vaʊtʃə]		(Hotel-)Gutschein, Voucher
pleasant ['plezənt]	Have a pleasant flight!	erfreulich, angenehm

COMPREHENSION TESTS / GRAMMATICAL EXERCISES

5

to rent sth [rent]	Vivian rented a flat in a London suburb.	etwas mieten
a package holiday ['pækɪdʒ]		eine Pauschalreise
a do-it-yourself holiday		eine Individualreise
to insure one's luggage [ɪn'ʃʊə]	Tony insured his car at ...	das Gepäck versichern
a video (film) ['vɪdiəʊ]		ein Video(-film)
times of departure and arrival [dɪ'pɑ:tʃə]		Abfahrts- und Ankunftszeiten

6

a picture story		eine Bildgeschichte

to interpret sth [ɪnˈtɜːprɪ̩t]		etwas interpretieren, deuten
to be suitable [ˈsuːtəbəl]	Would 8 p.m. be suitable for you? Yes.	geeignet sein, passen(d)
title [ˈtaɪtl]		Titel

7

to reserve sth [rɪˈzɜːv]		etwas reservieren
to change [ˈtʃeɪndʒ]	Where do I have to change? At Piccadilly Circus.	umsteigen
a direct (through) train [dɪ̩ˈrekt, daɪ-], [θruː]	Is that a direct train? Yes, it is.	ein durchgehender Zug
platform [ˈplætfɔːm]	Where is platform 2? It's over there.	Bahnsteig
to act out sth [ækt]		etwas spielen (im Sinne von etwas vorführen)
dialogue [ˈdaɪəlɒg]		Dialog

8

to enter sth		etwas betreten
store (department store) [stɔː]		Warenhaus
to cash a traveller's cheque		einen Reisescheck einlösen
to change sth into sth [kæʃ]	Claire changed euros into dollars.	etwas in etw. umtauschen
postal order [ˈpəʊstl]		Postanweisung (in G.B.)
trunk call [trʌŋk]	Is it a trunk or a local call?	Ferngespräch
(tele)phone box		Telefonzelle
coin [kɔɪn]		(Geld-)Münze
slot [slɒt]	Harry put 50 pence into the slot.	Schlitz (in einem Münzautomaten)
to dial the area code for ... [ˈdaɪəl], [ˈeərɪə], [kəʊd]		die Vorwahl(-nummer) von ... wählen
map of New York		Stadtplan von New York
guide [gaɪd]	Did they take a guide? No.	Fremdenführer

9

lady		Dame
colleague [ˈkɒliːg]		Kollege, Kollegin
actress [ˈæktrɪ̩s]	Is she a well-known actress? Yes.	Schauspielerin
youngsters		junge Leute

10

sights [saɪts]	Do you know the sights of London?	Sehenswürdigkeiten
love letter	Ronald knows how to write love letters.	Liebesbrief
express letter		Eilbrief
pocket money [ˈpɒkɪ̩t]		Taschengeld
Walkman		Walkman
to lend sth to sb	Can you lend me 60 pounds?	jemandem etwas leihen
waiter [ˈweɪtə]		Kellner
menu [ˈmenjuː]		Speisekarte
to hand sth to sb		hier: jemandem etwas geben

bill	Here's the bill, sir.	die Rechnung (im Hotel, Restaurant)
to give sb a tip		jemandem Trinkgeld geben

6 SHORT SCENES FROM EVERYDAY LIFE

trade fair [treɪd]		Handelsmesse
to land	The plane landed smoothly (glatt).	landen
constable [ˈkʌnstəbəl]		Polizist(in)
straight on [streɪt]	Go straight on. At the next crossing there's the post office.	geradeaus
traffic lights [ˈtræfɪk]		Verkehrsampeln
to turn left [tɜːn]		links abbiegen
to carry on [ˈkæri]		hier: weitergehen
to reach sth [riːtʃ]	The bus reached Dover at 4 p.m.	etwas erreichen
underground station		U-Bahnstation
taxi rank [ˈtæksi], [ræŋk]		Taxistand
to be in a hurry [ˈhʌri]		es eilig haben, in Eile sein
to be in the middle of sth [mɪdl]		inmitten von etwas sein
rush hour (traffic) [rʌʃ]		Berufsverkehr
fare [feə]	What's the fare to Brighton? £18.50	(Fahr-)Preis
keep the change.		Behalten Sie den Rest. (Wechselgeld)
vacancy [ˈveɪkənsi]	Do you have any vacancies? Yes, we do.	hier: freies Zimmer/ freie Stelle
receptionist [rɪˈsepʃənɪst]		Empfangschef (in)
to serve breakfast [sɜːv]		Frühstück geben (servieren)
exchange rate [ɪksˈtʃeɪndʒ], [reɪt]	What's the exchange rate of the pound?	Wechselkurs
to make up the bill		die Rechnung fertig stellen

COMPREHENSION TESTS / GRAMMATICAL EXERCISES

1

to present sth [prɪˈzent]		hier: etwas geben
stay [steɪ]	Did you enjoy your stay in the hotel? Yes.	Aufenthalt

2

to act out sth [ækt]		hier: etwas spielen

4

to reserve a seat [rɪˈzɜːv]		einen Platz reservieren
timetable	Can I get the timetable for trains to Bristol? Of course.	Fahrplan
passenger [ˈpæsɪndʒə]		Reisender, Passagier

5

to be polite/impolite [pə'laɪt]		höflich/unhöflich sein
to be ugly ['ʌgli]		hässlich sein
to be tall [tɔːl]		groß sein (in der Höhe)
to be fast [fɑːst]		schnell sein
to be slow [sləʊ]	He is a slow worker.	langsam sein, nachgehen (Uhr)

6

monetary unit ['mʌnɪtəri], ['juːnɪt]	What's the Italian monetary unit?	Währungseinheit
note [nəʊt]		Geldschein, Banknote
to be in circulation [ˌsɜːkjʊ'leɪʃən]		im Umlauf sein
foreign currency ['fɒrɪn], ['kʌrənsi]		ausländische Währung

8

to play bingo		Bingo spielen
to make love to sb	Would you make love to him? Perhaps.	mit jemandem schlafen
to swim in the (swimming) pool		im Swimmingpool schwimmen
to have a picnic ['pɪknɪk]		picknicken
forest ['fɒrɪst]	They made love in the forest.	Wald
to take one's dog for walkies		mit einem Hund Gassi gehen
to do the cooking ['kʊkɪŋ]	I like the French cooking.	kochen, Küche (die Zubereitung)
to collect stamps [kə'lekt]		Briefmarken sammeln
football stadium ['steɪdiəm]		Fußballstadion

9

ferry ['feri]	The passengers boarded the ferry.	Fähre, Fährschiff
to take off/the takeoff (plane)		starten, der Start (Abflug)
to check in [tʃek]	When do we have to check in? At 3.30 p.m.	einchecken
a couple ['kʌpəl]		ein Paar
to smuggle		schmuggeln
customs official ['kʌstəmz], [ə'fɪʃəl]	The customs official asked, "Do you have anything to declare (verzollen)"?	Zollbeamter
to examine the suitcases ['suːtkeɪsɪz]		die Koffer prüfen
to rent a caravan ['kærəvæn]		ein Wohnmobil mieten
a car-rental firm ['rentl] [fɜːm]		eine Autovermietung
freeway		Autobahn (USA)
accident ['æksɪdənt]	Who caused the accident? The driver of the Ford.	Unfall
ambulance ['æmbjʊləns]		Krankenwagen
hospital ['hɒspɪtl]	Mr Bent was sent to hospital.	Krankenhaus

7 SIGHTSEEING IN LONDON

I am sure [ʃʊəʳ], [ʃɔː]	I am sure that he will do it.	ich bin sicher
as soon as possible		so bald wie möglich
to go on a sightseeing tour		eine Stadtrundfahrt machen
a lively city ['laɪvli]		eine lebhafte Stadt
to pass sth	Did you pass Trafalgar Square? Yes, we did.	hier: an etwas vorbeikommen
neon signs ['niːɒn], [saɪnz]		Neonreklame
statue ['stætʃuː]		die Statue
foreigner	Are you a foreigner? Yes, I am.	Ausländer
to reach sth	We reached Bristol at 8 p.m.	etwas erreichen
to get out (off)		aussteigen
to take photos of sb	Sandra took photos of her child.	fotografieren
column ['kɒləm]		Säule
to feed the pigeons [fiːd], ['pɪdʒ₃ənz]		die Tauben füttern
a break [breɪk]	Let's have a break now.	Pause
to continue sth [kən'tɪnjuː]	Continue reading, please.	etwas fortsetzen
residence ['rezɪdəns]		Wohnsitz
to make a speech [spiːtʃ]		eine Rede halten
to listen to sb ['lɪsən]	We listened to the news.	jemandem zuhören
soapbox orator ['ɒrətə]		Seifenkistenredner
return		hier: die Wiederkehr
death penalty [deθ], ['penlti]		Todesstrafe
to turn into sth		in etwas einbiegen
to be busy ['bɪzi]	Don't disturb (stören) me. I am very busy.	hier verkehrsreich, belebt, beschäftigt sein
to be opposite ['ɒpəzɪt]		gegenüber sein
coronation church [kɒrə'neɪʃən]		Krönungskirche
a boat trip		eine Schiffs-(Boots-)Fahrt
to enjoy sth [ɪn'dʒɔɪ]	We enjoyed the party.	etwas genießen, sehr gefallen
to serve as [sɜːv]		dienen als
prison ['prɪzən]	The bank robbers were sent to prison.	Gefängnis
museum [mjuːˈziːəm]		Museum
to miss sth	Don't miss the plane.	etwas verpassen, versäumen
crown jewels [kraʊn], ['dʒuːəlz]		die Kronjuwelen
wedding ceremony ['wedɪŋ], ['serɪməni]		Hochzeitszeremonie (-feierlichkeit)
to take place	When does the football match take place? At 4 p.m.	stattfinden
the Docklands		die Docklands (neuer Londoner Stadtteil)
skyscraper [skaɪ], ['skreɪpə]		Wolkenkratzer
insurance company [ɪn'ʃʊərəns]		Versicherungsgesellschaft
atmosphere ['ætməsfɪə]		Atmosphäre
to get to know sth (sb)	I got to know (I met) Peter at Heathrow Airport.	etwas (jemanden) kennen lernen
dry humour ['hjuːmə]		trockener Humor
to be fantastic [fæn'tæstɪk]		fantastisch sein

COMPREHENSION TESTS / GRAMMATICAL EXERCISES

1

crime [kraɪm]		Kriminalität, Verbrechen
entertainment district [ˌentə'teɪnmənt]	Soho is London's entertainment district.	Vergnügungsviertel

6

Having lunch at a self-service restaurant

break [breɪk]	Pause
self-service restaurant ['restə-rɒnt]	Selbstbedienungsrestaurant
vegetable soup ['vedʒtəbl]	Gemüsesuppe
oxtail soup ['ɒksteɪl], [su:p]	Ochsenschwanzsuppe
onion rings ['ʌnjən]	Zwiebelringe
French fried potatoes [fraɪd]	Pommes frites
fried egg	Setzei
rasher ['ræʃə]	Streifen
bacon ['beɪkən]	Schinkenspeck
pork [pɔ:k]	Schweinefleisch
sausage ['sɒsɪdʒ]	Wurst
bean [bi:n]	Bohne
mashed potatoes [mæʃd]	Kartoffelbrei
filet of plaice ['fɪlɪ̩t], ['fɪleɪ], [pleɪs]	Schollenfilet
lamb cutlet [læm], ['kʌtlɪ̩t]	Lammkotelett
fried potatoes	Bratkartoffeln
pea [pi:]	Erbse
pineapple ['paɪnæpəl]	Ananas
roast beef [rəʊst]	Roastbeef
Yorkshire pudding ['pʊdɪŋ]	Yorkshirepudding
afters	Desserts, Nachspeisen
peach [pi:tʃ]	Pfirsich
cream [kri:m]	Sahne
fruit salad [fru:t], ['sæləd]	Obstsalat
chocolate sauce ['tʃɒklɪ̩t], [sɔ:s]	Schokoladensoße
strawberry ['strɔ:bəri]	Erdbeere
beverage ['bevərɪdʒ]	Getränk
lemon ['lemən]	Zitrone
soft drinks [sɒft]	alkoholfreie Getränke

8

to do one's homework		seine Hausaufgaben machen
to quarrel with sb ['kwɒrəl]	Who did you quarrel with? With Andrew.	mit jemandem streiten
a detective story [dɪ'tektɪv]		ein Krimi
to watch a video (film) ['vɪdɪəʊ]	Do you like watching videos? Yes.	sich ein Video ansehen
to crack jokes [kræk], [dʒəʊks]		Witze machen
to do a crossword puzzle ['pʌzəl]		ein Kreuzworträtsel lösen

9

to do the football pools [pu:lz]		im Fußballtoto spielen
postman		der Briefträger
solarium [səʊˈleəriəm]	Do you like going to the solarium? Yes, I do.	Solarium
to thunder (the thunder) [ˈθʌndə]	There is thunder (Gewitter) in the air.	donnern (Donner, Gewitter)
to puke [pju:k]		kotzen
to stroll around [strəʊl]		herumbummeln
to snow [snəʊ]		schneien
to catch sight of sb [saɪt]		jemanden erblicken
to try on sth	Where can I try on this jumper? In the changing room over there.	etwas anprobieren
the alarm system [əˈlɑ:m], [ˈsɪstəm]		die Alarmanlage
to rush into sth [rʌʃ]		in etwas hineinstürzen
to cross the zebra crossing [ˈzi:brə]		den Zebrastreifen überqueren
to run into sth (sb)	What car ran into yours? A Jaguar.	zusammenstoßen, hineinfahren
to go through the red traffic lights [ˈtræfɪk]		bei Rot über die Ampel fahren
to explode (a bomb) [ɪkˈspləʊd]		explodieren (eine Bombe)
wallet [ˈwɒlət]		Brieftasche

10

a bunch of keys [bʌntʃ]	Have you found your bunch of keys? No, I haven't.	ein Schlüsselbund
records [ˈrekɔ:dz]		Schallplatten
umbrella [ʌmˈbrelə]		Regenschirm
chess computer [tʃes]		Schachcomputer
electric shaver [ɪˈlektrɪk], [ˈʃeɪvə]	This electric shaver works very smoothly.	elektrischer Rasierapparat
gas lighter [gæs]		Gasfeuerzeug
to settle a bill		eine Hotelrechnung begleichen

8 ALWAYS TROUBLE WITH THE BOSS AND THE PARENTS

trouble [ˈtrʌbəl]	Do you have any trouble with Sarah? Yes, a lot.	Ärger, Schwierigkeiten
boss		Boss, Chef
to meet sb [mi:t]	I'm pleased to meet you./ I met him in London last year.	jemanden treffen, kennen lernen
to invite sb [ɪnˈvaɪt]		jemanden einladen
fortnight [ˈfɔ:tnaɪt]	How long will you stay in London? For a fortnight.	14 Tage
to be expensive [ɪkˈspensɪv]	What does that sweater cost? £65. Oh, that's expensive.	teuer sein
rent/to rent	Cars for rent?	Miete, mieten

to be independent of [ˌɪndɪˈpendənt]	In the 19th and 20th centuries, the English colonies wanted to become independent of Great Britain.	unabhängig sein von
to criticize sb [ˈkrɪtɪsaɪz] to stand sth/sb	What do you think about Tom? I can't stand him.	jemanden kritisieren etwas/jemanden ertragen
everywhere the same [seɪm]	Did you attend the same school? Yes, I did.	überall der, die dasselbe/gleiche
generation gap [dʒenəˈreɪʃən], [gæp] to be on good (better) terms with each other [tɜːmz]	Are you on good terms with him? Yes, I am.	Generationskluft gut (besser) miteinander auskommen („each other" bei 2 Personen, „one another" bei mehreren Personen)
counter [ˈkaʊntə] account [əˈkaʊnt] to pay in sth to withdraw [wɪðˈdrɔː]	I want to withdraw £100 from my account.	Schalter, Tresen hier: Konto etwas einzahlen hier: abheben/ sich zurückziehen
to be bad to grumble [ˈgrʌmbəl] to enjoy sth [ɪnˈdʒɔɪ]	That's really bad. Did you enjoy the picnic? Oh, yes. I really did.	schlecht, schlimm sein herumnörgeln, schimpfen etwas genießen, gern mögen
to be unemployed [ʌnɪmˈplɔɪd] at the moment [ˈməʊmənt]	Today a lot of people are unemployed in Britain. I can't do it now. I'm busy at the moment.	arbeitslos sein im Augenblick, zurzeit
a designer [dɪˈzaɪnə]		Designer, Musterzeichner, Entwerfer
textile factory [ˈtekstaɪl], [ˈfæktəri] to be bankrupt [ˈbæŋkrʌpt]	This firm went bankrupt last year.	Textilfabrik pleite sein
What a pity! [ˈpɪti] chance [tʃɑːns]	You haven't any chance to win the match.	Wie schade! Gelegenheit, Chance
to attend sth [əˈtend]	What kind of school did you attend? A grammar school.	etwas besuchen to visit (ein einmaliger Besuch)
a computer course demand [dɪˈmɑːnd]	There is a big demand for this product.	ein Computerkursus Bedarf, Nachfrage
to be a specialist [ˈspeʃəlɪst] I'll keep my fingers crossed for you. to intend to do sth [ɪnˈtend] to set off	I intend to set off early in the morning.	Spezialist sein Ich werde dir die Daumen drücken. etwas zu tun beabsichtigen aufbrechen
mountain valley [ˈvæli]		Berg Tal

COMPREHENSION TESTS / GRAMMATICAL EXERCISES

4
to take part in sth | | an etw. teilnehmen
to dial ['daɪəl] | First, dial the area code (Vorwahl) for York, then your phone number.

moonlight party ['muːnlaɪt] | | Mondscheinparty
(tele)phone directory [daɪ'rektəri] | May I have the phone directory? Yes, sir. | Telefonbuch

area code ['eəriə], [kəʊd] | | Vorwahl(-nummer)
coin [kɔɪn] | | Münze
slot [slɒt] | | Geldeinwurf bei Automaten

5
enquiry [ɪn'kwaɪəri] | What are you doing? I'm making enquiries about flights to New York. | Erkundigung, Anfrage
sale [seɪl] | Second-hand cars for sale. | der Verkauf, Absatz

6
to be universal [juːnɪ'vɜːsəl] | | allgemein gelten

7
to be glad [glæd] | I'm glad to hear that ... | sich freuen, froh sein
to get used to sth/to sb | | sich an etwas/jemanden gewöhnen

way of life | | Lebensart, Lebensweise
to complain about (of) sth [kəm'pleɪn] | What does he complain about? About the quality of the goods. | sich über etwas beschweren, beklagen (über)
to get on well | How have you been getting on so far? Thank you, very well. | gut gehen (es geht mir gut)

in the meantime ['miːntaɪm] | | inzwischen
to worry about sth ['wʌri] | Don't worry! It's all right. | sich Sorgen machen um etwas

probable (probably) ['prɒbəbəl] | The Rangers will probably win the football match. | wahrscheinlich

drug [drʌg] | | Droge, Rauschgift Medikament
to get over sth | | hier: etwas überwinden
MUM and DAD(DY) | | Mutter und Vater

8
title ['taɪtl] | | Titel
author ['ɔːθə] | What's your favourite (Lieblings-)author? Hemingway. | Schriftsteller, Autor

play | | Theaterstück
car park (parking) | Is there any parking? Just round the corner (Ecke). | Parkplatz

to be in a hurry ['hʌri] | | es eilig haben, in Eile sein

to give sb a wake-up call [weɪk ʌp]		jemanden telefonisch wecken

9
umbrella [ʌm'brelə]		Regenschirm
colleague ['kɒliːg]	She is a colleague of mine.	Kollege, Kollegin
stag party [stæg]		Abschiedsparty vom Junggesellenleben (nur unter Männern)
fiancé(e) [fi'ɒnseɪ]		Verlobter, Verlobte
meeting	Did you take part in this meeting? No.	hier: Versammlung

10
overcoat ['əʊvəkəʊt]		Mantel
to be expensive [ɪk'spensɪv]	Was your stay in Hawaii expensive? Yes, it really was.	teuer, kostspielig sein
to be reasonable in price ['riːzənəbəl]		preiswert sein
average quality ['ævərɪdʒ], ['kwɒlɪ̬ti]		Durchschnittsqualität
bag [bæg], to be heavy/to be light	The suitcase is heavy/light.	(Trage-)Tasche schwer/leicht sein (Gewicht)
a detective film [dɪ'tektɪv]		ein Kriminalfilm, Krimi
to be boring ['bɔːrɪŋ]	This novel is boring.	langweilig sein
a technical college		eine berufsbildende Lehranstalt (technisch)
diary ['daɪəri]	Do you have a diary? Yes, I do.	Tagebuch
to weigh [weɪ]		wiegen

11
calculator ['kælkjʊleɪtə]		Taschenrechner
to like	Do you like it? Yes, I do.	hier: gefallen
dress		Kleid
suit/to suit [suːt], [sjuːt]	Does it suit you? Yes, it does.	Anzug/gefallen/zu jemandem passen
travel agency ['trævəl]		Reisebüro

9   LET'S GO TO HARRODS
stationery department ['steɪʃənəri]		Schreibwarenabteilung
to be funny ['fʌni]		spaßig, lustig sein
to try to do sth [traɪ]	I'll try to find out what has happened.	etwas zu tun versuchen
toy department [tɔɪ]		Spielwarenabteilung
doll [dɒl]		Puppe
Red Indians, American Indians		Indianer
range [reɪndʒ]		Sortiment, Reihe, Serie
ladies' wear department		Damenkleiderabteilung

kilt		Schottenrock
to look for sth	What are you looking for? For a skirt (Rock).	nach etwas suchen
size [saɪz]		Größe
changing room		Ankleideraum
to try sth on	There is the changing room. Try it on, please.	anprobieren
to fit [fɪt]	The suit doesn't fit. It's too small.	passen (Anzug)
short back and sides		vorn und hinten kurz
to cut off		abschneiden
to have a shave		rasieren
to mind sth [maɪnd]	Mind the traffic rules!	etwas beachten, an etwas denken, auf etwas achten
skin [skɪn]		die Haut
to be sensitive ['sensɪtɪv]	He is a very sensitive man. The eyes are sensitive to light.	empfindlich sein

COMPREHENSION TESTS / GRAMMATICAL EXERCISES

1

to cry		schreien, weinen

3

to pick up sb	I'll pick you up at 7 p.m.	jemanden abholen
to invite sb for (to) sth		jemanden (zu etwas) einladen

4

to replace sth [rɪ'pleɪs]		etwas ersetzen
in bold type [bəʊld], [taɪp]		in Fettschrift
to indicate sth ['ɪndɪkeɪt]		etwas angeben
chat [tʃæt]		Gespräch, Geplauder
to drop (to fall) [drɒp]		fallen (Preise)
to be prepared, to be ready	I am prepared to help you with the translation.	bereit sein
to increase (to rise) [ɪn'kriːs]		steigen (Kosten)
to go on a tour		eine Reise machen
considerable(-ly) [kən'sɪdərəbəl]	This is a considerable amount (Betrag) of money.	beträchtlich
to pay (in) cash [kæʃ]	Do you want to pay (in) cash or by cheque? In cash.	bar zahlen

5

to reproduce sth [ˌriːprə'djuːs]		etwas wiedergeben
contents		Inhalt

8

to be engaged to sb [ɪn'geɪdʒd]	Is Irene engaged to Paul? Yes.	mit jemandem verlobt sein
to be in a hurry	I'm in a hurry.	in Eile sein, es eilig haben

9

to change	Where do I have to change? At Oxford Street.	hier: umsteigen
to get out		aussteigen
to rent a car		einen Wagen mieten
motel	Did you stay at a motel last night? Yes.	Motel (Hotel speziell für Autofahrer)
to be full (up)	The bus is full up.	(voll) besetzt sein
autumn ['ɔːtəm]		Herbst
to buy a guide to ... [gaɪd]	Do you have a guide to San Francisco? Yes.	einen Fremdenführer von ... kaufen
to enjoy sth [ɪnˈdʒɔɪ]		etwas genießen, jemandem gefällt etwas

10

to have one's hair shampooed and dyed [ʃæmˈpuːd], [daɪd]		die Haare waschen und färben lassen
wallet		Brieftasche
Lost Property Office [ˈprɒpəti]	Did you phone the Lost Property Office? No, but I'll do so.	Fundbüro
to be lucky		Glück haben
to make a date		sich verabreden
a delicious meal [dɪˈlɪʃəs]	Did you enjoy this delicious meal? Yes.	ein köstliches Essen

10 AN EXCITING FOOTBALL MATCH

to be exciting [ɪkˈsaɪtɪŋ]	That was an exciting film.	spannend sein
the Cup Final [ˈfaɪnəl]		das Pokalendspiel
to be dramatic [drəˈmætɪk]		dramatisch sein
to take the lead [liːd]		die Führung übernehmen
to score from a penalty [skɔː], [ˈpenlti]		einen Elfmeter schießen
to equalize [ˈiːkwəlaɪz]		ausgleichen
to be rough [rʌf]	The sea was very rough.	rauh, ruppig sein
to be lectured [ˈlektʃəd] severe(ly) [sᵻˈvɪə]		einen Verweis erhalten streng, scharf
to kick sb [kɪk]		jemanden mit dem Fuß stoßen, treten
TV viewer [ˈvjuːə]		Fernsehzuschauer
event [ɪˈvent]	That was a big event.	Ereignis
to launch sth [lɔːntʃ]	This product was launched on the market in April.	etwas starten, einführen
attack/to attack [əˈtæk]	The police were attacked by the gangsters.	Angriff/angreifen
to take the game [geɪm] into extra time [ˈekstrə]		es dazu bringen, dass nachgespielt wird
to score the winning goal [gəʊl]		das Siegestor schießen

to blast the ball into the net [blɑːst], [net]		den Ball ins Netz feuern
atmosphere ['ætməsfɪə]		Atmosphäre, Stimmung
to go mad [mæd]		durchdrehen, verrückt spielen
trophy ['trəʊfi]		Trophäe
national anthem ['næʃənəl], ['ænθəm]		Nationalhymne

COMPREHENSION TESTS / GRAMMATICAL EXERCISES

1

a summary ['sʌməri]	Would you please make a summary of the text? Okay.	eine Zusammenfassung

3

to be lucky ['lʌki]	You are lucky.	Glück haben
to be boring ['bɔːrɪŋ]	The film was boring.	langweilig sein
to be cheap		billig sein

4

to be predominant [prɪ'dɒmɪnənt]		vorherrschend sein
to regret	I regret that he failed the exam.	bedauern
a role [rəʊl]	What kind of role does Roy play? A predominant one.	eine Rolle
to miss sth		hier: etwas vermissen
sporting event [ɪ'vənt]		Sportereignis
to lose one's life	He lost his life in a catastrophe (Katastrophe).	umkommen, sterben

5

to be polite [pə'laɪt]		höflich sein
(horse)race		(Pferde-)Rennen
to be unique [juː'niːk]	Is it unique? Yes, it is.	einzigartig, einmalig sein
to forget one's good manners ['mænəz]		die guten Manieren vergessen
sometimes		manchmal
to be fashionable ['fæʃənəbəl]	It's fashionable to spend the holidays in tropical countries.	modern, modisch sein
meeting		Versammlung, Meeting
a social event ['səʊʃəl]		ein gesellschaftliches Ereignis
hat [hæt]		Hut
tennis championships		Tennismeisterschaften
boat race		hier: Ruderregatta
four times	How many times have you seen this film? Four times.	viermal
so far	Have you had any news from him so far? No, I haven't.	bis jetzt

6

to miss sth		hier: etwas versäumen
suggestion [sə'dʒestʃən]		Vorschlag
to complain about sth [kəm'pleın]	Jimmy complained about the bad quality.	sich über etwas beschweren, etwas beanstanden
to give one's word		sein Wort geben
proposal of marriage [prə'pəʊzəl]	Did he make a proposal of marriage? Yes, he did.	Heiratsantrag
to dial the area code ['daıəl], ['eərıə]		die Vorwahl (Nummer) wählen

7

a thriller ['θrılə]		ein Reißer, Krimi
the Tennis Finals		die Endrunde in den Tennismeisterschaften
to get an autograph (from) ['ɔ:təgrɑ:f]	May I get an autograph? With pleasure.	ein Autogramm von ... bekommen
to do the football pools [pu:lz]		im Fußballtoto spielen
to be seriously hurt ['sıərıəsli], [hɜ:t]		schwer verletzt werden
to die [daı]	She died of cancer (Krebs).	sterben
health [helθ]		Gesundheit

8

edition [ı'dıʃən]	This is the third edition of the book.	Auflage

11 GOING ON A TOUR OF SOUTH ENGLAND

to look for sth	What are you looking for? For my wallet.	etwas suchen
car-rental office ['rentl]		Autovermietung
to attract [ə'trækt]		anziehen, reizen, anlocken
to drive on the left (traffic)		Linksverkehr
to get used to sth	You will soon get used to it.	sich an etwas gewöhnen
to be ... from ...	Cheddam is about 2 miles from here.	entfernt sein von
to be well-known	This restaurant is well-known for its cooking.	sehr bekannt sein
later	I'll do it later.	später
to have a view of		einen Blick haben auf
lighthouse ['laıthaʊs]		Leuchtturm
beach	We had a lot of fun on the beach.	Strand
to be marvellous	That's marvellous.	wunderbar sein
to stroll (along)	We were strolling along Oxford Street when the accident happened.	(entlang-)bummeln, schlendern
village ['vılıdʒ]		Dorf
to be shocking		schockierend sein

experience [ɪkˈspɪərɪəns]	That was a great experience.	Erlebnis, Erfahrung
suddenly [ˈsʌdnli]		plötzlich
to turn into a street		in eine Straße einbiegen
to zigzag [ˈzɪgzæg]		im Zickzack fahren
to think (thought)		denken, glauben
fortunately [ˈfɔːtʃənətli]		glücklicherweise, Gott sei Dank
in time/on time	The train arrived on time.	rechtzeitig/ auf die Minute genau
destination [destɪˈneɪʃən]		Reiseziel, Bestimmungsort
coastline		die Küste
to be mild [maɪld]		mild sein
climate [ˈklaɪmɪt]	The climate is very mild here.	Klima
tropical vegetation [ˈtrɒpɪkəl]		tropische Vegetation
attraction [əˈtrækʃən]		Attraktion
as well as	Henry as well as Sarah is a good tennis player.	sowohl als auch
motorway		Autobahn
to end	The road ends here.	enden

COMPREHENSION TESTS / GRAMMATICAL EXERCISES

2

to set off for		aufbrechen nach
to take part in the excursion [ɪkˈskɜːʃən]		an dem Ausflug teilnehmen
to catch a cold	Be careful (vorsichtig) not to catch a cold.	sich erkälten
Chinese [tʃaɪˈniːz]		(die) Chinesen, chinesisch
delicious [dɪˈlɪʃəs]	The meal was delicious.	köstlich, lecker
duck [dʌk]		Ente

3

to interrupt sb (sth) [ɪntəˈrʌpt]	Please don't interrupt me.	jemanden/etwas unterbrechen
to knock (at) [nɒk]		anklopfen
moon		Mond
to become possible	One day this may become possible.	möglich werden

4

to do the cooking		die Speisen zubereiten
to disturb [dɪˈstɜːb]	Don't disturb me.	stören
umbrella		Regenschirm
suitcase [ˈsuːtkeɪs]	Is the suitcase heavy? Very heavy.	Koffer

6

road sign(s) [rəʊd], [saɪn]		Verkehrszeichen
to mean [miːn]	What does it mean?	bedeuten
maximum speed [ˈmæksɪ̥məm]		Höchstgeschwindigkeit
major road [ˈmeɪdʒə]		Haupt(verkehrs)straße
vehicle [ˈviːɪkəl]		Fahrzeug
scooter [ˈskuːtə]		Motorroller
to cycle [ˈsaɪkəl]		Rad fahren
pedestrian [pɪ̥ˈdestrɪən]		Fußgänger
entry [ˈentri]		Zufahrt, Eingang
vehicular traffic [viːˈhɪkjʊlə]		Fahrzeuge (~ verkehr)

7

colleague [ˈkɒliːg]		Kollege
to cancel sth [ˈkænsəl]	Was flight No 365 cancelled? Yes.	etwas stornieren, annullieren
tennis championships		Tennismeisterschaften
to relax [rɪˈlæks]		entspannen

8

to remit money to an account [rɪˈmɪt], [əˈkaʊnt]	What amount of money did you remit? 200 pounds.	auf ein Konto Geld überweisen
(small) parcel [ˈpɑːsəl]		Päckchen
penfriend		Schreibfreund(in)
furthermore, moreover [fɜːðəˈmɔː]		außerdem, ferner
recorded delivery [rɪkɔːdɪ̥d], [dɪˈlɪvəri]	Did you send it as recorded delivery? Yes.	Einschreiben
telephone box		Telefonzelle
coin [kɔɪn]		(Geld-)Münze
slot [slɒt]		Einwurf
to fax [fæks]	I faxed Charles at once.	faxen

9

hot		heiß
pleasant	That was a pleasant surprise. (Überraschung)	erfreulich, angenehm
to be exciting [ɪkˈsaɪtɪŋ]		hier: spannend sein
thin [θɪn]		dünn
to be famous for sth [ˈfeɪməs]		durch etw. berühmt sein

10

to weigh [weɪ]	What does this parcel weigh? 6.5 lbs.	wiegen
suit [suːt, sjuːt]		Anzug
size [saɪz]	What's the size of this suit? 42.	Größe
distance [ˈdɪstəns]	What's the distance from London to Oxford? About 100 miles.	Entfernung

12 HAVING AN ACCIDENT

bad luck	Did you win the game? No, I had bad luck.	Pech
while (Konj.), during (Präpos.)	While I was reading, she was knitting./During the break I'll have a drink.	während
the scene of accident [siːn]		die Unfallstelle
to bleed [bliːd]	Oh, my goodness. You are bleeding.	bluten
pain [peɪn]	Do you feel any pain? Yes, here.	Schmerz(en)
to hurt [hɜːt]	Where does it hurt? Here.	schmerzen
ambulance [ˈæmbjʊləns]	I'll call an ambulance.	Krankenwagen
to be injured [ˈɪndʒəd]	He was seriously injured in the accident.	verletzt sein
to run into sth	What happened? I ran into a car.	mit etwas zusammenstoßen
to overtake a car		ein Auto überholen
to have a headache [ˈhedeɪk]		Kopfschmerzen haben
to consult a doctor [kənˈsʌlt]		den Arzt aufsuchen
driving licence [ˈlaɪsəns]		Führerschein
witness [ˈwɪtnɪs]		der Zeuge
registration number [redʒɪˈstreɪʃən]		Zulassungsnummer
to question sb	She was questioned by the policeman.	jemanden befragen, vernehmen
to blame sb [bleɪm]	He was blamed for his bad behaviour (Benehmen).	jemandem die Schuld geben, jemandem Vorwürfe machen

COMPREHENSION TESTS / GRAMMATICAL EXERCISES

2

to appear on the scene [əˈpɪə], [siːn]		auf der Bildfläche erscheinen

4

village [ˈvɪlɪdʒ]		Dorf

7

to hurt [hɜːt]	Where does it hurt?	hier: Schmerzen haben, weh tun
to have a headache		Kopfschmerzen haben
to have a sore throat [sɔː], [θrəʊt]		Halsschmerzen haben
to have a temperature [ˈtemp(ə)rətʃə]		Fieber haben
to feel ill		sich schlecht fühlen
to feel dizzy [ˈdɪzi]		schwindlig sein
to have flu [fluː]		Grippe haben
to have a fall		stürzen

8

to drop a line to sb [drɒp]	When in N. Y. I'll drop a line to you.	an jemanden ein paar Zeilen schreiben
slide [slaɪd]		Dia
to do the gardening		Gartenarbeit(en) machen
to permit [pəˈmɪt]		erlauben
to go skating		Schlittschuhlaufen gehen
preparation	Have you made the necessary preparations? Not yet.	Vorbereitung
to swot up one's maths [swɒt], [mæθs]		Mathe pauken

9

to pick up sb		jemanden abholen
to stay	How long did you stay in Bombay? A fortnight.	sich aufhalten, bleiben
a couple of days [ˈkʌpəl]		ein paar Tage
musical [ˈmjuːzɪkəl]		Musical
favourite meal [ˈfeɪvərɪt]	What's your favourite meal?	Lieblingsmahlzeit
roast goose [rəʊst]		Gänsebraten
zoo [zuː]		Zoo
to have a lot of fun [fʌn]		viel Spaß haben
to take off	When does the plane take off? At 10.45 a.m.	hier: fliegen
to check in, to cancel [ˈkænsəl]		einchecken, annullieren, etwas streichen

10

importance [ɪmˈpɔːtəns]	Forget it. It is of no importance.	Bedeutung
doubt [daʊt]	I have no doubt that he will do it.	Zweifel
to save money [seɪv]		Geld sparen
overcoat		Mantel
sales [seɪlz]		Absatz, Umsatz
to refer to sth [rɪˈfɜː]	I refer to your letter of 9 June.	sich auf etwas beziehen
issue [ˈɪʃuː], [ˈɪsjuː]	This is the latest issue of the TIMES.	Ausgabe (Zeitung)
edition [ɪˈdɪʃən]	This is the first edition of the book.	Ausgabe, Auflage (Buch)
novel [ˈnɒvəl]		Roman
fiancé/fiancée [fiˈɒnseɪ]		Verlobter/Verlobte

13 SOME ASPECTS OF MODERN BRITISH LIFE

household		Haushalt
rent		die Miete
flat [flæt]		(Etagen-)Wohnung
trend [trend]		der Trend, die Tendenz
to mind (sth)	Do you mind me smoking? No, I don't.	hier: etwas dagegen haben, einzuwenden haben

to spend sth on sth	What do you spend your pocket money on? Very often on books.	etwas für eine Sache ausgeben
generation gap [dʒenəˈreɪʃən], [gæp]		die Kluft (der Spalt) zwischen den Generationen
to be due to sth [djuː]	The accident was due to careless driving.	auf etwas zurückzuführen sein
to be against sth	We are against this proposal (suggestion).	gegen etwas sein
to be materialistic [məˌtɪərɪəˈlɪstɪk]		materialistisch sein
lifestyle		Lebensstil (-art)
driving test		Fahrprüfung
driving school	I attended this driving school before taking the driving test.	Fahrschule
driving licence [ˈlaɪsəns]		Führerschein
in addition [əˈdɪʃən]		außerdem
plate [pleɪt]		das (Nummern-)Schild
the front and back		die Vorder- und Rückseite

COMPREHENSION TESTS / GRAMMATICAL EXERCISES

4

decision [dɪˈsɪʒən]	You must take (make) a decision now.	Entschluss, Entscheidung
fashion [ˈfæʃən]		Mode

5

eating habits [ˈhæbɪts]	He does it out of habit.	Essgewohnheiten
place		Ort, Stelle, Platz
to be boring		langweilig sein
to prefer sth	I prefer dogs to cats.	etwas bevorzugen
to be frozen (to freeze) [friːz]		gefroren sein
tin		Dose, Büchse
to be (to become) popular [ˈpɒpjʊlə]	This sportsman is very popular.	beliebt sein (werden)
self-service restaurant [ˈrestərɒnt]		Selbstbedienungsrestaurant
enormous(ly) [ɪˈnɔːməs]		enorm, gewaltig
lunch break [breɪk]		Mittags(essen)pause
a light meal		eine leichte Mahlzeit
since	I haven't seen him since Easter.	seit
Indian [ˈɪndɪən]		indisch
to offer specialities [ˌspeʃɪˈælɪtiːz]		Spezialitäten anbieten
to be reasonable in price [ˈriːzənəbəl]	Prices are reasonable here.	preiswert sein
to go out/to eat out		ausgehen/außerhalb essen

cooking	This restaurant is well-known for its good cooking.	Kochen, Küche
to be tasty ['teɪsti]	The cake is very tasty.	gut schmecken, schmackhaft sein
duck [dʌk]		Ente
to be exotic [ɪgˈzɒtɪk]		exotisch sein
to be traditional [trəˈdɪʃənəl]	It is traditional in GB to have turkey at Christmas.	traditionell sein
likewise		wie auch, so wie
turkey ['tɜːki]		Truthahn
Yorkshire pudding ['pʊdɪŋ]		Yorkshirepudding
to be true for		stimmen, zutreffen

7

to fall in love with sb	He has fallen in love with Joan.	sich in jemanden verlieben
to help sb out of a fix [fɪks]		jemandem aus der Klemme helfen
(to) dare [deə]		wagen

8

to be exciting [ɪkˈsaɪtɪŋ]		spannend sein
to be respected [rɪˈspektɪd]		geachtet sein
favourable ['feɪvərəbəl]		günstig
to taste [teɪst]	These biscuits taste good.	schmecken
to drink like a fish		wie ein Loch saufen

9

beach [biːtʃ]		Strand
to cause trouble [kɔːz], ['trʌbəl]	He caused a lot of trouble.	Ärger (Schwierigkeiten) bereiten
to earn money [ɜːn]		Geld verdienen
catalogue		Katalog
advertisement		Anzeige, Inserat
exhibition [ˌeksɪˈbɪʃən]	I met him at the exhibition.	Ausstellung

14 A VISIT TO AN ENGLISH SCHOOL

grammar school		Gymnasium
to be up to date	This book is up to date.	aktuell, zeitgemäß sein
teaching method ['meθəd]		Lehrmethode
lesson ['lesən]		Unterricht(sstunde)
to be welcome to do sth ['welkəm]	You are welcome to do it once again.	etwas gern tun dürfen
interest	He has a great interest in politics. (Politik)	das Interesse
shipping company		Reederei
vocational training [vəʊˈkeɪʃənəl]		Berufsausbildung

twice a week		zweimal in der Woche
the rest	Take what you want and throw the rest away.	der Rest
to have practical training ['præktɪkəl]		die praktische Ausbildung haben
to take an examination		eine Prüfung machen
to hold, held, held	The politician held a press conference.	hier: etwas abhalten
Chamber of Commerce ['tʃeɪmbə], ['kɒmɜːs]		Handelskammer
trainee [treɪˈniː]	Trainees have to post letters, to sort the correspondence, etc.	Auszubildende(r)
commerce and trade [treɪd]		Handel und Gewerbe
industry ['ɪndəstri]		Industrie
the College of Further Education in York ['fɜːðə]		das Institut für Fortbildung (z. B. Volkshochschule) in York
full-time		ganztägig, hier: Ganztagsunterricht
evening courses	Do you attend evening courses? Yes, I do.	Abendkurse
to be available [əˈveɪləbəl]	These goods are no longer available.	erhältlich, vorhanden, lieferbar sein
to prepare	Mother is preparing breakfast.	(sich) vorbereiten
to represent sth/sb [reprɪˈzent]	Mr Wilder represents the interests of the workers.	etwas/jemanden vertreten
to fish for compliments		nach Komplimenten haschen
laughter ['lɑːftə]		Gelächter
to be kind	That's very kind of you.	freundlich sein

COMPREHENSION TESTS / GRAMMATICAL EXERCISES

3

opposite meaning ['ɒpəzɪt]		entgegengesetzte Bedeutung
to be complete [kəmˈpliːt]	When will the work be complete(d)?	vollständig, fertig sein
to be popular		beliebt sein

4

to run the whole show	den Laden schmeißen
circus show ['sɜːkəs]	die Zirkusschau
to hit the nail on the head [neɪl]	den Nagel auf den Kopf treffen
to kill two birds with one stone [stəʊn]	zwei Fliegen mit einer Klappe schlagen

5

aspect [æspekt]		Aspekt, Gesichtspunkt
to be famous	Shakespeare was a famous poet.	berühmt sein
primary school* ['praɪməri]	What kind of school do you attend? A primary school.	Grundschule
middle school		entspricht etwa unserer Mittelschule
secondary education ['sekəndəri]		Unterricht in der Sekundarstufe
comprehensive school [kɒmprɪ'hensɪv]		Gesamtschule
to lead to [liːd]	This will lead to a catastrophe.	führen zu
to correspond to sth [kɒrɪ'spɒnd]		einer Sache entsprechen
A-levels ['levəlz]	Harry took the A-levels.	entspricht unserem Abitur
in contrast to ['kɒntrɑːst]		im Gegensatz zu
state school [steɪt]		Staatsschule
school fees [fiːz]		Schulgebühren
public school		Privatschule

6

to abolish sth [ə'bɒlɪʃ]	Exams should be abolished.	etwas abschaffen
to deal with sth [diːl]	This book deals with sports.	hier: etwas behandeln
round-table discussion		hier: Gesprächsrunde
to bring forward arguments [ɑːgjʊmənts]		Argumente vorbringen
psychologist [saɪ'kɒlədʒɪst]		Psychologe
to mark sth with a cross [mɑːk]		etwas ankreuzen
to motivate sb ['məʊtɪveɪt]	This advertisement motivates to buy.	jemanden motivieren
to commit suicide ['suːɪsaɪd]		Selbstmord begehen
talent ['tælənt]		Talent
application [æplɪ'keɪʃən]	Bob has made this application.	Bewerbung
success [sək'ses]	That's a great success.	Erfolg
to depend on sth [dɪ'pend]		von etwas abhängen
to satisfy ['sætɪsfaɪ]	This doesn't satisfy me.	zufrieden stellen, befriedigen
to compare oneself with sb		sich mit jemandem vergleichen

7

to pack one's suitcase [pæk]		den Koffer packen
road map	Do you have a road map of the region? Yes.	Straßenkarte
to fill up sth		etwas voll füllen
to check the oil		das Öl (den Ölstand) prüfen
radiator ['reɪdieɪtə]	There is no water in the radiator.	Kühler, Heizkörper
to hitchhike ['hɪtʃhaɪk]		per Anhalter fahren
caravan site ['kærəvæn], [saɪt]		der Campingplatz für Wohnwagen
chemistry ['kemɪstri]		die Chemie

* Wenn die Schularten nicht näher bezeichnet sind, werden sie klein geschrieben.

to queue up [kjuː]	Did you queue up for tickets? Yes.	anstehen, sich anstellen
ice revue [rɪˈvjuː]		Eisrevue
transmission [trænzˈmɪʃən]		hier: die Übertragung
Olympic Games [əˈlɪmpɪk]		die Olympischen Spiele
Football Cup Final		das Fußballpokalendspiel

8

to lose (lost, lost)	I lost all my money at the horse race.	verlieren
to lend sth	I have lent him a lot of money.	etwas ver(leihen)
to rise		steigen

9

tennis championships		Tennismeisterschaften
economics [ekəˈnɒmɪks]		Wirtschaftswissenschaften
the Bachelor of Arts degree [ˈbætʃələ], [dɪˈgriː]	Susan took the BA degree.	das 1. Staatsexamen an einer Universität
to look for sth (sb)	What are you looking for? For my credit card.	etwas (jemanden) suchen

10

for ages		seit Jahr und Tag

11

exhibition	Where did the exhibition take place? In Bristol.	Ausstellung
to drop a line to sb		an jemanden ein paar Zeilen schreiben
departure [dɪˈpɑːtʃə]		Abreise

15 WHAT TO DO AFTER SCHOOL?

to decide/decision	You must take a decision now.	sich entscheiden/ Entschluss
unskilled people [ʌnˈskɪld]		ungelernte Leute
youth unemployment rate [reɪt]		Jugendarbeitslosenzahl
to introduce [ˌɪntrəˈdjuːs]	This book introduces you to business English.	einführen
Modern Apprenticeships [əˈprentɪsʃɪps]		moderne Lehrlingsausbildung
training system		Ausbildungssystem
opportunity [ˌɒpəˈtjuːnɪti]		Gelegenheit
skills/qualifications [ˌkwɒlɪfɪˈkeɪʃənz]	What skills are required for this job?	hier: Fachkenntnisse/ Qualifikationen
to require sth		etwas brauchen, benötigen
technician [tekˈnɪʃən]		Techniker
vocational training [vəʊˈkeɪʃənəl]		Berufsausbildung
telecommunications [ˌtelikəmjuːnɪˈkeɪʃənz]		Telekommunikation
florist/floristry [ˈflɒrɪst]		Florist, Blumenhandel

in favour of ['feɪvə]	I voted in favour of Labour.	zugunsten von
training agreement		Ausbildungsvertrag
apprentice [ə'prentɪs]	I work as an apprentice for this company.	Auszubildender (im hand-werklichen Bereich)
employer [ɪm'plɔɪə]		Arbeitgeber
to get wages ['weɪdʒɪz]		(Arbeits-)Lohn erhalten
certificate [sə'tɪfɪkət]		hier: Zeugnis
standard ['stændəd]		Standard
industry ['ɪndəstri]		Industrie
to earn money [ɜːn]		Geld verdienen
chances	What are his chances? They are promising.	Chancen, Aussichten
to take advantage of sth [əd'vɑːntɪdʒ]	Will you take advantage of this offer? Yes.	von etwas Gebrauch machen
working life		Arbeitsleben

COMPREHENSION TESTS / GRAMMATICAL EXERCISES

3

to draw a salary [drɔː], ['sæləri]	Clerks draw a salary.	Gehalt beziehen
to be qualified ['kwɒlɪfaɪd]		qualifiziert sein
to be liberal ['lɪbərəl]	He is a very liberal man.	liberal (eingestellt) sein
commercial correspondence [kə'mɜːʃəl], [kɒrɪ'spɒndəns]		Handelskorrespondenz
to remain up to date		auf dem Laufenden bleiben
a full-time job	Do you have a full-time or a part-time job?	eine Vollzeitbeschäftigung

4

economics		Wirtschaftswissenschaften
to apply for sth [ə'plaɪ]	Have you applied for this job? No.	sich um etwas bewerben

5

housewife	Is Mrs Brown a housewife? Yes.	Hausfrau
insurance company [ɪn'ʃʊərəns]		Versicherungsgesellschaft
electrician [ɪˌlek'trɪʃən]		Elektriker
engineer [ˌendʒɪ'nɪə]		Ingenieur
programmer ['prəʊgræmə]	What's your job? I'm a computer programmer.	Programmierer
optician [ɒp'tɪʃən]		Optiker
shipping company		Reederei
to construct machines [kən'strʌkt], [mə'ʃiːnz]		Maschinen bauen
to install electrical equipment [ɪn'stɔːl], [ɪ'lektrɪkəl], [ɪ'kwɪpmənt]		Elektrogeräte installieren
goods [gʊdz]	What sort of goods do you sell?	Waren
glasses ['glɑːsɪz]	Does Ann wear glasses? Yes.	Brille

to do the housework		die Hausarbeit machen
to insure risks [ɪnˈʃʊə]		Risiken versichern

7

to drive off		losfahren
to pick up sb		jemanden abholen
to do the gardening	What's Maureen doing? She is doing the gardening.	Gartenarbeiten tun
solarium [səʊˈleəriəm]		Solarium
to take one's dog for walkies		mit dem Hund Gassi gehen
detective story/thriller [dɪˈtektɪv]		Krimi
to seize sb [siːz]	The police seized the criminal.	ergreifen, fassen
to pay a fine [faɪn]		eine Geldstrafe zahlen
to become suspicious [səˈspɪʃəs]		Verdacht schöpfen
to shadow sb [ˈʃædəʊ]	Scotland Yard shadowed this man.	jemanden beschatten

8

to be careful	Be careful with this dog.	sorgfältig, vorsichtig sein
distinct(ly) [dɪˈstɪŋkt]		deutlich
to be punctual [ˈpʌŋktʃʊəl]		pünktlich sein
to miss sth	You should not miss this golden opportunity.	etwas versäumen, verpassen
to be probable [ˈprɒbəbəl]		wahrscheinlich sein
to celebrate sth [ˈselɪbreɪt]	Let's celebrate his success.	etwas feiern

9

to go fishing		angeln gehen
vacation [vəˈkeɪʃən]	Mr Gibb is on vacation.	Ferien, Urlaub
break	Let's have a break now.	Pause
refreshment [rɪˈfreʃmənt]		Erfrischung
to press one's trousers [ˈtraʊzəz]		die Hosen bügeln
to iron one's shirts [ˈaɪən], [ʃɜːts]		die Hemden bügeln

16 COMMUNICATING IN BUSINESS

to communicate with sb [kəˈmjuːnɪkeɪt]	We usually communicate by e-mail.	mit jemandem kommunizieren
the Technical College in Leeds		die berufsbildende Lehranstalt (techn.) in Leeds
to pass		hier: vorbeikommen
workplace		Arbeitsplatz
second	It won't take a second.	Sekunde
to depend on	Will you come with me? That depends on Burt.	abhängen von
fax user		Faxbenutzer (Teilnehmer)

to transmit sth [trænz'mɪt]	Did he transmit the message by fax? Yes.	etwas übermitteln
head		Leiter, Chef
export department [dɪ'pɑːtmənt]		Exportabteilung
homepage		Homepage
screen (monitor) [skriːn]		Bildschirm (Monitor)
to launch sth (on) [lɔːntʃ]	Have they launched a new video camera on the market? Yes.	etwas einführen (auf)
cordless telephone ['kɔːdləs]		schnurloses Telefon
to print sth out		etwas ausdrucken
an order/to order sth		ein Auftrag/ etwas bestellen,
guest [gest]		Gast
innovation [ɪnə'veɪʃən]	Innovation is important to be successful in business life.	Innovation, Erneuerung
to demonstrate sth ['demənstreɪt]		etw. demonstrieren, vorführen

COMPREHENSION TESTS / GRAMMATICAL EXERCISES

1
addressee [ˌædre'siː]		Adressat(in), Empfänger(in)

2
sales letter		Werbebrief

3
to be employed by		angestellt sein bei
to be dependent on sth (sb)		von etwas (jemandem) abhängig sein
distance	What's the distance to London? 82 miles.	Entfernung

4
fax machine		Faxgerät

6
enquiry		Anfrage
advertisement [əd'vɜːtɪsmənt]		Anzeige, Inserat
magazine [ˌmægə'ziːn]		Zeitschrift, Magazin
issue ['ɪʃuː, 'ɪsjuː]	Is this the latest issue of the Times? Yes.	Ausgabe
to be grateful ['greɪtfəl]		dankbar sein
sample	Is this article up to sample? No, it isn't.	Probe, Muster
yours faithfully ['feɪθfəli]		hochachtungsvoll

7

to submit a quotation [səb'mɪt], [kwəʊ'teɪʃən]		ein Angebot unterbreiten
cover ['kʌvə]		Deckblatt
to have much pleasure in doing sth ['pleʒə]		Freude daran haben, etwas zu tun
illustrated calatogue ['ɪləstreɪtɪd], ['kætəlɒg]		illustrierter Katalog
the current price list ['kʌrənt]		die gültige Preisliste
to call the attention to sth	May I call your attention to our new video recorder?	die Aufmerksamkeit auf etwas lenken
instant camera ['ɪnstənt], ['kæmərə]		Sofortbildkamera
to be dead easy		kinderleicht sein
to load sth [ləʊd]		hier: etwas laden
to shoot [ʃuːt]	Did he shoot that man? Yes.	schießen, erschießen
to be dry		trocken sein
marvellous ['mɑːvələs]	Isn't it marvellous? Yes, it is.	wunderbar, fantastisch
to develop [dɪ'veləp]		(sich) entwickeln
to welcome sb	Did the fans heartily welcome the pop star? Yes, they did.	jemanden begrüßen, empfangen
customer ['kʌstəmə]		Kunde
to assure that [ə'ʃʊə]		versichern, dass
to receive one's prompt and careful attention		hier: etwas wird sofort und sorgfältig ausgeführt

8

nurse [nɜːs]	Which nurse is on duty? Anne.	Krankenschwester
to speak slang		Slang sprechen
to organise a safari [sə'fɑːri]		eine Safari organisieren
to be engaged to sb	Who is Mandy engaged to? To Mark.	mit jemandem verlobt sein
foreign correspondent ['fɒrɪn]		Auslandskorrespondent(in)
to glitter ['glɪtə]		glitzern
to be talented ['tæləntɪd]		begabt, talentiert sein
actor/actress ['æktə], ['æktrɪs]		Schauspieler(in)
power	That isn't in my power.	hier: Macht(befugnis)

9

stalls [stɔːlz]		Parkett
to have trouble with sb		mit jemandem Ärger haben
change		hier: Wechselgeld
I'm afraid that	I'm afraid that he failed the exam.	ich (be)fürchte, dass
suggestion [sə'dʒestʃən]	Has he made an acceptable suggestion? No.	Vorschlag
records ['rekɔːdz]		Schallplatten
to lend sth to sb (oder: sb sth)	Would you lend me £100? Yes.	jemandem etwas leihen
to be wrong		hier: in Unordnung sein
definitely ['defɪnɪtli]		bestimmt

17 THE MEDIA

The Times, please!

classical ['klæsɪkəl]		klassisch
it's true that [truː]		es stimmt, dass
to be fond of doing sth	Are you fond of reading books? Yes, I am.	etwas gern tun
copy ['kɒpi]		hier: Zeitungsexemplar
circulation [ˌsɜːkjʊˈleɪʃən]		hier: die Auflage (einer Zeitung)
to fall sharply [ˈʃɑːpli]		stark fallen
to deal with sth [diːl]	What does the film deal with? This film deals with the colour problem.	sich befassen mit, etwas behandeln
politics ['pɒlɪtɪks]		Politik
economics [ˌekəˈnɒmɪks]		hier: Wirtschaftsthemen, -fragen
current affairs ['kʌrənt], [əˈfeəz]		Tagesgeschehen
murder ['mɜːdə]		Mord
bank robbery ['rɒbəri]		Bankraub
drugs [drʌg]		Drogen
to publish sth ['pʌblɪʃ]	When will the book be published? Next year.	etwas veröffentlichen
letters to the editor ['edɪtə]		Leserbriefe
to print sth [prɪnt]	Do you intend to have your speech printed?	etwas drucken
this is also true for (of)	This is also true for (of) the letter you have written.	das trifft ebenfalls auf ... zu, das gilt ebenfalls für ...
regional newspaper ['riːdʒənəl]		Regionalzeitung
area ['eəriə]		Gebiet
periodical [ˌpɪəriˈɒdɪkəl]		Zeitschrift
profit ['prɒfɪt]		Gewinn, Profit
to reduce sth [rɪˈdjuːs]	Prices were reduced by about 5% last week.	etwas senken, reduzieren
to modernize sth ['mɒdənaɪz]		etwas modernisieren
plant [plɑːnt]		Betriebsanlagen
staff [stɑːf]		Personal
to lead to sth	This will lead to a catastrophe.	zu etwas führen
conflict ['kɒnflɪkt]		der Konflikt
trade union [treɪd], [ˈjuːnjən]		Gewerkschaft
print worker [prɪnt]		Setzer, Drucker
to set		hier: setzen
to replace sth	The wrong goods will be replaced by those you have ordered.	etwas ersetzen
computer system ['sɪstəm]		Computersystem

COMPREHENSION TESTS / GRAMMATICAL EXERCISES

3

to replace sth [rɪˈpleɪs]
in bold type [bəʊld]
to occur [əˈkɜː] — The accident occurred in the morning.

reputable [ˈrepjʊtəbəl]
to be compelled to [kəmˈpeld]

etwas ersetzen
in Fettschrift
sich ereignen, geschehen

angesehen, seriös
gezwungen sein

4

issue

to advertise [ˈædvətaɪz] — If you want to sell your car, you should advertise.

customer
to be silly [ˈsɪli] — Don't be so silly.
to believe in sth [bɪˈliːv]
horoscope [ˈhɒrəskəʊp] — Do you believe in horoscopes? No.

editor [ˈedɪtə]
common [ˈkɒmən] — That's of common interest.
print worker

Ausgabe (z. B. einer Zeitung)
inserieren

Kunde
albern, verrückt
an etwas glauben
Horoskop

Herausgeber
gemeinsam, allgemein
Setzer (im Verlagswesen)

5

Virgo [ˈvɜːgəʊ]
social life
to miss sth — You shouldn't miss this opportunity. It will never come again.

to grab an opportunity [græb]
relation [rɪˈleɪʃən]
to urge sb to do sth [ɜːdʒ] — He urged me to lend him some money.
to join sb in doing sth [dʒɔɪn] — I joined them in playing golf (going for a walk).

Jungfrau
gesellschaftliches Leben
etwas versäumen, verpassen

hier: eine Gelegenheit ausnutzen
Verwandte(r)
jemanden drängen etwas zu tun
etwas mit jemandem zusammen tun

6

astrology [əˈstrɒlədʒi]
Aquarius [əˈkweəriəs] — Under which star sign were you born? Under Aquarius.

to be energetic [enəˈdʒetɪk]
to be ambitious [æmˈbɪʃəs]
to be creative [kriˈeɪtɪv]
to dominate [ˈdɒmɪneɪt]
to be successful [səkˈsesfəl] — If you want to be successful, you must work harder.

company
to be sensitive [ˈsensɪtɪv]

romance [rəʊˈmæns]

Astrologie
Sternzeichen: Wassermann

tatkräftig, energisch sein
ehrgeizig sein
kreativ, schöpferisch sein
dominieren, herrschen
Erfolg haben, erfolgreich sein

Gesellschaft
sensibel, feinfühlig, empfindlich

Liebesromanze

sign of the zodiac ['zəʊdiæk] | | Sternzeichen
description [dɪ'skrɪpʃən] | | Beschreibung
to match | It doesn't match. | hier: (zusammen)-passen
personality [ˌpɜːsə'næləti] | | Persönlichkeit

7

to be unthinkable | | undenkbar sein
in fact | | tatsächlich
to be enthusiastic about sth [ɪnˌθjuːzi'æstɪk] | I'm enthusiastic about this idea. | von etwas begeistert sein
to choose a channel ['tʃænl] | | einen (Fernseh-)Kanal wählen
major ['meɪdʒə] | Is this the major problem? Yes. | Haupt-, bedeutend

lighter entertainment | | leichtere Unterhaltung
humour ['hjuːmə] | | Humor
serious ['sɪəriəs] | You should take it more seriously. | ernst

documentaries [ˌdɒkjʊ'mentəriːz] | | Dokumentarfilme
opera ['ɒpərə] | | Oper
current affairs | | Tagesgeschehen
advertising | | Werbung
choice | | Wahl, Auswahl
satellite and cable television ['sætəlaɪt] | | Satelliten- u. Kabelfernsehen
to dislike sth | I dislike his behaviour. (Benehmen) | etwas nicht mögen

current programme | | das laufende Programm
to be currently informed | | laufend informiert sein
traffic jam ['træfɪk], [dʒæm] | | Verkehrsstau
result [rɪ'sʌlt] | Are you satisfied with this result? No. | Ergebnis

8

extract [ɪk'strækt] | | Auszug
inside | | hier: innen, drin in
debate [dɪ'beɪt] | Did you listen to the debate? Yes. | Debatte

guest [gest] | | Gast
genius ['dʒiːniəs] | | Genie
highlight | | Höhepunkt
safari [sə'fɑːri] | Did you go on safari? Yes. | Safari
sports news | | Sportnachrichten
close | | (Sende-)Schluss
national anthem ['ænθəm] | | Nationalhymne

9

main [meɪn] | | Haupt-
to specialize ['speʃəlaɪz] | Do you want to specialize? Yes. | sich spezialisieren

specific subject [spə'sɪfɪk] | | spezifisches Thema
favourite ['feɪvərət] | What's your favourite meal? Duck. | Lieblings-

10

bank holiday		öffentlicher Feiertag
to enjoy sth	Did you enjoy your stay in New York? Oh yes.	etwas genießen, gefallen
bomb alarm [əˈlɑːm]		Bombenalarm
village [ˈvɪlɪdʒ]	Is it true that life in a village is boring? I think so.	Dorf
health [helθ]		Gesundheit
wealth [welθ]		Reichtum
crime [kraɪm]		Verbrechen
violence [ˈvaɪələns]	Are crime and violence increasing? Yes, they are.	Gewalt
member	He is a member of this club.	Mitglied
to claim sth [kleɪm]		hier: auf etwas Anspruch erheben, beanspruchen
century [ˈsentʃəri]		Jahrhundert
to differ from [ˈdɪfə]	I differ from you in this matter.	sich unterscheiden von
to play a role [rəʊl]		eine Rolle spielen

11

pilot [ˈpaɪlət]		Pilot
Baptist [ˈbæptɪ̩st]		Baptist
Catholic [ˈkæθəlɪk]	Is she a Catholic? Yes, she is.	Katholik
to go bowling [ˈbəʊlɪŋ]		bowlen gehen
material [məˈtɪərɪəl]		Material, Stoff

12

to need sth		etwas brauchen
crossing		Kreuzung
advice [ədˈvaɪs]	Did he give you some good advice? Yes, he did.	Rat
shelf [ʃelf]		Regal
to spend money on sth		für etwas Geld ausgeben
lottery [ˈlɒtəri]		Lotterie

18 HOW GREAT BRITAIN IS GOVERNED

to govern [ˈgʌvən]		regieren
monarchy [ˈmɒnəki]		Monarchie
monarch		Monarch
role [rəʊl]	The monarch plays no important role in Britain.	Rolle
to be representative [reprɪˈzentətɪv]	These results are not representative.	repräsentativ sein
to reign [reɪn]		herrschen
head of government		Regierungschef
diplomatic representative [dɪpləˈmætɪk]		diplomatischer Vertreter
state visit		Staatsbesuch
abroad [əˈbrɔːd]	Peter has gone abroad.	ins Ausland
to appoint sb [əˈpɔɪnt]	Mr Sherman was appointed sales manager of this firm.	jemanden ernennen

to dismiss sb [dɪsˈmɪs]	He was dismissed for being lazy and dishonest. (unehrlich)	jemanden entlassen
advice/to advise sth	That was good advice./ I advise you to accept this offer.	der Rat/etwas raten
Prime Minister [praɪm]		Premierminister
Commander-in-Chief [kəˈmɑːndə]		Oberbefehlshaber
Navy/Army/Air Force [ˈneɪvi], [ˈɑːmi], [ˈeəfɔːs]		Marine/Armee/Luftwaffe
a Bill		eine Gesetzesvorlage
to pass a Bill		eine Gesetzesvorlage verabschieden
Parliament [ˈpɑːləmənt]	The Bill was passed by Parliament.	Parlament
to consist of sth	The United Kingdom consists of Great Britain and Northern Ireland.	aus etwas bestehen
member		Mitglied
a political party	What political party do you belong to?	eine Partei
to be independent		unabhängig sein
at least [liːst]		mindestens
to elect sb [ɪˈlekt]		jemanden wählen
general elections	When do the next general elections take place? Next month.	allgemeine Wahlen
main function [ˈfʌŋkʃən]		Hauptaufgabe
to represent sth [repriˈzent]		etwas repräsentieren
opinion [əˈpɪnjən]	What's your opinion?	Meinung
economic affairs		hier: Wirtschaftsfragen
public affairs		öffentliche Angelegenheiten
to be in a state of change	There will be a change in the political system.	hier: es gibt eine Veränderung
automatically [ɔːtəˈmætɪkli]		automatisch
in the course of time [kɔːs]		im Laufe der Zeit
power	I'll do everything in my power.	Macht
to restrict sth		etwas einschränken
whereas		wohingegen, während
immense(ly) [ɪˈmens]		immens, ungeheuer
to regard sth as [rɪˈgɑːd]	This is regarded as a catastrophe.	etwas ansehen als, halten für
pure [pjʊə]		rein
debating club		Debattierklub
transitional phase [trænˈzɪʃənəl], [feɪz]		Übergangsphase
to abolish sth [əˈbɒlɪʃ]	Should the death penalty (Todesstrafe) be abolished? Yes.	etwas abschaffen
Cabinet [ˈkæbɪnɪt]		Kabinett

Chancellor of the Exchequer ['tʃɑ:nsələ], [ɪks'tʃekə]		Finanzminister
Home Secretary ['sekrᵊtəri]		Innenminister
Foreign Secretary		Außenminister
to be responsible for sth [rɪ'spɒnsᵻbəl]	You are responsible for the bad results.	für etwas verantwortlich sein
growth [grəʊθ]		Wachstum
prosperity [prɒ'sperᵻti]		Prosperität
as a rule [ru:l]		in der Regel
vote/to vote for sb [vəʊt]	I voted for Mrs Harris.	Stimme (z. B. bei einer Wahl), für jemanden stimmen

COMPREHENSION TESTS / GRAMMATICAL EXERCISES

1

official title [ə'fɪʃəl], ['taɪtl]	What's his official title?	offizieller Titel

2

social class ['səʊʃəl]		Gesellschaftsschicht

4

to make a brilliant ['brɪljənt] speech [spi:tʃ]		eine brillante Rede halten
Money Bill	Was the Money Bill passed by Parliament? Yes.	Finanzvorlage
inflation [ɪn'fleɪʃən]		Inflation
debate [dɪ'beɪt]		Debatte
Strangers' Gallery ['gæləri]		die Zuschauertribüne
politician [pɒlᵻ'tɪʃən]	Would you like to become a politician? Yes, I would.	Politiker
to defeat the enemy [dɪ'fi:t] ['enəmi]		den Feind schlagen
battle ['bætl]		Schlacht

6

election campaign [ɪ'lekʃən], [kæm'peɪn]		Wahlkampagne
election meeting	Did you take part in the election meeting? Yes, I did.	Wahlversammlung
counterargument ['kaʊntərˌɑ:gjʊmənt]	What are your counterarguments?	Gegenargument
opposition [ɒpə'zɪʃən]		Opposition
economy [ɪ'kɒnəmi]		Wirtschaft
to prosper ['prɒspə]		blühen, gedeihen
(youth) unemployment [ju:θ]		(Jugend-)Arbeitslosigkeit
to decline [dɪ'klaɪn]	The birth rate has considerably declined in the last few years.	fallen

National Health Service | | staatlicher Gesundheits-dienst
to be in a bad way | | schlecht gehen
equal opportunities [ˈiːkwəl], [ˌɒpəˈtjuːnᵻtiːz] | Everybody should have equal opportunities. | Chancengleichheit, gleiche Chancen
social services | | Sozialleistungen
to improve [ɪmˈpruːv] | Has the situation on the labour market improved? Yes, it has. | (sich) bessern, verbessern

police force | | Polizei
to protect sb [prəˈtekt] | | jemanden schützen
crime and violence [ˈvaɪələns] | | Verbrechen und Gewalt
crime rate [kraɪm], [reɪt] | | Verbrechensrate, Kriminalitäts-
pollution [pəˈluːʃən] | | Umweltverschmutzung
danger | | Gefahr
to develop [dɪˈveləp] | | (sich) entwickeln

8

to cancel sth [ˈkænsəl] | Was the order cancelled? Yes. | etwas stornieren
to lease sth [liːs] | | etwas leasen
to iron shirts | | Hemden bügeln
to press trousers | | Hosen bügeln
to offer sb a post [pəʊst] | | jemandem eine Stelle anbieten

to reduce prices [rɪˈdjuːs] | | Preise senken
considerable | | beträchtlich
to accept conditions | | Konditionen annehmen
to sign a contract [saɪn] | | einen Vertrag unterschreiben

to submit an offer [səbˈmɪt] | | ein Angebot annehmen

9

to attend a holiday course | | einen Ferienkurs besuchen

part board [bɔːd] | | Teilpension
full board | Do you take part board or full board? Neither. Just bed and breakfast. | Vollpension

10

news | What's the news? | Nachrichten, Neuigkeiten
to believe [bᵊˈliːv] | | glauben
to take sth seriously | | etwas ernst nehmen
I don't have the foggiest idea. [aɪˈdɪə] | | Ich habe nicht den blassesten Schimmer.
I don't care. | | Es ist mir egal.
truth [truːθ] | Tell me the truth. | die Wahrheit

19 A BLOODY DAY

to be bloody/blood ['blʌdi]		blutig sein/Blut
to explode/explosion [ɪkˈspləʊd]		explodieren/Explosion
supermarket [ˈsuːpəˌmɑːkɪt]		Supermarkt
terrorist [ˈterərɪst]		Terrorist
to place sth		etwas setzen, stellen, legen
curtain [ˈkɜːtn]	Would you please draw the curtain?	der Vorhang
to warn sb/warning [wɔːn]		jemanden warnen/ die Warnung
responsible [rɪˈspɒnsəbəl]	You are responsible for the safety of these people.	verantwortlich
to scream [skriːm]		schreien
hole [həʊl]		das Loch
to be cut off	His leg was cut off.	hier: abgerissen sein
to tear, tore, torn	The clothes were torn.	etwas zerreißen
sympathy [ˈsɪmpəθi]		hier: Mitgefühl
victim [ˈvɪktɪm]		das Opfer (einer Katastrophe)
bomb outrage [ˈaʊtreɪdʒ]		Bombenattentat
rigid [ˈrɪdʒɪd]		starr, hier: strikt
death penalty [ˈpenlti]	Are you for or against the introduction of the death penalty?	die Todesstrafe
to reintroduce sth		etwas wiedereinführen
to frighten sb off		jemanden abschrecken
to frighten sb [ˈfraɪtn]	Don't frighten me.	jemanden in Schrecken versetzen, Angst machen
coward [ˈkaʊəd]		Feigling
to beat sb		hier: jemanden bekämpfen/ schlagen/vernichten

COMPREHENSION TESTS / GRAMMATICAL EXERCISES

3

to succeed in doing sth [səkˈsiːd]	The inspector succeeded in seizing the criminal.	gelingen
to fascinate [ˈfæsɪneɪt]		faszinieren
to exhibit sth [ɪgˈzɪbɪt]		etw. ausstellen

4

idea	Do you have any idea what's wrong with him. No, I don't.	Idee, Ahnung, Vorstellung
column [ˈkɒləm]		Säule

5

county [ˈkaʊnti]		Grafschaft
to belong to sth	What political party does he belong to? To the Conservatives.	zu etwas gehören, etwas angehören
capital		Hauptstadt

7

to welcome sb rapturously [ˈræptʃərəsli]		jemanden stürmisch empfangen, begrüßen
to give sb an autograph [ˈɔːtəɡrɑːf]		jemandem ein Autogramm geben
to do sth most readily		etwas sehr gern tun
obvious(ly) [ˈɒbviəs]	It is obvious that she has left him for good (für immer).	offensichtlich
to arrest sb [əˈrest]		jemanden einsperren
robber [ˈrɒbə]	Has the police caught the bank robbers? Yes.	Räuber
jewellery [ˈdʒuːəlri]		Schmuck
inspector		Inspektor
to question sb		jemanden befragen
to interrogate sb [ɪnˈterəɡeɪt]	Who questioned/ interrogated you? Inspector Morse.	jemanden verhören
football boots		Fußballschuhe
to settle an invoice [ˈɪnvɔɪs]		eine Rechnung begleichen

8

to think something over	You should do it. I'll think it over.	etwas überdenken
to help sb out of his difficulties		jemandem aus den Schwierigkeiten heraushelfen
to suppose [səˈpəʊz]		vermuten
to change for the better/ for the worse	His state of health (Gesundheitszustand) has changed for the better (for the worse)	sich zum Besseren/ Schlechteren wenden, sich verbessern, verschlechtern
cancer [ˈkænsə]		Krebs
to send for sb		jemanden holen lassen
to care for	I'll care for the children when you are going out.	sich kümmern um
to settle a matter		eine Angelegenheit regeln
to sb's full satisfaction [ˌsætɪsˈfækʃən]		zur vollen Zufriedenheit einer Person
to leave no stone unturned		nichts unversucht lassen

20 GREAT BRITAIN AND ITS ETHNIC MINORITIES

ethnic [ˈeθnɪk]		ethnisch, völkisch
above all [əˈbʌv]		vor allem
Commonwealth of Nations [ˈkɒmənwelθ]		Commonwealth (Völkergemeinschaft)
various [ˈveərɪəs]	I have done it for various reasons.	verschiedene, mehrere
unemployment rate		die Arbeitslosenzahl
standard of living [ˈstændəd]	The standard of living has risen in the last few years.	Lebensstandard
citizen [ˈsɪtɪzən]		(Staats-)Bürger

to flood into sth [flʌd]		zu etwas hinströmen, hineinfluten
economic situation	The economic situation of this country has changed for the better (worse).	die wirtschaftliche Lage
to get worse and worse		immer schlechter werden
to emigrate ['emɪɡreɪt]	He decided to emigrate to Canada.	auswandern, emigrieren
immigrant ['ɪmɪɡrənt]		Einwanderer, Immigrant
to try one's luck		sein Glück versuchen
to realize that ['rɪəlaɪz]	I realized that there was no hope for the injured man.	hier: feststellen, erkennen, dass
however		jedoch
accommodation [əˌkɒməˈdeɪʃən]		Unterkunft
to be discriminated against [dɪˈskrɪmɪneɪtɪd]		diskriminiert werden
to be due to sth [ˈdjuː]	This is due to mismanagement.	auf etwas zurückzuführen sein
custom		Sitte, Brauch
language barrier [ˈbæriə]		Sprachbarriere
social unrest [ʌnˈrest]	Everything should be done to avoid social unrest.	soziale Unruhe(n)
bitterness [ˈbɪtənəs]		Verbitterung
to grow, grew, grown		wachsen
to fail to do sth [feɪl]	He failed to warn us of the danger.	versäumen, etwas zu tun
to protect sb [prəˈtekt]		jemanden schützen
to create sth [kriˈeɪt]		etwas schaffen
law [lɔː]	The law forbids stealing.	Gesetz
to continue to increase	Unemployment continued to increase.	weiter ansteigen

COMPREHENSION TESTS / GRAMMATICAL EXERCISES

1

mass(es) [mæs]	Masses of people had come to the demonstration.	Masse(n)

3

dustman [ˈdʌstmən]		Müllmann
tobacconist's shop [təˈbækənɪsts]		Tabakwarenladen
discrimination [dɪˌskrɪmɪˈneɪʃən]		Diskriminierung
unless [ənˈles]		wenn nicht

4

to dislike sth		etwas nicht mögen
behaviour [bɪˈheɪvjə]		Benehmen
to be tired	I must go to bed. I'm tired.	müde sein
hard-earned money		schwer verdientes Geld

5

to have a glance at sth [glɑːns]		einen Blick auf etwas werfen
to obtain sth [əbˈteɪn]	I haven't been able to obtain this book anywhere.	etwas erhalten, erlangen
to recognize sb/sth [ˈrekəgnaɪz]	I last saw her three days ago. I didn't recognize her.	jemanden/etwas anerkennen, jemanden wiedererkennen
to establish sth [ɪˈstæblɪʃ]/ to found sth	The Pilgrim Fathers established settlements in North America.	etwas errichten/ gründen
colony [ˈkɒləni]		Kolonie
economically [ekəˈnɒmɪkli]		wirtschaftlich
to return sth	I returned the money I had borrowed from him.	etwas zurückgeben
member [ˈmembə]		Mitglied
the ties [taɪz]		die Bindungen, Bande
to become looser and looser [ˈluːsə]		immer loser (lockerer) werden
to link sth/sb together		etwas/jemanden miteinander verbinden

6/7

to play chess [tʃes] — Schach spielen
mouse — Maus

9

exhibition [ˌeksɪˈbɪʃən]	How did you find the exhibition? Very good.	Ausstellung
to pay (in) cash [kæʃ]	Do you pay (in) cash? No, I pay by credit card.	(in) bar zahlen
earth		Erde
to be out of one's mind [maɪnd]		nicht bei Trost sein
my goodness		Meine Güte!
to give sb the sack [sæk]		jemanden feuern
horse race	Did you see the horse race on TV? No, I didn't.	Pferderennen
to hurt [hɜːt] (oneself)		(sich) verletzen

21 LET'S HAVE A LOOK AT THE BRITISH ECONOMY

the Group of Seven [gruːp]		die Siebener Gruppe
economic/industrial country [ɪnˈdʌstriəl]		Wirtschafts-/Industrieland
structure [ˈstrʌktʃə]		Struktur
aerospace company		Raumfahrtgesellschaft
electronic(s) [ɪˌlekˈtrɒnɪks]		elektronisch (Elektronik)
to enjoy a worldwide reputation [repjʊˈteɪʃən]	Do the managers of this firm enjoy a good reputation? Yes.	einen weltweiten Ruf genießen
to settle	The English settled (sich ansiedeln) on all continents.	hier: sich niederlassen
heavy industry		Schwerindustrie

the shipbuilding industry ['ɪndəstri]		die Werften
to lose in importance		an Bedeutung verlieren
mainly	This is mainly due to bad management.	hauptsächlich
the Far East		der Ferne Osten
cost(s)		Kosten
in contrast to this ['kɒntrɑːst]		im Gegensatz hierzu
expansion [ɪkˈspænʃən]		Expansion
chemical industry [ˈkemɪkəl]		chemische Industrie
engineering industry [ˌendʒɪˈnɪərɪŋ]		Maschinenindustrie
telecommunications [ˌtelikəmjuːnɪˈkeɪʃənz]	The development of telecommunications is progressing (voranschreiten) very rapidly.	Telekommunikation
technologies [tekˈnɒlədʒiːz]		Technologien
to revolutionize [revəˈluːʃənaɪz]		revolutionieren
stiff competition [stɪf], [kɒmpəˈtɪʃən]	Most companies have to face stiff competition on the market.	harte Konkurrenz
trend		Trend
to merge [mɜːdʒ]	Many companies are compelled (gezwungen) to merge in order to survive (überleben)	fusionieren, sich zusammenschließen
to swallow sth (up) [ˈswɒləʊ]		etwas schlucken (hier: aufkaufen)
takeover		die Übernahme (von Firmen)
to be sufficient evidence of sth [səˈfɪʃənt], [ˈevɪdəns]		genügend Beweis für etwas sein
development [dɪˈveləpmənt]		Entwicklung
globalization [ˌgləʊbəlaɪˈzeɪʃən]		Globalisierung
challenge [ˈtʃælɪndʒ]		Herausforderung
production cost(s) [prəˈdʌkʃən]	Production costs are continuously increasing.	Produktionskosten
investment [ɪnˈvestmənt]		Investition
to master sth	I'm sure you will master it.	etwas meistern

COMPREHENSION TESTS / GRAMMATICAL EXERCISES

1

to belong to	India belongs to the Commonwealth of Nations.	gehören zu
to take place		stattfinden

3

to be located [ləʊˈkeɪtɪd]	Silicon Valley is located in California.	gelegen sein
to lose in importance		an Bedeutung verlieren

to be substituted by ['sʌbstɪ̣tju:tɪ̣d]		ersetzt werden durch
natural gas ['nætʃərəl], [gæs]		Erdgas
to move from ... to [mu:v]	Henry moved from London to Bristol, didn't he? Yes.	umziehen von ... nach
to become unemployed		arbeitslos werden
trade fair [treɪd], [feə]		Handelsmesse

4

You are splitting hairs.	Sie treiben Haarspalterei.
She is my cup of tea.	Sie ist mein Fall.
All that glitters is not gold. ['glɪtə]	Es ist nicht alles Gold, was glänzt.
A bird in a hand is worth two in the bush. [bɜ:d], [wɜ:θ], [bʊʃ]	Der Spatz in der Hand ist besser als eine Taube auf dem Dach.
He killed two birds with one stone. [stəʊn]	Er schlug zwei Fliegen mit einer Klappe.

5

to study economics [ˌekəˈnɒmɪks]	Wirschaftswissenschaften studieren
plant [plɑ:nt]	Werkgelände
press shop	Stanzerei
front and rear body sections [rɪə], ['sekʃənz]	Vorder- und Hinterteil
to fit sth together	etwas zusammenfügen
automation [ɔ:təˈmeɪʃən]	Automation
to join sth to [dʒɔɪn]	etwas ineinanderfügen
the bare body [beə]	das nackte (unlackierte) Gestell
paint shop [peɪnt]	Lackiererei
conveyor(er) belt [kənˈveɪə]	Fließband
interior equipment [ɪnˈtɪərɪə]	Innenausstattung
bumper ['bʌmpə]	Stoßstange
electrical equipment [ɪˈlektrɪkəl]	elektrische Ausrüstung
to become mobile ['məʊbaɪl]	fahrbar sein
final assembly stage [əˈsemblɪ], [steɪdʒ]	Endmontagestufe
chassis [ʃæsi]	Chassis, Fahrgestell
engine ['endʒɪ̣n]	Motor
to add sth	etwas hinzufügen

6

to insert sth [ɪnˈsɜ:t]		etwas einsetzen
probable (ly)		wahrscheinlich
surprise [səˈpraɪz]	That was a big surprise.	Überraschung
tea set		Teeservice
truth	Is that the whole truth? Yes.	Wahrheit
to mention sth ['menʃən]		etwas erwähnen
behaviour [bɪˈheɪvjə]		Benehmen
shorthand and typing		Kurzschrift und Schreibmaschine

beach		Strand
to bath [bɑːθ]		baden
a good knowledge of French [ˈnɒlɪdʒ]	Does he have a good knowledge of French? Yes.	gute Französischkenntnisse
to be satisfactory	These results are satisfactory.	zufrieden stellend sein
to be exhausted [ɪgˈzɔːstə̣d]		erschöpft sein
to reach one's goal [gəʊl]		das Ziel erreichen
to go bankrupt [ˈbæŋkrʌpt]	Did the firm go bankrupt? Yes.	Pleite gehen
to be injured [ˈɪndʒəd]		verletzt sein
to pay a fine [faɪn]		eine Geldstrafe zahlen

7

prize [praɪz]		Preis (z. B. in der Lotterie)
solution [səˈluːʃən]	I think this is the best solution.	Lösung
to overlook sth	Damn, I overlooked this mistake.	etwas übersehen
to be exciting [ɪkˈsaɪtɪŋ]		spannend sein
to land smoothly [ˈsmuːðli]		glatt landen
rapturous(ly) [ˈræptʃərəs]		stürmisch
to be remarkable [rɪˈmɑːkəbəl]	He is a remarkable man.	bemerkenswert sein
unemployment rate [reɪt]		Arbeitslosenzahl
surprising(ly)		überraschend

22 IS THE WORLD FACING AN ENVIRONMENTAL CATASTROPHE?

to face sth		hier: konfrontiert sein
environmental catastrophe [ɪnˌvaɪərənˈmentl], [kəˈtæstrəfi]	Will this lead to an environmental catastrophe? No.	Umweltkatastrophe
I'm afraid	I'm afraid it is going to rain.	ich fürchte
danger		Gefahr
environment		Umwelt
mankind [mænˈkaɪnd]		Menschheit
pollution [pəˈluːʃən]		Umweltverschmutzung
ozone hole [ˈəʊzəʊn]		Ozonloch
global warming [ˈgləʊbəl]		Erderwärmung
deforestation [diːfɒṛəˈsteɪʃən]		Abholzung
sufficient(ly) [səˈfɪʃənt]	Is there sufficient evidence (Beweise) that he is the thief (Dieb)?	genügend, ausreichend
to warn sb	I have warned you of him.	jemanden warnen
Earth Summit [ˈsʌmə̣t]		Erdgipfel
to be aware [əˈweə]	I'm aware that I must act now.	wissen
to take common action [ˈkɒmən]		gemeinsam handeln
to save [seɪv]		hier: retten
to take steps	Did you take steps against him? Yes.	Schritte unternehmen
greenhouse gases		Treibhausgase
carbon-dioxide emissions [ˈkɑːbən], [daɪˈɒksaɪd], [ɪˈmɪʃənz]		Kohlendioxidemissionen

to extend sth	Can you extend your stay for a few weeks? I'm sorry, but I can't.	sich vergrößern, etwas verlängern
to endanger sth [ɪnˈdeɪndʒə] to be aware of sth		etwas gefährden, sich einer Sache bewusst sein
health		Gesundheit

COMPREHENSION TESTS / GRAMMATICAL EXERCISES

1

to deal with sth [diːl]	This book deals with pollution.	etwas behandeln

2

to decrease [dɪˈkriːs]	The danger has decreased.	abnehmen
prospects [ˈprɒspekts]		Aussichten
environmental project [ˈprɒdʒekt]		Umweltprojekt

3

nuclear power station [ˈnjuːklɪə]		Atomkraftwerk
to be located [ləʊˈkeɪtɪd]	This company is located in Cumberland.	liegen, gelegen sein
to be comparable with sth [ˈkɒmpərəbəl]		mit etwas vergleichbar sein
to be polluted [pəˈluːtɪd]	Many rivers, lakes and seas are polluted.	(umwelt-)verschmutzt sein

5

Energy – important for all of us

energy [ˈenədʒi]		Energie
for private use [ˈpraɪvɪt]		für den privaten Gebrauch
Industrial Revolution [ɪnˈdʌstrɪəl], [ˌrevəˈluːʃən]		die industrielle Revolution
natural resources [ˈnætʃərəl], [rɪˈzɔːsɪz]		Bodenschätze
natural gas [gæs]		Erdgas
price increase [ˈɪnkriːs], [ˈɪŋ-]		Preiserhöhung
source(s) of energy		Energiequelle(n)
to solve sth [sɒlv]	Did he manage to solve the problem? Yes, he did.	etwas lösen
nuclear power station [ˈnjuːklɪə]		Atomkraftwerk
to replace sth [rɪˈpleɪs]	Coal has been largely replaced by oil and natural gas.	etwas ersetzen
coalition government [ˌkəʊəˈlɪʃən]		Koalitionsregierung
to make efforts [ˈefəts]	They have made great efforts to save the life of the injured man.	sich bemühen

solar energy ['səʊlə]		Solarenergie
wind energy ['enədʒi]		Windenergie
plenty of	He is said to have plenty of money.	viel, eine Menge
to be available [ə'veɪləbəl]	These goods are no longer available.	erhältlich, lieferbar sein
to be unable		nicht in der Lage sein
to prove [pru:v]		sich erweisen
advantage [əd'vɑ:ntɪdʒ]		Vorteil

6

to introduce oneself	I introduced myself to Mr Gibbs.	sich vorstellen
driving test		Fahrprüfung
to pass sth		etwas bestehen
invoice ['ɪnvɔɪs]		Rechnung

7

to miss sth		etwas verpassen
to take a decision [dɪ'sɪʒən]	That was a good decision.	eine Entscheidung treffen
to be reasonable in price ['ri:zənəbəl]	Are prices reasonable? Yes.	preiswert sein

8

speech [spi:tʃ]	He made a speech about environmental pollution.	Rede

23 SOCIAL ASPECTS OF GREAT BRITAIN

social aspects ['æspekts]		soziale Aspekte
trade union [treɪd], ['ju:njən]		Gewerkschaft
economics [ˌekə'nɒmɪks]	What did you study? Economics.	Wirtschaftswissenschaften
social problems		soziale Probleme
to welcome sb	At the airport they were heartily welcomed by Sarah.	jemanden begrüßen
to make oneself comfortable ['kʌmftəbəl]		es sich bequem machen
fire(place)	They were sitting round the fire(place).	Kamin
influence ['ɪnfluəns]		Einfluss
greatly		sehr
to restrict sth		etwas ein(be-)schränken
power	I'll do everything in my power.	Macht
to suffer from sth ['sʌfə]	He suffered from a heart attack.	an etwas leiden, etwas erleiden
endless		endlos
wildcat strike ['waɪldkæt]		wilder Streik
coal miner ['maɪnə]		Bergmann
to cause damage ['dæmɪdʒ]		Schaden verursachen
to solve a problem	Could the problem be solved? Yes.	ein Problem lösen

a secret vote [vəʊt]		eine geheime Abstimmung
effective [ɪˈfektɪv]	The contract becomes effective tomorrow.	effektiv, wirksam
to take steps		Schritte unternehmen
Employment Act [ækt]		Beschäftigungsgesetz
to join sth [dʒɔɪn]	Did he join this club? Yes.	etwas beitreten
closed shop/compulsory membership [kəmˈpʌlsəri]		Zwangsmitgliedschaft/ obligatorische Mitgliedschaft
social security [sɪˈkjʊərɪti]		soziale Sicherheit

COMPREHENSION TESTS / GRAMMATICAL EXERCISES

5

to seize the bull by the horns [siːz], [bʊl]		den Stier bei den Hörnern packen
to take the opportunity [ɒpəˈtjuːnɪti]	If I were you, I would take this opportunity.	die Gelegenheit ergreifen
to trick sb		jemanden hereinlegen
to fire sb		jemanden feuern, rausschmeißen
to hang sb [hæŋ]		jemanden hängen
to pull sb's leg	Are you just pulling my leg?	jemanden auf den Arm nehmen
to fall in love with sb		sich in jemanden verlieben
to make fun of sb [fʌn]		sich über jemanden lustig machen
in a playful way	Did he do it in a playful way? Difficult to say.	aus Spaß

6

social services		soziale Dienstleistungen
to become unemployed		arbeitslos werden
income [ˈɪŋkʌm], [ˈɪn-]		Einkommen
to decrease [dɪˈkriːs]	Prices have decreased.	fallen, abnehmen
rent		Miete
flat		Wohnung

7

working hours	What are the working hours in the factory?	Arbeitszeit
to create sth [kriˈeɪt]		etwas kreieren, schaffen
to have a definite opinion [ˈdefɪnɪt]	I have no definite opinion.	eine feste Vorstellung haben
to be available		vorhanden sein
to be dissatisfied [dɪˈsætɪsfaɪd]	Are you dissatisfied with these results? Yes.	unzufrieden sein
to be aggressive [əˈgresɪv]		aggressiv sein
wages and salaries [ˈweɪdʒɪs], [ˈsæləriːz]		Löhne und Gehälter
dispute [dɪˈspjuːt], [dɪ-]	Was the dispute between them settled? No.	Streit
divorce [dɪˈvɔːs]		Scheidung
activity [ækˈtɪvəti]		Aktivität

10

to settle a matter	Has he settled the matter to your full satisfaction? Yes.	eine Angelegenheit regeln
proposal [prəˈpəʊzəl], [ˈdɪ-]	Has he made a proposal of marriage (Heiratsantrag)?	Vorschlag
to settle a dispute [dɪˈspjuːt], [ˈdɪ-]		einen Streit schlichten
to deliver goods [dɪˈlɪvə], [gʊdz]		Waren liefern
to execute an order [ˈeksɪkjuːt]		einen Auftrag ausführen

24 BRITAIN AND THE WORLD

capital goods		Investitionsgüter
electronic equipment [ɪˈkwɪpmənt]		elektronische Geräte
telecommunications products		Telekommunikations-erzeugnisse
chemicals [ˈkəmɪkəlz]		Chemikalien
the sterling area [ˈstɜːlɪŋ], [ˈeərɪə]	What countries belong to the sterling area?	der Sterling Block (ihm gehören Länder an, die das Pfund Sterling als Währung haben)
to change	Has anything changed in the British way of life? A lot.	hier: sich ändern
reason [ˈriːzən]		Grund
sale(s) [seɪl]		Absatz, Verkauf
to realize [ˈrɪəlaɪz]	Have you realized that he is blind (blind)? No.	hier: etw. erkennen, wahrnehmen
to create sth [kriˈeɪt]		etwas schaffen, kreieren
to join sth [dʒɔɪn]	Are you going to join a political party? No.	etwas beitreten
European Community [kəˈmjuːnɪti]		Europäische Gemeinschaft
globalization [gləʊbəlaɪˈzeɪʃən]		Globalisierung
challenge [ˈtʃælɪndʒ]	This job is a challenge.	Herausforderung
keen competitors [kiːn], [kəmˈpetɪtə]		harte Konkurrenten
to make every effort [ˈefət]	We will make every effort to execute your order in time.	große Anstrengungen machen
to keep pace with [peɪs]		Schritt halten mit
condition		Bedingung
economic growth [grəʊθ]		Wirtschaftswachstum
labour market		Arbeitsmarkt
to improve [ɪmˈpruːv]	His knowledge of French has improved.	sich (ver-)bessern
to master sth		etwas meistern

COMPREHENSION TESTS / GRAMMATICAL EXERCISES

3

to warn sb [wɔːn]	I have warned you of this danger.	jemanden warnen
to explode [ɪkˈspləʊd]		explodieren

4

to decline [dɪˈklaɪn]	Exports declined last year.	fallen, zurückgehen
major [ˈmeɪdʒə]		Haupt-...
to establish sth [ɪˈstæblɪʃ]	Mark is going to establish a new firm.	etwas errichten, gründen
to found sth		
to change for the better		sich bessern, verbessern

5

Towards a united Europe

agricultural [ˌægrɪˈkʌltʃərəl]		landwirtschaftlich
to date back sth		etwas zurückdatieren
century [ˈsentʃəri]		Jahrhundert
an effective step [ɪˈfektɪv]	Have effective steps been taken to create a political union?	ein wirksamer Schritt
to set up sth		etwas errichten
Coal and Steel Community [stiːl]		Montanunion
common market		der gemeinsame Markt
to restrict sth to [rɪˈstrɪkt]	The Coal and Steel Community was restricted to coal and steel.	etwas beschränken auf
to extend sth [ɪkˈstend]		etwas erweitern
Rome treaty [ˈtriːti]		der Römische Vertrag
the European Economic Community		die Europäische Wirtschaftsgemeinschaft
to avoid sth [əˈvɔɪd]	The catastrophe could not be avoided.	etwas vermeiden
to remove sth [rɪˈmuːv]		etwas beseitigen, entfernen
customs barrier [ˈbæriə]		Zollbarriere
decisive [dɪˈsaɪsɪv]		entscheidend
Single Market	They decided to establish a Single Market.	Binnenmarkt
capital		Kapital
services		Dienstleistungen
to move freely [muːv]		sich frei bewegen
European Union		die Europäische Union
common [ˈkɒmən]		gemeinsam
monetary unit [ˈmʌnɪtəri], [ˈjuːnɪt]		Währungseinheit
negotiation [nɪˌgəʊʃiˈeɪʃən]	Are you going to enter into negotiations with them? Yes.	Verhandlung
membership		Mitgliedschaft
Poland [ˈpəʊlənd]		Polen
the Czech Republic [tʃek]		die Tschechische Republik
Hungary [ˈhʌŋɡəri]		Ungarn
to come true		wahr werden

6

compartment [kəmˈpɑːtmənt]	You must not smoke in this compartment.	Abteil
to make out a cheque		einen Scheck ausstellen
to sign a contract [saɪn]	Did you sign the contract? No.	einen Vertrag unterschreiben

7

to run the whole show		den Laden schmeißen
to raise the salary [reɪz], [ˈsæləri]		das Gehalt erhöhen
a job on the side	Do you have a job on the side? No.	einen Nebenverdienst haben
to cross the border [ˈbɔːdə]		die Grenze überschreiten
visa [ˈviːzə]		Visa
to be duty-free [ˈdjuːti]	Here is the list of duty-free goods.	zollfrei sein
to overdraw an account [ˌəʊvəˈdrɔː], [əˈkaʊnt]		ein Konto überziehen
sales contract	Have they concluded (schließen) a sales contract? Yes.	Kaufvertrag
to cancel an agreement [ˈkænsəl]		einen Vertrag (Abkommen) stornieren (lösen)

8

to refuse [rɪˈfjuːz]		sich weigern
exhibition [ˌeksəˈbɪʃən]	Do you have a stand at the exhibition? Yes.	Ausstellung
to go out to eat		Essen gehen (auswärts)
to settle		hier: sich niederlassen

25 NEW YORK

sales manager		Verkaufsleiter
to decide to do sth	He decided to visit the Niagara Falls.	sich entschließen etwas zu tun
to receive landing permission [pəˈmɪʃən]		Landeerlaubnis erhalten
to circle [ˈsɜːkəl]		kreisen
to have a view of [vjuː]		einen Blick haben auf
skyline [ˈskaɪlaɪn]		Skyline, Stadtsilhouette
skyscraper [ˈskaɪˌskreɪpə]		Wolkenkratzer
financial center [fəˈnænʃəl], [faɪ-]		Finanzzentrum
Stock Exchange	Do you speculate on the Stock Exchange?	die Börse
to commemorate sth [kəˈmeməreɪt]		an etwas erinnern
anniversary [ˌænəˈvɜːsəri]	When does the firm celebrate its 100th anniversary?	Jahrestag
southern tip [ˈsʌðən]		die südliche Spitze
to be well worth a visit [wɜːθ]		einen Besuch wert sein
to live on better terms with one another [tɜːmz]		besser miteinander auskommen
dirty [ˈdɜːti]	What dirty weather!	schmutzig
public authorities [ɔːˈθɒrətiːz]		Behörden
to touch down [tʌtʃ]		aufsetzen (Flugzeug)
to land smoothly [ˈsmuːðli]		glatt landen

COMPREHENSION TESTS / GRAMMATICAL EXERCISES

2
headquarters [ˈhedˌkwɔːtəz]		hier: Sitz

4
to stroll		herumbummeln
colo(u)rful [ˈkʌləfəl]	This picture is very colorful.	bunt, farbenfroh
style [staɪl]		Stil
playground		Spielplatz
entire [ɪnˈtaɪə]	Tell me the entire story.	ganz, vollständig

5
to be hectic [ˈhektɪk]		hektisch sein
to be crowded [ˈkraʊdɪd]		überfüllt sein
rush hour [rʌʃ]	Buses are crowded in the rush hour.	Berufsverkehr
packed trains		volle Züge
pay		Bezahlung
cost of living	The cost of living has increased in the last few months.	Lebenshaltungskosten
rent for apartments		Wohnungsmiete
crime/violence		Verbrechen/Gewalt
pollution		Umweltverschmutzung
close to nature [ˈneɪtʃə]		dicht an der Natur

7
distinct(ly) [dɪˈstɪŋkt]	Speak more distinctly, please.	deutlich
serious [ˈsɪərɪəs]	His state of health is serious.	ernst
to consult (sb) (sth)		(jemanden) befragen (etwas) nachschlagen
to give up sth	You should give up smoking.	etwas aufgeben
a nasty soup [ˈnɑːsti]		eine scheußliche Suppe
buggy		Buggy (Kinderwagen)
to obey/disobey the traffic rules [əʊˈbeɪ], [ruːl]		die Verkehrsregeln beachten/missachten
at least [liːst]		mindestens

8
to worry about [ˈwʌri]	Don't worry about it.	sich Sorgen machen über
to tell lies [laɪz]		lügen
to be frightened [ˈfraɪtnd]		Angst haben
to crib from sb [krɪb]		von jemandem abschreiben
neighbour [ˈneɪbə]	You must not crib from your neighbour.	Nachbar

26 IMPRESSIONS OF THE UNITED STATES

settler		Siedler
to require sth [rɪˈkwaɪə]	Do you require any help? No, thank you.	etwas benötigen
population [ˌpɒpjʊˈleɪʃən]		Bevölkerung
capital		Hauptstadt
a melting pot		ein Schmelztiegel
five times		fünfmal
seaside resort [rɪˈzɔːt]		Seebad
a testing and launching center		ein Test- und Startzentrum
space rocket [speɪs], [ˈrɒkɪt]		Weltraumrakete
empty [ˈempti]	The bottle is empty.	leer sein
desert [ˈdezət]		die Wüste
snow [snəʊ]		Schnee
cattle ranch		Viehfarm
culture [ˈkʌltʃə]		Kultur
education		Bildung, Erziehung
to be fascinated by [ˈfæsɪneɪtɪd]	I was fascinated by the wonderful sunset.	begeistert, fasziniert sein von
Memorial [mɪˈmɔːriəl]		Denkmal, Ehrenmal
classical [ˈklæsɪkəl]		klassisch
architecture [ˈɑːkɪtektʃə]		Architektur

COMPREHENSION TESTS / GRAMMATICAL EXERCISES

1

distance	What's the distance from New York to San Francisco? About 2500 miles.	Entfernung

6

to range from ... to	At the flea market offers range from a pin (Stecknadel) to an elephant.	reichen von ... bis
to regard sth/sb as [rɪˈgɑːd]	He is regarded as the best dentist in town.	jemanden/etwas betrachten als, halten für
experience [ɪkˈspɪəriəns]	That was a great experience.	Erlebnis, Erfahrung
for this purpose [ˈpɜːpəs]		zu diesem Zweck
iron ore [ˈaɪən], [ɔː]		Eisenerz
pearl [pɜːl]	Venice is the pearl of Italy.	Perle
to be prosperous [ˈprɒspərəs]		blühen(d), wohlhabend
to process sth/[ˈprəʊses]	Iron is processed into steel.	etwas verarbeiten/ das Verarbeiten
processing		das Verarbeiten
marketing		das Vermarkten
aircraft [ˈeəkrɑːft]		Flugzeug
reservation [ˌrezəˈveɪʃən]		Reservat
silver [ˈsɪlvə]		Silber
copper [ˈkɒpə]		Kupfer

7

to hitchhike	I'll hitchhike to Washington tomorrow.	per Anhalter fahren
refreshments [rɪˈfreʃmənts]		Erfrischungen
I have been getting on well.		Mir geht es gut.

8

to pay (in) cash [kæʃ]		bar zahlen
to raise a loan [reɪz], [ləʊn]		ein Darlehen aufnehmen
to repay sth/ to pay back sth		etwas zurückzahlen
a four-star hotel [stɑː]		ein Viersternehotel
to grant credit [grɑːnt]		Kredit gewähren
receptionist [rɪˈsepʃənɪst]		Empfangschef
single/double room		Einzel-/Doppelzimmer
to give sb a wake-up call	The receptionist gave me a wake-up call at 7 o'clock.	jemanden wecken
to rent a car		einen Wagen mieten
fully comprehensive [kɒmprɪˈhensɪv] insurance (full insurance)	Do you want fully comprehensive (full) insurance? Yes.	Vollkasko

9

son-in-law [ɔː]		Schwiegersohn
father-in-law		Schwiegervater
sister-in-law		Schwägerin
daughter-in-law		Schwiegertochter
in-laws		Schwiegereltern
to retire		in Pension gehen
to go bowling		Bowling spielen gehen

10

to apologize for sth [əˈpɒlədʒaɪz]		sich für etwas entschuldigen
to mention [ˈmenʃən]		erwähnen
to treat sb [triːt]	Which doctor is treating you? This one.	jemanden behandeln
to blackmail sb [ˈblækmeɪl]		jemanden erpressen
to bother [ˈbɒðə]	Don't bother. That's all right.	sich Sorgen machen
cancer [ˈkænsə]	Does she have cancer? Yes.	Krebs
to support sb [səˈpɔːt]		jemanden unterstützen
to be rude [ruːd]	Don't be so rude to Paul.	grob, unverschämt sein
the will		der Wille
to wonder [ˈwʌndə]		sich wundern, gespannt sein

27 SOME ASPECTS OF MODERN AMERICAN LIFE

to afford sth [əˈfɔːd]	I can't afford to spend more money on cars.	sich etwas leisten
to share sth [ʃeə]	He would share the last penny with me.	etwas teilen
apartment [əˈpɑːtmənt]		(Etagen-)Wohnung (amerik.)

emancipation [ıˌmænsɪ̩ˈpeɪʃən]		Emanzipation
to make progress [ˈprəʊgres]	Has he made any progress? Oh yes.	Fortschritte machen
divorce rate [dɪ̩ˈvɔːs]		die Scheidungsrate
to divorce from, to get divorced from	Is it true that Miriam got divorced from Henry? Yes, it is.	sich scheiden lassen von, geschieden werden von
further education		Fortbildung
to change sth	He changes cars every two years.	hier: etwas wechseln
to earn money		Geld verdienen
to be everlasting		ewig, immerwährend
the music scene [ˈmjuːsɪk], [siːn]		die Musikszene
folk song [fəʊk]		Volkslied

COMPREHENSION TESTS / GRAMMATICAL EXERCISES

2

gambler [ˈgæmblə]		Spieler
to be worth a visit [wɜːθ]	The zoo is worth a visit.	einen Besuch wert sein

3

favo(u)rable [ˈfeɪvərəbəl]	Have you got some favo(u)rable information? Yes.	günstig

5

vocational [vəʊˈkeɪʃənəl]	Are you going to your vocational training course (Berufsausbildungskurs)?	Berufs-...
event [ɪˈvent]		Ereignis
to wear sth [weə]	Does she wear hats? Yes.	etwas tragen (z. B. Kleidungsstücke)
elementary school [elɪ̩ˈmentəri]		Grundschule
high school		Oberschule (In den USA)
to take a test		sich einem Test unterziehen
to fail	Did he fail the exam? Yes.	durchfallen (Prüfung)
grade [greɪd]		Schulklasse (In den USA)
diploma [dɪ̩ˈpləʊmə]		Diplom
law [lɔː]	What do you study? Law.	hier: Jura
to play a role		eine Rolle spielen
pitcher [ˈpɪtʃə]		Werfer
batter [ˈbætə]		Schlagmann
to hit	Did he hit you? Yes.	hier: schlagen
baseball bat [bæt]		Baseballkeule (...schläger)
to touch [tʌtʃ]		berühren
to push		stoßen
game [geɪm]		Spiel
helmet [ˈhelmɪ̩t]		Helm

7

engineer [ˌendʒɪˈnɪə]		Ingenieur
a part-time job	Do you have a part-time job or a full-time one?	Teilzeitbeschäftigung
to enjoy a good reputation [ɪnˈdʒɔɪ], [ˌrepjʊˈteɪʃən]		einen guten Ruf genießen
to attend a technical college	What type of college does Jack attend? A technical college.	eine berufsbildende Lehranstalt (technisch).
to be successful [səkˈsesfəl]		erfolgreich sein
to apply for a post		sich um eine Stelle bewerben

8

actor		Schauspieler
to be popular	Is he very popular? Yes.	beliebt sein
to be efficient [ɪˈfɪʃənt]		tüchtig sein
spare parts [speə]		Ersatzteile
to deliver goods		Waren liefern

9

to pick up sb		jemanden abholen
to post letters	Who has posted the letters today? Henry.	Briefe aufgeben

10

fare [feə]		(Fahr-)Preis
to enquire about sth	What did he enquire about? About the fare?	sich nach etwas erkundigen
to send a telegram		ein Telegramm aufgeben
to submit an offer [səbˈmɪt]		ein Angebot unterbreiten
acceptable [əkˈseptəbəl]	This offer is not acceptable.	annehmbar, akzeptabel
to make a proposal [prəˈpəʊzəl] (suggestion) [səˈdʒestʃən]		einen Vorschlag machen
to make (take) a decision [dɪˈsɪʒən]	You should take a decision now.	sich entscheiden, eine Entscheidung treffen
to settle an invoice [ˈɪnvɔɪs]		eine Rechnung begleichen

11

to be careful	Be careful!	hier: vorsichtig sein
alcohol [ˈælkəhɒl]		Alkohol
to take care of sth		sich um etwas kümmern
in advance [ədˈvɑːns]	Have you booked in advance? No.	im Voraus

12

to run a risk	Would you run this risk? No.	ein Risiko eingehen
to think sth over		etwas überdenken
to consult a doctor		zum Arzt gehen (konsultieren)
to take something seriously		etwas ernst nehmen
to follow an advice [ədˈvaɪs]	Did he follow your advice? Yes.	einen Rat befolgen

SPECIFIC TEXTS DEALING WITH COMMERCE AND TRADE

1   WORKING IN AN EXPORT FIRM

to be employed	beschäftigt sein
trainee [treɪˈniː]	Auszubildende(r)
to sort/to file sth [sɔːt], [faɪl]	etwas sortieren/ablegen
correspondence	Korrespondenz
business letter	Geschäftsbrief
to calculate prices [ˈkælkjʊleɪt]	Preise kalkulieren
vocational training [vəʊˈkeɪʃənəl]	Berufsausbildung
to deal with sth [diːl]	sich mit etwas befassen, behandeln
to receive an enquiry [ɪnˈkwaɪəri]	eine Anfrage erhalten
refrigerator [rɪˈfrɪdʒəreɪtə]	Kühlschrank
to contact sb [ˈkɒntækt]	mit jemandem Verbindung aufnehmen
to receive offers	Angebote erhalten
to work out sth	etwas ausarbeiten
to quote prices [kwəʊt]	Preise nennen, angeben
terms of payment and delivery	Zahlungs- und Lieferbedingungen
discounts [ˈdɪskaʊnts]	Preisnachlässe (Skonti, Rabatte)
delivery date	Liefertermin
to enclose leaflets (brochures) [ɪnˈkləʊz], [ˈliːflə̩ts], [ˈbrəʊʃəz]	Prospekte beifügen
to give sb an idea of sth [aɪˈdɪə]	jemandem von etwas eine Vorstellung vermitteln
to place an order with sb	jemandem einen Auftrag erteilen
shipping agent [ˈeɪdʒənt]	Spediteur
to request sb to do sth [rɪˈkwest]	jemanden bitten etwas zu tun
advice of despatch [dɪˈspætʃ]	die Versandanzeige
date of arrival	der Ankunftstermin
to settle an invoice	eine Rechnung begleichen

2   AT THE PORT OF LONDON

to be busy	rege, beschäftigt sein
dockworkers [ˈdɒk...]	Hafenarbeiter
to load and unload sth [ləʊd]	etwas be- und entladen
cargo [ˈkɑːgəʊ]	Warenladung, Fracht
warehouse [ˈweəhaʊs]	Lager-(Haus)
lorry [ˈlɒri]	Lastkraftwagen
customer [ˈkʌstəmə]	Kunde
wholesaler [ˈhəʊl,seɪlə]	Großhändler
quay [kiː]	Kai
to pass through customs	den Zoll passieren
to pack sth [pæk]	etwas packen, verpacken

seaworthy case(s) [ˈsiːwɜːði], [keɪs] — seefeste Kiste(n)
to stow sth in containers [stəʊ] — etwas in Containern verstauen

to examine the shipping documents [ˈdɒkjʊmənt] — die Verschiffungsdokumente (nach-)prüfen
Bill of Lading [ˈleɪdɪŋ] — Seefrachtbrief, Konnossement
to make sure — sich vergewissern
to be properly stowed [ˈprɒpəli] — ordnungsgemäß verstaut sein

field of occupation [ˌɒkjʊˈpeɪʃən] — Arbeitsbereich
port of destination [ˌdestɪˈneɪʃən] — der Bestimmungshafen
means of transport [miːnz] — Transportmittel

3 A BUSINESS TALK

department store — Warenhaus
to receive sth — etwas erhalten
circular [ˈsɜːkjʊlə] — Rundschreiben
to attract a person's interest — das Interesse einer Person auf sich ziehen

sales manager — Verkaufsleiter
... speaking — am Apparat
collection [kəˈlekʃən] — Kollektion
tropical wear [ˈtrɒpɪkəl], [weə] — Tropenkleidung
to extend sth [ɪkˈstend] — etwas erweitern
range [reɪndʒ] — hier: Sortiment
representative [ˌreprɪˈzentətɪv] — Vertreter
to call on sb — jemanden aufsuchen
to make sb familiar with sth [fəˈmɪljə] — jemanden mit etwas vertraut machen
to suggest [səˈdʒest] — vorschlagen
to be convenient [kənˈviːnɪənt] — angenehm sein
call — Anruf

4 A BUSINESS LETTER
   (Making a counterproposal)

to make a counterproposal [ˈkaʊntə] — einen Gegenvorschlag machen
quotation [kwəʊˈteɪʃən] — Angebot
to appeal to sb [əˈpiːl] — hier: jemandem gefallen
to point out that [pɔɪnt] — darauf hinweisen, dass
customer [ˈkʌstəmə] — Kunde
to be acceptable — annehmbar sein
in these circumstances [ˈsɜːkəmstænsɪz] — unter diesen Umständen
to place an order with sb — jemandem einen Auftrag erteilen
to grant a reduction [grɑːnt] — einen Preisnachlass gewähren
list price — Listenpreis
to look forward to sth [ˈfɔːwəd] — sich auf etwas freuen
Yours sincerely (engl. und amerik.) [sɪnˈsɪəli] — Mit freundlichen Grüßen

5 A BUSINESS LETTER
(Making a complaint)

complaint [kəmˈpleɪnt]	Reklamation, Beanstandung
the execution of an order [ˌeksəˈkjuːʃən]	die Ausführung eines Auftrags
a guidebook	ein Reiseführer
to be currently out of stock [ˈkʌrəntli]	zurzeit nicht auf Lager sein
to hold sth at the disposal of [dɪˈspəʊsəl]	etwas zur Verfügung halten

6 VISITORS AT THE HANOVER FAIR

to visit a fair	eine Messe besuchen
manufacturer [ˌmænjʊˈfæktʃərə]	Hersteller, Fabrikant
engineer [ˌendʒəˈnɪə]	Ingenieur, Techniker
mechanic [mɪˈkænɪk]	Mechaniker
tradesman	hier: Handwerker
wholesaler [ˈhəʊlˌseɪlə]	Großhändler
retailer [ˈriːteɪlə]	Einzelhändler
to display products [dɪˈspleɪ]	Erzeugnisse (Waren) ausstellen
sales manager	Verkaufsleiter
the head of the sales department	der Chef der Verkaufsabteilung
he has to see that	er muss darauf achten, dass
incoming letters	eingehende Post (Briefe)
to be competitive [kəemˈpetətɪv]	konkurrenzfähig sein
customer [ˈkʌstəmə]	Kunde
to get the best possible service	den bestmöglichen Service erhalten
to settle a complaint [kəmˈpleɪnt]	eine Beanstandung (Reklamation) regeln
to the customer's satisfaction [ˌsætəsˈfækʃən]	zur Zufriedenheit des Kunden
mechanical engineer [mɪˈkænɪkəl]	Maschineningenieur
to design tools [dɪˈzaɪn], [tuːlz]	Werkzeug(e) konstruieren (entwerfen)
to construct machinery [məˈʃiːnəri]	Maschinen bauen
to be engaged [ɪnˈgeɪdʒd]	tätig sein
manufacturing plant [plɑːnt]	Herstellwerk, Produktionsbetrieb
aircraft [ˈeəkrɑːft]	Flugzeug, Maschine
locomotive [ˌləʊkəˈməʊtɪv]	Lokomotive
crane [kreɪn]	Kran
drilling machine	Bohrmaschine
combustion engine [kəmˈbʌstʃən]	Verbrennungsmotor
electrical engineer [ɪˈlektrɪkəl]	Elektroingenieur
generator [ˈdʒenəreɪtə]	Generator
electricity [ɪˌlekˈtrɪsəti]	Elektrizität

7 WHAT DO YOU KNOW ABOUT MODERN COMMUNICATIONS SYSTEMS?

communications system [kəˌmjuːnɪ̩ˈkeɪʃənz]	Kommunikationssystem
to take the final examination [ˈfaɪnəl]	sich der Abschlussprüfung unterziehen
to deal with sth [diːl]	etwas behandeln
fax [fæks]	Telefax, Fax
satellite [ˈsætl̩aɪt]	Satellit
to transmit sth [trænzˈmɪt]	etwas übertragen
by means of [miːnz]	mittels
fax user	Telefaxbenutzer
to communicate	kommunizieren, übermitteln
fax machine [məˈʃiːn]	Faxgerät
to be connected to sth	an etwas angeschlossen sein
to be composed of [kəmˈpəʊzd]	sich zusammensetzen aus
keyboard [ˈkiːbɔːd]	Tastatur
central processing unit [ˈjuːnɪ̩t]	die Zentraleinheit
monitor [ˈmɒnɪ̩tə]	Monitor, Bildschirm
printer [ˈprɪntə]	Drucker
software	Software
to instruct [ɪnˈstrʌkt]	hier: Anweisung geben
to carry out an order	einen Auftrag ausführen
advantage [ədˈvɑːntɪdʒ]	Vorteil
to work economically [ˌekəˈnɒmɪkli]	wirtschaftlich arbeiten
space [speɪs]	Raum
to store data [stɔː]	Daten speichern
to take (make) a decision [dɪˈsɪʒən]	eine Entscheidung treffen, einen Entschluss fassen
to be successful [səkˈsesfəl]	erfolgreich sein, Erfolg haben
to revolutionize sth [ˌrevəˈluːʃənaɪz]	etwas revolutionieren
telecommunications [ˌtelɪkəmjuːnɪ̩ˈkeɪʃənz]	Telekommunikation
homepage	Homepage
to transfer sth [trænsˈfɜː]	etwas transferieren, überweisen
and the like	und dergleichen

8 HOW A HOUSE IS BUILT

bricklayer [ˈbrɪkˌleɪə]	Maurer
building site [saɪt]	Baugrundstück
on the outskirts [ˈaʊtskɜːts]	am Stadtrand
architect [ˈɑːkɪ̩tekt]	Architekt
to make construction plans [plænz]	Baupläne entwerfen
to discuss sth in detail [dɪˈskʌs], [ˈdiːteɪl]	etwas im Einzelnen besprechen
to lay the bricks	mauern
carpenter [ˈkɑːpɪ̩ntə]	Zimmermann, Tischler
tiler [ˈtaɪlə]	Dachdecker
roof [ruːf]	das Dach
plumber [ˈplʌmbə]	Klempner
to fit the gas and water pipes [fɪt], [gæs]	die Gas- und Wasserleitung installieren

electrician [ɪˌlekˈtrɪʃən]   Elektriker
to do the electrical wiring [ˈwaɪərɪŋ]   die elektrischen Leitungen legen
to install the electrical equipment [ɪnˈstɔːl]   die elektrische Ausstattung installieren
to plaster the walls [ˈplɑːstə]   die Wände verputzen
the central heating system [ˈsentrəl], [ˈhiːtɪŋ], [ˈsɪstɪ̣m]   die zentrale Heizungsanlage
radiator [ˈreɪdieɪtə]   Heizkörper
gas boiler [ˈbɔɪlə]   Gasboiler (-erhitzer)
fitter [ˈfɪtə]   Installateur, Monteur
joiner [ˈdʒɔɪnə]   Schreiner, Tischler
to fit in the window frames [freɪmz]   die Fensterrahmen einsetzen
glazier [ˈgleɪzɪə]   Glaser
to glaze the windows [gleɪz]   die Fenster verglasen
painter   Maler
tradesman [ˈtreɪdzmən]   hier: Handwerker
to whitewash the ceiling [ˈsiːlɪŋ]   die Decke weißen
to paper the walls   (die Wände) tapezieren

Tools

tools [tuːlz]   Handwerkszeug
trowel [ˈtraʊəl]   (Maurer-)Kelle
plane [pleɪn]   Hobel
saw [sɔː]   Säge
paintbrush [brʌʃ]   Pinsel
workbench [ˈwɜːkbentʃ]   Werkbank
roof tile   Dachpfanne
nail [neɪl]   Nagel
screwdriver [ˈskruːdraɪvə]   Schraubenzieher
a pair of pliers [ˈplaɪəz]   Zange
hammer [ˈhæmə]   Hammer
drill [drɪl]   Bohrer
ruler [ˈruːlə]   Zollstock
plug [plʌg]   Stecker
(plug) socket [ˈsɒkɪ̣t]   Steckdose

9   A FARMER'S ACTIVITIES

to rake [reɪk]   harken, rechen
to plough the land [plaʊ], [lænd]   das Land pflügen
to sow wheat/barley/oats [səʊ], [wiːt], [ˈbɑːli]   Weizen/Gerste/Hafer säen
to fertilize the soil [ˈfɜːtɪ̣laɪz], [sɔɪl]   den Boden düngen
to harvest potatoes [ˈhɑːvɪ̣st]   Kartoffeln ernten
to harvest the crop [krɒp]   die Ernte einbringen
to thresh grain [θreʃ], [greɪn]   das Korn dreschen
to feed cattle [fiːd], [ˈkætl]   das Vieh füttern
to milk cows [kaʊ]   Kühe melken

10 SARAH LEARNS HOW TO COOK

to cook [kʊk]	kochen
trainee [treɪˈniː]	Auszubildende(r)
to have a lot of trouble	viel Ärger (Schwierigkeiten) haben
to go wrong	schiefgehen
the head cook	der Küchenchef
to be satisfied with sb [ˈsæt̬sfaɪd]	mit jemandem zufrieden sein
spice [spaɪs]	Gewürz
ingredients [ɪnˈgriːdɪənts]	die Zutaten
to practise sth [ˈpræktɪ̬s]	etwas praktizieren
yogurt soup [ˈjɒgət]	Joghurtsuppe
duck with pears [dʌk], [peəz]	Ente mit Birnen
chocolate mousse	Mousse au chocolat
menu [ˈmenjuː]	Speisekarte
tablespoon	Esslöffel
chicken stock	Hühnerbrühe
pepper and salt [sɔːlt]	Pfeffer und Salz
egg yolk [jəʊk]	Eigelb
dried mint [mɪnt]	getrocknete Minze (Pfefferminze)
two teaspoons of paprika [ˈpæprɪkə]	zwei Teelöffel Paprika
olive oil [ˈɒlɪ̬v]	Olivenöl
pears	Birnen
to be unripe/ripe	unreif/reif sein
to peel sth [piːl]	etwas schälen
cinnamon stick [ˈsɪnəmən]	Zimtstange
to slice onions [slaɪs], [ˈʌnjənz]	Zwiebel schneiden
carrot [ˈkærət]	Karotte
a pinch of dried thyme [taɪm]	eine Prise getrockneter Thymian
semi-sweet [ˈsemɪ]	halb süß, nur leicht gesüßt
liqueur [lɪˈkjʊə]	Likör
whipped cream [wɪp]	Schlagsahne

Yogurt soup

to boil (in water) [bɔɪl]	kochen
to be soft	weich (gar) sein
to add sth	etwas hinzutun
to pour sth into [pɔː]	etwas hineingießen
mixture [ˈmɪkstʃə]	Gemisch, Mischung
to stir sth [stɜː]	etwas rühren, umrühren
to thicken [ˈθɪkən]	dicker werden, eindicken
to melt sth [melt]	etwas schmelzen
to serve	hier: servieren
to sizzle [ˈsɪzəl]	brutzeln

Duck with pears

to brown sth	etwas anbraten
frying pan [pæn]	Bratpfanne
to be liquid [ˈlɪkwɪ̬d]	flüssig sein
sauce [sɔːs]	Soße

to soften sth ['sɒfən] — etwas garen, gar kochen
to simmer sth ['sɪmə] — etwas sieden lassen
to cook gently ['dʒentli] — hier: sachte kochen lassen
to be tender ['tendə] — hier: zart sein
to decorate ['dekəreɪt] — hier: garnieren

Chocolate mousse
to chop sth [tʃɒp] — etwas klein schneiden
to be frothy ['frɒθi] — locker, weich sein
to be thoroughly combined ['θʌrəli] — völlig vermischt sein
bowl [bəʊl] — Schüssel
to fold in remaining cream — hier: den Rest Sahne „vorsichtig" hineinrühren

FOR FURTHER STUDY

THE PREPOSITIONS
taxi stand [stænd], taxi rank [ræŋk] — der Taxistand
to flow [fləʊ] — fließen
river bank — Flussufer
ground floor — Erdgeschoß
burglar ['bɜːglə] — Einbrecher

THE CONJUNCTIONS
to pick up sb from the station — jemanden vom Bahnhof abholen
to be clumsy ['klʌmzi] — ungeschickt, unbeholfen, schwerfällig sein
to catch a cold — sich erkälten
to be fined — eine Geldstrafe zahlen
to observe the traffic rules [əb'zɜːv] — die Verkehrsregeln beachten
to drop sb — jemanden fallen lassen
to break into a house — in ein Haus einbrechen
to pinch [pɪntʃ] — klauen, stehlen
to question sb — jemanden befragen
constable — Polizist
to drop a line — ein paar Zeilen schreiben
to hear a pack of lies — sich einen Haufen Lügen anhören
to wonder ['wʌndə] — sich wundern, neugierig sein
the penny has dropped — der Groschen ist gefallen
to seize the bull by the horns [siːz], [bʊl] — den Stier bei den Hörnern packen
to cause a storm in a tea cup [stɔːm] — einen Sturm im Wasserglas verursachen
to polish up sth ['pɒlɪʃ] — etwas auffrischen, aufpolieren
to be short of money — wenig Geld haben, knapp an Geld sein
to be modest ['mɒdɪ̜st] — bescheiden sein

THE IF-CLAUSES

1

to get into trouble	Schwierigkeiten bekommen
to book sth in advance	etwas im Voraus buchen
to reach one's goal	sein Ziel erreichen
to do the football pools	im Fußballtoto spielen

5

to take part in a stag party [stæg]	an einer Junggesellenparty teilnehmen (Abschied vom Junggesellendasein)
to try one's luck	sein Glück auf die Probe stellen
to be angry with sb [ˈæŋgri]	auf jemanden ärgerlich sein
to waste money [weɪst]	Geld verschwenden
to have a hangover	einen „Kater" haben
to come across difficulties	auf Schwierigkeiten stoßen
It's raining cats and dogs.	Es regnet Bindfäden.
to blackmail sb	jemanden erpressen
to report sb to the police	jemanden bei der Polizei anzeigen
to bribe sb [ˈbraɪb]	jemanden bestechen
to insult sb [ɪnˈsʌlt]	jemanden beleidigen
to get into a fix	in der Klemme sein (geraten)
to stand the test	sich bewähren
to launch sth on the market [lɔːntʃ]	etwas auf dem Markt einführen
to get a guarantee [ˌgærənˈtiː]	Garantie erhalten

6

to interfere in sth [ˌɪntəˈfɪə]	sich in etwas einmischen
to go on a tour around the world	eine Weltreise machen
to accept conditions	Bedingungen annehmen
to grant credit	Kredit gewähren
information	die Auskunft
to be unfavourable	ungünstig sein

THE INDIRECT SPEECH

1

to be merry	angeheitert sein
caravan [ˈkærəvæn]	Wohnwagen
to take photos of sb	jemanden fotografieren
to apply for a job	sich um eine Stelle bewerben
to have good luck	Glück haben
to arrange a party	eine Party arrangieren
to accept the invitation	die Einladung annehmen

2

tube [tjuːb]	Londoner U-Bahn
to celebrate sth [ˈselɪbreɪt]	etwas feiern

3

package holiday	eine Pauschalreise
to make the necessary arrangements	die notwendigen Vorkehrungen treffen
exchange rate	der Wechselkurs
to be worth a visit [wɜːθ]	einen Besuch wert sein
to be a great experience [ɪkˈspɪərɪəns]	ein großes Erlebnis sein

THE INFINITIVE

1

to control oneself	sich beherrschen
to be advisable [ədˈvaɪzəbəl]	ratsam sein
to be risky [ˈrɪski]	riskant sein
to be frivolous [ˈfrɪvələs]	leichtsinnig sein
to trust sb [trʌst]	jemandem (ver)trauen
to be unwise (stupid) [ˈʌnwaɪz]	unklug (dumm) sein
to provoke sb [prəˈvəʊk]	jemanden provozieren
to come to an agreement	sich einigen
to reach a compromise [ˈkɒmprəmaɪz]	einen Kompromiss schließen
to cancel an order [ˈkænsəl]	einen Auftrag stornieren
to refuse sth [rɪˈfjuːz]	etwas ablehnen

2

to expect that [ɪkˈspekt]	erwarten, dass
to advise sth	etwas raten
to think sth over	etwas überdenken
to change one's mind [maɪnd]	seine Meinung ändern
to keep sth to oneself	etwas für sich behalten
to order sth	etwas anordnen
the injured woman [ˈɪndʒəd]	die verletzte Frau
to take sb to	jemanden (hin-)bringen zu
to lend money to sb	jemandem Geld leihen
to raise a loan	einen Kredit aufnehmen
to settle a bill	eine (Hotel-)Rechnung begleichen

3

to tell the truth [truːθ]	die Wahrheit sagen
to execute an order	einen Auftrag ausführen

4

to quarrel with sb [ˈkwɒrəl]	mit jemandem streiten
to cry	hier: weinen
to seize sb [siːz]	jemanden fassen, ergreifen
to escape [ɪˈskeɪp]	entkommen, entwischen

5

to explain sth to sb	jemandem etwas erklären
to pick sb up	jemanden abholen
to remember sth	sich an etwas erinnern

THE PARTICIPLE/THE GERUND

1

to recommend sth [rekəˈmend]	etwas empfehlen
to be air-conditioned [-kənˈdɪʃənd]	klimatisiert sein
to fill in a registration form [ˌredʒɪˈstreɪʃən], [fɔːm]	einen Anmeldeschein ausfüllen
cashier [kæˈʃɪə]	Kassierer(in)
to injure [ˈɪndʒə]	verletzen
to be exciting [ɪkˈsaɪtɪŋ]	spannend sein
victory [ˈvɪktəri]	Sieg
to celebrate sth [ˈselɪbreɪt]	etwas feiern
to congratulate sb on sth [kənˈgrætʃʊleɪt]	jemandem zu etwas gratulieren

2

to be enjoyable [ɪnˈdʒɔɪəbəl]	Spaß machen
to be advisable [ədˈvaɪzəbəl]	ratsam sein
to be frivolous [ˈfrɪvələs]	leichtsinnig sein
to be foolish [ˈfuːlɪʃ]	töricht sein
to quarrel/quarrel [ˈkwɒrəl]	sich streiten, der Streit
to skate [skeɪt]	Schlittschuh laufen
to stick one's nose into other people's business	die Nase in anderer Leute Sachen stecken
to be risky [ˈrɪski]	riskant sein
to speculate [ˈspekjʊleɪt]	spekulieren (z. B. an der Börse)
Stock Exchange [stɒk]	Börse
to lead sb by the nose	jemanden an der Nase herumführen

3

to look forward to sth	einer Sache entgegensehen, sich freuen (auf)
to apologize for sth [əˈpɒlədʒaɪz]	sich für etwas entschuldigen
to be afraid of [əˈfreɪd]	(be)fürchten
to be tired of	hier: etwas satt sein (haben)
to be used to	gewohnt sein, pflegen
to be rude to sb [ruːd]	grob, unverschämt sein
to hurt somebody's feelings	jemanden verletzen
to talk sb into a matter	jemanden zu etwas überreden

4

to be tipsy ['tɪpsi]	beschwipst sein
sports news	Sportnachrichten
to make a speech [spi:tʃ]	eine Rede halten
to faint [feɪnt]	ohnmächtig werden
to have a heart attack [ə'tæk]	einen Herzanfall haben (erleiden)

5

to insult sb [ɪn'sʌlt]	jemanden beleidigen
places of interest	Sehenswürdigkeiten
to be skimmed [skɪmd]	gestreift werden
surfer	Surfer

6

to be rapturously welcomed ['ræptʃərəsli]	stürmisch begrüßt werden
to bath, to have a bath [bɑ:θ]	baden
to knit [nɪt]	stricken
to overtake sb	jemanden überholen
to run into sb	mit jemandem zusammen-stoßen
the injured (man, woman)	der/die Verletzte
ambulance ['æmbjʊləns]	Krankenwagen

7

to notice sth ['nəʊtɪ̯s]	etwas bemerken
to be tired	müde sein
to do the housework	die Hausarbeit machen

8

to drive downtown	in die Innenstadt fahren
to pass the driving test	die Fahrprüfung bestehen

9

to catch sight of sb [saɪt]	jemanden erblicken
to do a crossword puzzle	ein Rätsel raten
to have a shave [ʃeɪv]	sich rasieren
to watch a video ['vɪdiəʊ]	sich ein Video ansehen
weather forecast ['fɔ:kɑ:st]	Wettervorhersage
to have a cognac ['kɒnjæk]	einen Cognac trinken
sauna ['saʊnə]	Sauna
to play chess [tʃes]	Schach spielen

KEY TO PRONUNCIATION AND STRESS – Die Zeichen der Lautschrift

ʌ	kurzes „a", wie glatt	to run [rʌn]
æ	offener „ä"-Laut, mehr zum „a" hin, z. B. kämmen	black [blæk]
ɑː	langes „a", etwa wie Hahn	bar [bɑː]
ɒ	kurzes, offenes „o", etwa wie flott, Motte	not [nɒt]
aɪ	wie rein, mein	five [faɪv]
aʊ	etwa wie Haus, Maus	house [haʊs]
ɔː	langes, offenes „o", etwa wie Horn	ball [bɔːl]
ɔɪ	etwa wie deutsch	boy [bɔɪ]
e	kurzes „e" wie nett	leg [leg]
eɪ	nicht wie das deutsche „Eis", sondern e-i, d. h., von „e" zum „i" übergleiten	make [meɪk]
ə	kurzes, unbetontes „e", wie danke	under [ˈʌndə]
ᵊ	bedeutet, dass „ə" angewendet, aber auch nicht angewendet werden kann.	
əʊ	von „ə" zu „u" übergleiten	to show [ʃəʊ]
ɜː	etwa wie Dörrgemüse	bird [bɜːd]
i	etwa wie in niedlich	pretty [ˈprɪti]
iː	langes „i", etwa wie Tier	three [θriː]
ɪ	kurzes „i", etwa wie Kitt	to sit [sɪt]
ɪə	von kurzem „i" zu „ə" übergleiten	near [nɪə]
iə	von „i" zu „ə" übergleiten	peculiar [pɪˈkjuːliə]
j	j wie Junge	yet [jet]
uː	langes „u", etwa wie Kuh	shoe [ʃuː]
ʊ	kurzes „u", etwa wie Futter	to put [pʊt]
ʊə	etwa wie Uhr	poor [pʊə]
ŋ	etwa wie Gong	song [sɒŋ]
r	Zunge an den Gaumen bringen und leicht zurückbiegen	railway [ˈreɪlweɪ]
s	wie beißen, küssen	to kiss [kɪs]
z	wie Eisen, leise	nose [nəʊz]
θ	wie ein gelispeltes „s"; die Zungenspitze an die oberen Vorderzähne	mouth [maʊθ]
ð	wie ein schwaches gelispeltes „s"; die Zungenspitze an die oberen Vorderzähne	then [ðen]
f	wie ein schwaches gelispeltes „s"; die Zungenspitze an die oberen Vorderzähne	then [fen]
ʃ	wie Tisch	fish [fɪʃ]
tʃ	„t" gleitet zu „ʃ" über	church [tʃɜːtʃ]
ʒ	wie Garage	pleasure [ˈpleʒə]
dʒ	wie Ingenieur	to jump [dʒʌmp]
v	wie Wetter, Visum	to visit [ˈvɪzˌɪt]
w	nicht wie das deutsche „w", sondern mit vorgestülpten Lippen ein kurzes „u" bilden, vor dem man schnell zum nachfolgenden Laut übergleitet	wine [waɪn]
ᵊ	bedeutet, dass manche Sprecher bei der Aussprache das „i" und andere das „ə" benutzen	
ˈ	steht dieser Haken, so wird die nachfolgende Silbe stärker betont! „Main stress!"	window [ˈwɪndəʊ]
ˌ	steht dieser Haken, so wird die nachfolgende Silbe schwächer betont! „Secondary stress!"	examination [ɪɡˌzæmɪˈneɪʃən]
ː	bedeutet, dass der vorangehende Laut lang gesprochen wird.	shoe [ʃuː]

GRAMMATICAL TERMS – Grammatische Ausdrücke

active (voice) ['æktɪv, 'vɔɪs]	Aktiv (Tatform)
adjective ['ædʒɪktɪv]	Adjektiv (Eigenschaftswort)
adverb ['ædvɜːb]	Adverb (Umstandswort)
adverb of manner ['mænə]	Adverb der Art und Weise
adverb of place ['ædvɜːb, 'pleɪs]	Adverb des Ortes
adverb of time [taɪm]	Adverb der Zeit
adverbial clause [əd'vɜːbiəl, 'klɔːz]	adverbialer Nebensatz
article ['ɑːtɪkəl]	Artikel (Geschlechtswort)
definite article ['defənət]	bestimmter Artikel
indefinite article [ɪn'defənət]	unbestimmter Artikel
attributive [ə'trɪbjʊtɪv]	attributiv
auxiliary (verb) [ɔːg'zɪljəri]	Hilfsverb (Hilfszeitwort)
cardinal number ['kɑːdənəl]	Grundzahl
comparative [kəm'pærətɪv]	Komparativ (1. Steigerungsstufe)
comparison [kəm'pærəsən]	Steigerung
conditional [kən'dɪʃənəl]	Konditional I (Bedingungsform)
conditional perfect ['pɜːfɪkt]	Konditional II
conjunction [kən'dʒʌŋkʃən]	Konjunktion (Bindewort)
continuous form [kən'tɪnjʊəs, 'fɔːm]	Verlaufsform (des Verbs)
consonant ['kɒnsənənt]	Konsonant (Mitlaut)
definite article	bestimmter Artikel (Geschlechtswort)
demonstrative pronoun [dɪ'mɒnstrətɪv 'prəʊnaʊn]	Demonstrativpronomen (hinweisendes Fürwort)
direct object ['ɒbdʒɪkt]	direktes Objekt
direct speech ['daɪrekt, 'spiːtʃ]	direkte Rede
future tense ['fjuːtʃə, 'tens]	Futur I (Zukunft)
future perfect	Futur II (vollendete Zukunft)
genitive ['dʒenətɪv]	Genitiv (Wesfall)
gerund ['dʒerənd]	Gerundium
if-clause	if-Satz
imperative [ɪm'perətɪv]	Imperativ (Befehlsform)
indefinite article	unbestimmter Artikel (Geschlechtswort)
indirect object [ɪndə'rekt[aɪ], 'ɒbdʒɪkt]	indirektes Objekt
indirect speech ['spiːtʃ]	indirekte Rede
infinitive [ɪn'fɪnətɪv]	Infinitiv (Grundform)
infinitive construction [kən'strʌkʃən]	Infinitivkonstruktion
interrogative pronoun [ɪntə'rɒgətɪv]	Interrogativpronomen (Fragefürwort)
irregular verb [ɪ'regjʊlə]	unregelmäßiges Verb
main clause ['meɪn, klɔːz]	Hauptsatz
modal auxiliary ['məʊdl, ɔːg'zɪljəri]	modales Hilfsverb
negation	Verneinung
noun [naʊn]	Substantiv (Hauptwort)
object ['ɒbdʒɪkt]	Objekt (Satzergänzung)
ordinal number ['ɔːdənəl]	Ordnungszahl
participle ['pɑːtəsɪpəl]	Partizip (das Mittelwort)
participle structure ['strʌktʃə]	Partizipialkonstruktion
passive (voice) ['pæsɪv, 'vɔɪs]	Passiv (Leideform)
past (tense)	Imperfekt (Präteritum, Vergangenheit)
past participle	2. Partizip, Partizip Perfekt
past perfect ['pɑːst, 'pɜːfɪkt]	Plusquamperfekt (vollendete Vergangenheit)
personal pronoun ['pɜːsənəl]	Personalpronomen (persönliches Fürwort)

plural [ˈplʊərəl]	Plural (Mehrzahl)
position	Stellung (z. B. des Adverbs)
possessive pronoun [pəˈzesɪv]	Possessivpronomen (besitzanzeigendes Fürwort)
predicative [prɪˈdɪkətɪv]	prädikativ
preposition [prepəˈzɪʃən]	Präposition (Verhältniswort)
present participle [ˈprezənt]	Partizip Präsens (1. Partizip)
present perfect [ˈpɜːfɪkt]	Perfekt (vollendete Gegenwart)
present (tense) [tens]	Präsens (Gegenwart)
pronoun [ˈprəʊnaʊn]	Pronomen (Fürwort)
prop word [ˈprɒp, wɜːd]	Stützwort
question tag [ˈkwestʃən, tæg]	Bestätigungsfrage (Kurzfrage)
question word	Fragewort
reflexive pronoun [rɪˈfleksɪv]	Reflexivpronomen (rückbezügliches Fürwort)
regular verb [ˈregjʊlə]	regelmäßiges Verb
relative pronoun [ˈrelətɪv]	Relativpronomen (bezügliches Fürwort)
reported speech [rɪˈpɔːtɪd, ˈspiːtʃ]	indirekte Rede
sequence of tenses [ˈsiːkwəns]	Zeitenfolge
short form	Kurzform
simple form	einfache Form
singular [ˈsɪŋgjʊlə]	Singular (Einzahl)
statement [ˈsteɪtmənt]	Aussagesatz
subject [ˈsʌbdʒɪkt]	Subjekt (Satzgegenstand)
subordinate clause [səˈbɔːdɪnət]	Nebensatz
substitute	Ersatzform
superlative [suːˈpɜːlətɪv]	Superlativ (2. Steigerungsstufe)
verb [vɜːb]	Verb (Zeitwort)
vowel [ˈvaʊəl]	Vokal (Selbstlaut)
word order	Wortstellung

LIST OF GRAMMATICAL SUBJECTS

The verb

	page
the present simple	9
the present continuous	15
the past simple	38
the past continuous	44
the "WILL"-future	68
the "going to"-future	73
the conditional	79
the conditional perfect	190
the present perfect	85
the past perfect	90
Short forms	188
to do (negative and interrogative sentences)	57
the passive voice	108/114
the irregular verbs	120/191
the use of the tenses (revision)	119
participles	181
gerund	183
modal auxiliaries	135
can	136
may	140
must	145
shall	154
will	149
the infinitive	178
if-clauses	173
the indirect speech	176

The pronouns

personal pronouns	32
possessive adjectives	17
demonstrative adjectives	21
possessive pronouns	45
demonstrative pronouns	52
relative pronouns	95
interrogative pronouns	62
reflexive pronouns	129
indefinite pronouns	
some – any	97
every – each	103/104
many – much	81
little – few	131

The numbers

the cardinal numbers	9/25
the ordinal numbers	9/63

The noun

	page
the plural	9
irregular plurals	21/126
the word order	33/39/125
the "of"-genitive	50
the "s"-genitive	51
the direct, indirect object (word order)	33

The article

the definite article	15/101
the indefinite article	15/103

The adjective/adverb/ predicative complement

the adjective	69/75
comparison	
with "er" and "est"	69
with "more" and "most"	69
irregular comparison	75
as ... as, not as ... as, etc.	80
the adverb	91/124/130
comparison of the adverb	125
word order	125
the predicative complement	124

Prepositions and Conjunctions

Prepositions	170
Conjunctions	172

Miscellaneous

since – for	87
ago – before	87
during – while	91
nicht wahr?	10
ich auch – ich auch nicht	109/110
little – few	131
hard – hardly	124
usually – used	150
need – dare	151
must – need not	146
as well as – both	141

HOW TO FIND THE WORDS IN THE VOCABULARY

                              page

1. Working for Fowler & Co 194
2. What to do at the weekend? ... 196
3. By caravan to the seaside 199
4. Great Britain and its geography 202
5. Making travel enquiries to London 203
6. Short scenes from everyday life 206
7. Sightseeing in London 208
8. Always trouble with the boss and the parents 210
9. Let's go to Harrods 213
10. An exciting football match 215
11. Going on a tour of South England 217
12. Having an accident 220
13. Some aspects of modern British life 221
14. A visit to an English school ... 223
15. What to do after school? 226
16. Communicating in business ... 228
17. The Media 231
18. How Great Britain is governed . 234
19. A bloody day 238
20. Great Britain and its ethnic minorities 239
21. Let's have a look at the British economy 241
22. Is the world facing an environmental catastrophe? ... 244
23. Social aspects of Great Britain 246
24. Britain and the world 248
25. New York 250
26. Impressions of the United States 252
27. Some aspects of modern American life 253

                              page

Specific texts dealing with commerce and trade

1. Working in an export firm 256
2. At the port of London (Shipping goods) 256
3. A business talk 257
4. A business letter 257
5. A business letter 258
6. Visitors at the Hanover Fair ... 258
7. What do you know about modern communications systems? 259
8. How a house is built? 259
9. A farmer's activities 260
10. Sarah learns how to cook 261

For further study

1. The prepositions 262
2. The conjunctions 262
3. The if-clauses 263
4. The indirect speech 263
5. The infinitive 264
6. The participle/the gerund 265

BILDQUELLENVERZEICHNIS

Bilder des Autors:
S. 19, 28, 29 (2), 36 (1), 42 (1), 44, 89 (3), 98, 99 (1), 117 (2), 144

BTA British Tourist Authority:
S. 36 (1), 40 (2), 41, 48, 54, 61, 65, 66, 77 (2), 78, 105 (1), 116

Deutsche Presse-Agentur, Frankfurt:
S. 14 (3), 22 (2), 24, 35 (2), 37, 42 (1), 59, 60, 72, 82, 83, 105 (1), 106 (2), 111, 113, 118, 121, 122 (2), 123, 127 (2), 128 (3), 134, 139, 142, 143, 147 (1), 148 (3), 149, 152, 153, 154 (2)

Europcar Autovermietung GmbH: S. 67

Hannover Messe: S. 162

Her Majesty's Stationery Office: S. 67

Interfoto, München: S. 100

Westermann: S. 138

Illustrationen: Birgit Ackermann

© Winklers Verlag Darmstadt